The Law of Sovereign Wealth Funds

The words ‘good’ and ‘bad’ are meaningless.
This is based on science and not on opinion.
R. Buckminster Fuller
‘Critical Path’

The Law of Sovereign Wealth Funds

Fabio Bassan

Professor, Faculty of Economics, Roma Tre University, Italy and Founding Director, Sovereign Wealth Funds Law Centre

Edward Elgar

Cheltenham, UK • Northampton, MA, USA

Published by
Edward Elgar Publishing Limited
The Lypiatts
15 Lansdown Road
Cheltenham
Glos GL50 2JA
UK

Edward Elgar Publishing, Inc.
William Pratt House
9 Dewey Court
Northampton
Massachusetts 01060
USA

A catalogue record for this book
is available from the British Library

Library of Congress Control Number: 2011925762

FSC
www.fsc.org
MIX
Paper from
responsible sources
FSC® C018575

ISBN 978 0 85793 235 8

Typeset by Servis Filmsetting Ltd, Stockport, Cheshire
Printed and bound by MPG Books Group, UK

Contents

Foreword

Franco Bassanini

No one doubts that Sovereign Wealth Funds (SWFs) must nowadays be recorded among the major players in the international financial markets and in the global economy. They contribute to global growth and financial stability, by maintaining open flow of resources for long-term investments, by providing liquidity to stabilise rising fiscal deficits, by contributing to recapitalise crisis-stricken banks, by supporting economic activities, by boosting productivity, and by investing in strategic financial institutions in critical situations.

In 2009, commodity funds (managing portfolios of financial assets and income coming from the sale of raw materials) hold assets equal to \$2 trillion and account for 61 per cent of global sovereign funds, while the assets of non-commodity funds (managing portfolios of financial assets derived from the income of foreign exchange balance of trade surplus and/or payments) amounted to \$1.5 trillion and account for 39 per cent of global sovereign funds.[1] Before the crisis, the SWFs assets were expected to reach \$12 trillion by 2015, but nowadays, according to some reliable estimates, they are expected to reach between \$6 trillion and \$10 trillion by the same year.[2]

The phenomenon of SWFs is very complex. In principle, they are special investment vehicles with long-term horizons, created or owned by a sovereign state. All of them belong to the family of Foreign Government Controlled Investors (FGCI), which include similar public entities like state-owned enterprises (SOEs). They are, however, a non-homogeneous category, with varied and multiple possible purposes. They represent an original mix between government and market, public and private instruments, with different risk profiles.

The complexity of the SWFs' economic and legal issues depends to

---

1 Sovereign Wealth Fund Institute, 2009.

2 A. Quadrio Curzio, *Sovereign Wealth Funds. A complete guide to state-owned investment funds* (Harriman House, 2010) pp. 39–46. The author analyses the different SWF growth scenarios.

a large extent on the more or less protectionist reaction of the recipient states which host foreign investments. The host states are interested in boosting foreign direct investment but at the same time they are often worried about foreign investment decisions that could be driven by political objectives, affecting strategic national issues. Obviously, the main host state concern is that a foreign state may take indirect control of (mostly) private companies working in strategic industry or financial sector, like the case of Libyan funds and Unicredit Bank. As a consequence, a potential conflict of interests and laws between home and host states may arise.

The work of Fabio Bassan contributes significantly to the debate and literature on SWFs, investigating the legal matter as a whole.

The book focuses on the central issue of the complexity of SWFs' regulatory framework. It starts from the assumption that SWFs are a 'genus' in the family of FGCI and their common denominator is that they are not only public, but sovereign entities, sometimes with a separate legal personality. The other relevant distinguishing feature of SWFs is the investment element, prominently foreign and with a long-term horizon.

Many scholars talk about a new form of 'state capitalism' or recall in mind the public intervention in economy. Bassan rightly stresses out the original mechanism of 'State as an investor', in which the state has, at the same time, the role of regulator and shareholder and acts, through the vehicle of SWFs, as a private operator, investing both internally and abroad in foreign companies and banks.

The definition of SWFs proposed by Bassan ('funds established, owned and operated by local or central governments, with investments strategies including the acquisition of equity interest in companies listed in international markets operating in sectors considered strategic by their countries of incorporation') is functional to the application of specific rules for SWFs, at least partially different from those applicable to other similar entities, like central banks, pension funds, SOEs, development banks, hedge or private equity funds or other investors.

When a state invests as a private entity it should be treated as such, but the SWFs are characterised by the element of 'sovereignty' and their purposes are at the same time private (creating the most value for investors) and public (for instance, stabilising price volatility or developing resources of the country). So, there is a particular cross-relationship between public and private law, well analysed in the first chapters.

The author analyses in detail also the problematic legal issue of the cross-relationship between international and national law of home and host states, in the framework of European law. At global level, the multilateral approach has been chosen, with the direct involvement of the IMF and the OECD. The former has drawn up 24 guiding Generally Accepted

Principles and Practices (GAPPs), also called the 'Santiago principles' and has created an International Working Group (IWG) evolved in an international forum (IFSWF). The OECD has provided guidelines and principles mainly for recipient countries, like non-discrimination of foreign investors, transparency and predictability, progressive liberalisation of capital movement, not conditioned on the principle of reciprocity, or commitment to avoid new restrictions. However, GAPPs and OECD guidelines represent a voluntary framework without any sanction in case of failure to comply with. Therefore, as Bassan points out, the multilateral framework is inadequate and SWFs remain subject to national measures. So, there might be a potential problem of regulatory asymmetry or a too high level of host state discretion in allowing foreign investments in domestic economies: both could be negative for sound long-term investment flows.

Very remarkable is also Bassan's study on bilateral relationship between the investment's home state and the host state. On the one hand, he investigates in depth the questions whether the home state can invoke state immunity for its SWF's operations and whether an SWF can challenge – on the grounds of immunity – the restrictive measures adopted by a host state. On the other hand, Bassan examines the question whether bilateral investment treaties (BITs) can be invocated for the SWFs' investments' protection.

In order to avoid limitations that would distort investment regimes and affect free flow of capital across borders, it will be crucial also the new European legal framework for SWFs, based on free movement of capital (one of the pillars of the single market), the new Lisbon Treaty provisions[3] and the new Commission communications about foreign investments in EU.[4] Going forward, a multilateral agreement on investment – agreed by both major developed and emerging countries – could represent the first best solution in the long run in order to favour cross border investment at the global level.[5]

The main geographical destinations of SWFs' stock of capital investment is directed towards Asia (31 per cent), to EU (30 per cent), to US (20 per cent) and to remaining regions (19 per cent). From a geographical

[3] Arts. 206 and 207 TFEU.

[4] COM (10) nos. 343 and 344.

[5] See the G8 Declaration of L'Aquila, *Responsible Leadership for a Sustainable Future,* 2009 ('52. To this end, we commit to enhance cooperation with our major partners to agree upon shared principles which may serve as the basis for a more structured and wider process towards an agreed common multilateral framework in the long run creating a predictable and stable climate for investment.').

point of view, Europe remains the main destination of sovereign wealth fund investment in term of value, while Asia is the first destination in terms of deals. The investment vehicles portfolio is composed mostly by equity (50 per cent), followed by fixed income securities (35–40 per cent) and in only a residual from other forms of investment alternatives and more risky, such as hedge funds or derivatives. In Italy, foreign SWFs' investments are mainly concentrated in sensitive fields such as energy and infrastructures, followed by finance, real estate and telecommunications. The SWFs are also active in financing long-term projects in research and technological innovation, green economy, environment, alternative energy sourcing. These are all sectors which themselves may yield high investment returns, stimulate follow-on investment and, as a result, create growth and jobs. Investment in such strategic sectors could enhance competitiveness and productivity.

Therefore, SWFs are crucial long-term investors: they could favour a rebalancing of capital flows from surplus to deficit countries and contribute to re-allocate huge amounts of money towards long-term investments (LTIs) in national economies' strategic sectors, without weighing on troubled public finances and budgets. These kinds of investments should play a key role for the global, European and national exit strategies from the economic and financial crisis, because they can stimulate a sustainable growth and contribute to fiscal consolidation and financial stability.

Thus, the role of SWFs is going to rise in the coming years, as well as the role of other long-term investors, with which they can establish important working relationships and partnerships. I refer, in particular, to development banks and public saving banks (such as the EIB, the German KfW, the French CDC and the Italian CDP), pension funds and insurance companies which are involved in long-term investments too.

SWFs' direct investments should be encouraged by an appropriate regulatory framework. This legal framework could be constrained by national protectionist barriers, due to the lack of transparency of some SWFs' asset allocation, some foreign government practices and more or less sensitive sector in which they invest. These concerns are important and they should be regulated, doing so, however, that the protection of their host countries will not stop the flow of foreign SWFs' investments. In fact, SWFs have much to offer not only to their sponsor countries but also to recipient countries, in terms of capital injections for long-term investments essential to boost fiscal recovery, business activity and the job market.

Although some specific rules for SWFs are needed, I think that a common legal framework for long-term investors and/or for long-term investments should be provided. It should be based on few shared principles. In particular, it is important to keep markets open to foreign capital and create a friendly LTI regulatory framework (or, at least, a regulatory framework not discriminatory against LTI).

The new framework should involve accounting standards, prudential principles and corporate governance rules, as well as new rules and incentives for PPPs and PFIs, and an *ad hoc* system of fiscal incentives, as proposed by the de Larosière Group Report on European Financial Supervision[6] and more recently by the Mario Monti Report on European Single Market.[7]

From a fiscal policy point of view, in many European countries the strategic LTI are disadvantaged compared to financial short-term investments. These discriminatory tax disincentives should be abolished. Considering the important positive externalities of the strategic long-term investments, we may envisage *ad hoc* incentives for financial products and firms investing in the long-term initiatives of general interest, on the lines of the fiscal incentives granted to the US Project Bonds by the American Administration Stimulus Plan and of the incentives awarded to the renewable energy projects by many European tax systems.[8] Following the same logic, however, higher tax rates are frequently provided for the selling back of real estate assets bought few years before (usually less than 3–5 years), presuming a speculative transaction.

Tax expenditures for LTI should not be considered in the Maastricht criteria. Moreover, in the rethinking of the European Growth and Stability Pact, some kind of new 'Golden Rule' should be applied to the duration of investments. Long-term strategic investment with a time span of over 25–30 years, and/or the related guarantee schemes, should be considered not under primary spending, but as a fixed investment having a special accounting treatment within the European statistical framework.

As for the accounting standards, the 'mark to market' principle, if applied to typical long-term investors, does not permit distinctions between short-term and long-term investment values in balance sheets. There is need to: (i) introduce accounting criteria that reflect long-term investors' specific business model; (ii) distinguish between different temporal durations/matching liabilities and investments; and (iii) take into

---

6 *The High-Level Group on Financial Supervision in EU*, chaired by J. de Larosière, Report, 25 February 2009.

7 Mario Monti, *A new strategy for the single market at the service of Europe's economy and society,* May 2010.

8 The very rapid growth of European private investment in renewable energy plants is commonly attributed to these tax or price incentives: *quod erat demonstrandum*!

account the value of future cash flow over the long-term. Appropriate accounting rules for long-term investors would also make a substantial contribution towards stabilising global financial markets and reducing short-term volatility.

The prudential treatment of financial assets giving priority to their mark to market value is also standing in the way of long-term investment. The mark to market accounting rules applied to typical long-term investors do not incorporate in their ALM distinctions between short-term and long-term investments. Therefore, a change in the prudential principles might be recommended. Due to the mark to market rule, the contingencies affecting the value of these investments over the short-term are having repercussions over time on the financial statements – higher earnings volatility and additional solvency requirements – although the actual horizon for these investments goes beyond that for the publication of the accounts.

Similar proposals have been put forward – after the de Larosière and Mario Monti Reports – by the Eurofi Financial Forum 2010,[9] by the two conferences organised by the Long Term Investors' Club and the OECD in Rome and in Venice,[10] and by a working paper presented to the EU Commissioner Michel Barnier by four prominent European long-term public investors (EIB, KfW, CDC and CDP) in September 2010.[11]

At the international level, in the recent New York Conference on SWFs and other Long-term Investors,[12] Augustin de Romanet, the CEO of CDC, announced that the need of a more favourable regulatory framework for the LTI will be supported by the French Government and will be included in the G20 Agenda of the 2011 French Presidency. The Italian

---

[9] *Optimizing EU financial reforms for achieving resilience, growth and competitiveness. What priorities? What roadmap?*, 27–30 September 2010, Brussels. See especially the paper *For an EU action plan to remove the disincentives to long-term investment.*

[10] *The Long-term Investment in the Age of Globalisation,* Rome, 17 June 2010 (all papers available at: http://www.astrid-online.it/Dossier--d1/DISCIPLINA/The-Long-T/index.htm (accessed 4 April 2011)) and *Towards a Sustainable Future: The Role of Long-Term Investment,* Venice, 28–29 October 2010 (all papers available at: http://www.astrid-online.it/Dossier--d1/DISCIPLINA/Studi--ric/index.htm (accessed 4 April 2011)).

[11] Letter to Mr. Barnier, *Proposals to adapt the EU's financial regulatory framework to long-term investments requirements*, 20 September 2010, with annex *Proposals to promote Long-term investments in Europe – Conclusions of European long-term financial institutions' working group on banking supervision.*

[12] Conference, *Wealth Funds and Other Long-Term Investors,* 4–5 October 2010, New York.

Government shares the same opinion.[13] In fact, without substantial changes in prudential, accounting and tax regulations, the objectives set in the EU 2020 strategy and in the Mario Monti strategy on the Single Market could not be reached.

At the European political level, the need of a new regulatory framework, more favourable to LTI, has been strongly emphasised by the European Commission in the recent Communications on *A New Single Market Act*,[14] on *A Comprehensive European international investment policy*,[15] and on *The EU Budget Review*.[16] The EU Commission political choice on this issue is therefore explicit and may be very important for a sound European long-term investment policy, but there is, of course, the need of a strong and durable political commitment and of a coherent follow up.

However, critics have objected that the European Union has no powers to decide in this matter, since it relates specifically to the introduction of some exceptions and additions to the set of rules laid down by Basel III, Solvency II and the IAS 39. But the rules of Basel III will be implemented in Europe by a European Union directive (CRD IV) and Solvency II is itself a European directive. As for the international accounting standards, though they are defined by an independent NGO (the IASB), they can be effective only if they are recalled by the European and national legislation. So the EU institutions have in fact some power to influence and even to negotiate with the IASB less penalising rules for LTI, and to directly enact better rules for insurance companies and pension funds through changes to Solvency II.

More difficulties must be faced as regards Basel III. In principle, the European Commission is not obliged to transpose the Basel rules mechanically, but could provide for exceptions and integrations, as the U.S. did for Basel I and II. However, strong political and practical reasons suggest not to reopen the Pandora's box of Basel III, the result of a difficult and complex negotiation. A compromise solution may perhaps be found in

---

[13] Giulio Tremonti, *The Crisis, Europe and the Long-term Investors,* LTIC Venice Forum *Towards a Sustainable Future: The Role of Long-Term Investment*, organised by Cassa Depositi e Prestiti – Venice, 28–29 October 2010. See also, F. Bassanini and E. Reviglio, 'A New Regulatory Framework and Instruments for European Long Term Investments after the Crisis', in *Astrid Rassegna* no. 20/2010 (www.astrid.eu).

[14] European Commission Communication, 'Towards a New Single Market Act' COM (10) 608, 27 October 2010.

[15] European Commission Communication, 'Towards a Comprehensive European International Investment Policy' COM (10) 343, 7 July 2010.

[16] European Commission Communication, 'The EU Budget Review' COM (10) 700, 19 October 2010.

the framework of the new mission given by the Seoul G20 summit to the Financial Stability Board, to propose the extension of the Basel rules to other parties (shadow banks). An integrative protocol could perhaps be envisaged, that, without changing the Basel III rules as regards banks, could integrate and refine them in respect of long-term investors. *Stricto jure*, in fact, the rules of Basel III apply to banks, but do not apply to long-term investors such as insurance, pension funds, SWFs and public savings and development banks (like EIB, CDC, CDP, KfW). But, *de facto* and by default, the same rules are frequently applied by the markets to these investors, dramatically reducing their firepower in the financing of long-term investment. There is good reason to fill the void, with an additional or integrative protocol to Basel III establishing special rules adapted to the specific mission and business model of these institutions.

Aside of new International and European sets of rules to favour LTI (and to attract SWF's investments), new financial instruments such as Project Bonds, European equity Funds and Guarantee Schemes may be contemplated.

Many SWFs invest most of their resources in U.S. bonds, while at European level they find only fragmented markets. So, it is clear that the lack of a European bond market is now an obstacle for attracting foreign investments. Thus, the construction of a European sovereign debt market by issuing E-bonds would be an interesting opportunity for SWFs investment in EU. Moreover, EU would ensure a significant flow of foreign capital, especially from emerging economies, essential for long-term investments in strategic areas. The issuance of E-bond would enrich the positive experience of other new financial instruments, such as the 2020 European Fund for Energy, Climate Change and Infrastructure ('Marguerite'), set up in 2009.

The world's financial markets will likely show an extraordinary growth in the quantity of savings of emerging economies. During the recent crisis, there has been a marked intensification of competition for funds by governments of economically-advanced countries seeking to finance swelling public debt. In this competition, sound, socially-cohesive economies boasting achievements in technology and environmental stewardship will have the advantage, inspiring global investors' confidence and so attracting resources. In this context, the solid reputation of Europe as a reliable economic area – partly a result of the Stability and Growth Pact and the ECB's rigorous anti-inflation policy – will play to the EU's favour.

However, the demand for infrastructure, energy, climate change, strategic and urban infrastructure is very large all over the world and will grow rapidly in the next years. For instance, the overall cost of the Trans-European Transport Network (TEN-T) still to be financed has been assessed at around €500 billion by 2020. The overall cost of the European investments in Energy and Climate Change is estimated in over €2,500 billion by 2020. To finance such an ambitious programme the EU needs to increase its capability to attract long-term private and public–private capital from global markets, the SWFs' investment included.

For doing so, the EU should bolster the euro's leverage, providing for LTI a new favourable regulatory framework and using a better combination of long-term capital and debt instruments (such as EU equity funds, project bonds and common guarantee schemes) issued by large European funds and other similar long-term public and private financial institutions and investors. These actions, together with the issuance of European Sovereign Debt securities, will also strengthen the alliance of European peoples and secure the political cohesion of the Union.

PART I

SWFs: New actors in the international scene. A definition and classification

1. Sovereign entities investing abroad as private entities: limits of the conventional framework

1. STATE INVESTORS BETWEEN PUBLIC AND PRIVATE, NATIONAL AND INTERNATIONAL LAW

The economic crisis which started in 2008 emphasised a significant return of national states in the economies, viewed suspiciously as a relic of the past. In the second half of the last century, states have been gradually losing their economic sovereignty (that was either expressly transferred to international organisations or materially lost) and participating in an advanced *jus comune* environment where domestic legal systems gradually lose their relevance. Conversely, in the first decade of the 21st Century national states have regained their central position as regulators and as shareholders, both internally (coming into the ownership of big national companies and banks) and internationally (investing abroad in foreign companies and banks). This was due to contingent factors (including the economic crisis) but above all to structural factors.

Observers usually view the issue as a Manichaean confrontation between public and private: private companies that interfere with the states' regulatory or economic sovereignty; public companies that act (abroad) as private ones. According to some authors, the challenge today arises from the usurpation of public power by private companies, and of private power by states. Others argue instead that it arises from foreign public actors wielding public power that reaches across borders, in the form of sovereign investing through instruments of private commerce and in direct (but potentially unfair) competition with private actors.

Actually, one should admit that there are not separate political and economic playing fields where states and companies operate respectively. Transnational corporations increasingly regulate the markets in which they participate, and states participate in (both domestic and international) economic markets as operators. They both make a political use of financial power trying to influence the market they operate in.

Nevertheless, there are some differences. Firstly, states regulate their domestic markets but operate abroad (through state-owned enterprises – SOEs – or sovereign wealth funds – SWFs), in (recipient state) markets they cannot regulate, while large corporations use their influence irrespective of the market.[1] Secondly: private companies are accountable to shareholders, and use their power mainly to maximise their profits (the private welfare), while investing states are also accountable to stakeholders (at the end, their citizens) and can be interested also in pursuing other goals, as public welfare encloses a wider range of interests.[2] If these are the premises, there are at least three direct consequences. First: the finalistic element (the purpose of the investment) plays an important role and deserves a close attention.[3] Second: both the subjective and the objective element (sovereignty and investment, respectively) of state action are necessary to understand what SWFs are, how they operate and what is their role in the current scenario, as none of those elements by itself can answer to the question about purposes. Third: the opposition between formalists and functionalists, that use to advantage the sovereignty and the investment element respectively, and suggest again a public/private dualism (SWFs would be formally public but functionally private), does not explain properly the current situation, as they both miss the relevance of purposes.[4]

Hence, the phenomenon can be interpreted rather as an integration than a confrontation between public and private law. States act as enterprises

[1] This is an important difference that observers often do not take in due consideration. Indeed, it is possible that SWFs try to influence recipient state laws, but they can do it in a far less effective way than transnational corporations do. Because the latter act in all recipient states and markets in the same way, while SWFs act each time in a very specific country; because they pursue different interests; because investing states raise a great diffidence in recipient states. Hence, unlike transnational corporations, states investing abroad are nothing but operators in a market they can not regulate, while transnational corporations decisively contribute to regulating investment activities in many countries.

[2] SWFs' accountability is a complex matter. We deal with it in Ch.3, para. 1.

[3] SWFs' investment purposes are the pivot originating many effects regarding definitions (Ch.2), regulation (both active and passive, Ch.3 and Ch.4) and state immunity (Ch.5).

[4] L. Catà Backer ('Sovereign Investing in Times of Crisis: Global Regulation of Sovereign Wealth Funds, State Owned Enterprises and the Chinese Experience' [2009] *Transnational Law and Contemporary Problems* 101–228) replaces the classical dichotomy between public and private with a new classification (participation/regulation) that, as we will see (Ch.3, para. 1), is a good starting point (because the author traces a line between states participating in and regulating markets), but not the solution of the conundrum (because he does not admit the decisive relevance of purposes).

that invest resources in their own territories and abroad. However, while states regulate internally, in the international scenario, they are only operators in a market they cannot regulate. Sovereign Wealth Funds are an old form – although recently re-appeared stronger and in different forms – by which states participate in international trade, and represent a most evident outcome of a sharp contradiction: they are sovereigns and they make investments (also) abroad; therefore, they can only be studied within the framework of the bigger picture.

SWFs are one of the vehicles by which states make investments, including – but not only – abroad. If we were to use the taxonomic classifications of biology, we might define a SWF as a 'genus', belonging to the 'family' of foreign government-controlled investors (FGCIs) – which include, for instance, also SOEs.[5] FGCIs are in turn one of the instruments used by states to interact in domestic and international trade, which we might group into an 'order', that of Foreign Investments.[6] We propose to review the SWF 'genus' and identify its 'species', by definition and classification. In doing this, we cannot neglect the need to reconstruct a broader 'family', in order to determine whether the discipline we are focusing on would apply to the SWF 'genus' only or also to other genera in the same family. The answer to this question is an interesting one, because the need for specific rules for SWFs may only be justified if the characteristics that make this 'genus' different from the others are such as to make it actually impossible to apply the discipline to the entire 'family'.

2. SPECIFIC ISSUES RAISED BY SWFS

To begin with, we may assume that the feature FGCIs have in common is the public factor: states operate in the markets, following their rules, and they are subject to private law. Hence the general conflict between the application of private or public law, depending on the objective (the investment) or subjective (state sovereignty) element stressed, respectively. However, the controversy appears to be mostly ideological. In fact, on one hand, in national regulations the separation between public and private tends to be superseded by a cross-relation that is perhaps more complex but certainly more in line with present trends. On the other hand, in international law,

[5] See Ch.2, para 1.2 for a comparison between SWFs and SOEs.

[6] According to the taxonomic classifications of biology, 'species' that share elements in common are grouped into a 'genus'. Genera with similar characteristics belong to the same 'family'. Similar families are grouped into an 'order' and similar orders into 'classes'.

this separation has always had a different meaning and has generated different consequences. But with SWFs, a new factor was added to the framework, which characterises the 'genus' compared to the 'family' of FGCIs: the 'sovereign' factor. With SWFs we do not have mere investments by states in national or foreign enterprises: here states invest by means of a 'sovereign' instrument. This factor overcomes the typical conflict of interest, with the state both regulator and operating in the market it regulates: it engenders a different relationship between regulator (internally) and regulated (externally, when states operate abroad as investors). This relationship is new by form (it is a foreign investment, sovereign) and consequences, and therefore deserves to be studied carefully. How much can the 'sovereign' factor make SWFs different from other FGCIs – such as, for instance, SOEs – is one of the aspects that this work wishes to investigate.

2.1 The Recent and Quick Growth of the Phenomenon: A Review of Causes and Consequences

The question of sovereign wealth funds is a very hot one at national and international level. While these funds have been around for some years, their management has changed fast recently. In the past, state-owned funds had a low risk propensity, played a passive role in the companies participated, and were used mostly to ensure domestic stabilisation,[7] even if, as purposes and instruments used often coincide, it is not always easy to make distinctions and classifications.[8] Conversely, recent sovereign investments are characterised by higher risk propensity and active role in the management of participated companies;[9] furthermore, the resources

---

[7] Like, for instance, the Kuwait Investment Board, created in 1953 and transferred in 1960 to the Kuwait Investment Authority, established with the purpose of stabilising domestic economy with respect to oil price fluctuations. Or, similarly, the funds created in the 1970s, and again in 1990, with the Pension Fund of the Norwegian government. On the other hand, the phenomena that have been occurring in the last half decade are different, and due mostly to raw material prices, oil in particular.

[8] The difficulties in making a classification have led some to believe that as 'each of these mechanisms may involve elements of reserve management, stabilization, and the transfer of wealth across generations . . . this mix of motivations reinforces the case for considering sovereign wealth funds in a broader context of the external investment activities of governments': E. Truman, *Sovereign Wealth Funds: the Need for Greater Transparency and Accountability* (Peterson Institute for International Economics, 2007).

[9] Some SWFs (Brunei, Canada, China, Kuwait, Malaysia, The Netherlands, Qatar, Singapore, The United Arab Emirates, and Vietnam) state that their investment strategies involve the acquisition of significant or controlling stakes in

managed by SWFs have recently grown significantly.[10] The system has progressed quickly, though the economic crisis started in 2008 has slowed down its growth.[11]

The number of SWFs and the resources they can make use of have raised due mostly to two events, one structural and one contingent. As for the former, the increase in savings volumes in South-East Asian countries after the 1997 crisis (a precautionary strategy of crisis prevention, a self insurance against exchange volatility), together with the concomitant reduction in internal investments caused by the weakness of their respective economies, has enhanced foreign investments from those countries.[12] As for the latter, the rise of raw material prices (especially oil and gas) has

---

companies: E. Truman, *Sovereign Wealth Funds: Threat or Salvation?* (Peterson Institute for International Economics, 2010) p. 42.

[10] According to some studies, the governments of India, China, Thailand, Indonesia, Korea, Malaysia, controlled already in 2005 at least 60% of their foreign direct investments for aggregate values of several billion dollars (see E. Truman, n. 9 above, the figures for which are based on *International Financial Statistics* estimates). According to recent data (see E. Truman, table 1) the following funds have resources in excess of 100 billion dollars: Abu Dhabi Investment Authority (established in 1976 by the United Arab Emirates); Government of Singapore Investment Corporation (established in 1981); Government Pension Fund-Global (established by Norway in 1990); Future Generation Fund (established by Kuwait in 1976); Stabilization Fund of the Russian Federation (established in 2004); Temasek Holdings (established in 1974 by Singapore).

[11] S. Jen, *How big could Sovereign Wealth Funds be by 2015?*, Morgan Stanley, May 2007 Report. The estimates are obviously very rough: the lack of transparency of the funds prevents analysts from making accurate assessments. Furthermore, such variables as a reduction in oil prices or a weakness of national economies might reduce investments significantly. As many scholars have observed, the aggregate figure is bigger than the one managed by hedge funds and private equity funds, but is remarkably smaller than the one managed by pension funds and mutual funds (see, inter alia, P. Hildebrand, *The challenge of sovereign wealth funds*, report presented to the International Center for Monetary and Banking Studies, Geneva, 18 December 2007, p. 2, and R. Kimmitt, 'Public footprints in private markets – sovereign wealth funds and the world economy' [2008] *Foreign Affairs* n. 1, pp. 119–30). As a consequence, the comparison with either the former or the latter will overstress or understate their size. However, SWFs have now acquired relevance as a system, and the resources under their management are bound to grow.

[12] See A. Monk, *Sovereignty in the era of global capitalism: the rise of Sovereign Wealth Funds*, Working Paper, pp. 5 *ff.*; D. Park, *Capital outflows, Sovereign Wealth Funds and domestic financial instability in developing Asia*, Asia Developing Bank Working Paper Series, 2008, n. 129; D. Park – G. Estrada, *Developing Asia's Sovereign Wealth Funds and Outward Foreign Direct Investment*, Asia Developing Bank Working Paper Series, 2009, n. 169.

assured producer countries a significant increase in export revenues, not counterbalanced (for reasons that vary depending on the country) by an increase in internal investments.[13] This has made available huge amounts of funds, sometimes managed by state-owned companies, more often managed directly by governments, when surpluses were channelled to central banks that used them to increase their reserves, or when producer countries maintained (or resumed) control of raw material extracting companies.[14]

These two circumstances have had four main consequences at both quantitative and qualitative level. The first one is the increase in the investments (both portfolio and foreign direct investments –FDIs) of many states operated through specific funds that benefit from sizeable and growing financing.

The second one is the structural change in investment flows: they are no longer one-way (from industrialised to less developed countries) but two-way flows: countries traditionally considered as less developed are now exporting capitals too, not just raw materials.[15] However, the reciprocity is not symmetrical: the new flows are not made up of private (as it is in many developed countries) but of state investments. Therefore, at least at this early stage of progress, there is no longer a clear-cut separation between states that make foreign investments with specific funds (home states) and states whose national enterprises are the recipients of foreign investments (host states).

The third consequence is that the type of investments made by SWFs has changed: they are much more flexible today than in the past, and characterised by a greater propensity to risk. Investment objectives have also changed in part, from shares in major listed companies to banks; from derivatives to bonds, from the real estate market to hedge funds.[16]

---

13 These two causes are at the origin of the classical distinction between excess rate and commodity fund.

14 Some scholars believe that behind the rise of SWFs are mainly changes in the international monetary system: see X. Ping-C. Chao, *The theoretical logic of Sovereign Wealth Funds*, China Investment Corporation Paper, 2009.

15 The irony of this new context is highlighted by Y. Lee, 'A reversal of neo-colonialism: the pitfalls and prospects of Sovereign Wealth Funds' [2009] *Georgetown International Law Journal*, 1103–49, at 1106, where he says that 'western countries . . . are reminiscent of claims raised by former developing countries regarding their right to regulate foreign investment in accordance with their national laws, objectives and priorities'.

16 See the paper by M. Weiss: Congressional Research Service – Report for Congress: *Sovereign Wealth Funds: Background and policy issues for Congress*, January 2008, p. 2.

The fourth consequence, perhaps the less studied so far, is still embryonic and relates to the change in SWF strategies, that are no longer aiming at mere portfolio investments but at real FDIs. Indeed, some SWFs are changing their original strategy, based on acquiring minority interests in order to achieve financial goals, and are acquiring – also (this is the recent trend) together with other SWFs – greater and greater shares of interest, if not dominant influence; this implies a shift from a substantially passive attitude towards taking responsibility for (and therefore getting involved in) the management of the companies held.

The issue has recently gained relevance in international politics: many SWF investments have in part minimised the adverse effects of the so-called subprime loans,[17] and have also acted as market stabilisers.[18] Nevertheless, the quick development of the phenomenon has caused diverse reactions worldwide, mostly protectionist ones, ranging from a demand for greater transparency in the management and organisation of SWF to proposals for a mere prohibition of their operation in certain areas. The undisguised concern is that a foreign state may take indirect control of (mostly) European or US private companies working in strategic industry sectors.

These reactions, one-sided at first, came from important international community players: the United States passed an act on this matter in July 2007, the German government presented a bill in 2008, other countries have started a serious internal debate. Other similar initiatives pushed the G7 to ask the International Monetary Fund (IMF) to review the case and make recommendations. The European Commission also evaluated (but did not take) specific measures.

The discussion that followed the adoption of these first one-sided actions has focused mostly on two profiles. On one hand, the legitimacy of intervening in investment fund markets financed and managed, directly or indirectly, by sovereign states, characterised by a degree of transparency considered insufficient and by purposes that are feared to go beyond

---

17 Among SWF operations in 2007/8 are those with Citigroup (4.9% of which was purchased in November 2007 by the UAE Fund Abu Dhabi Investment Authority – ADIA); with UBS AG (9% of which was purchased in December 2007 by the Fund of the Singapore government); with Morgan Stanley (where China Investment Corporation purchased 9.9% in December 2007); with Merrill Lynch (where Singapore Temasek invested 6.2 billion dollars in December 2007), with Citibank (an investment by the Singapore and Kuwait funds for 14.5 billion in January 2008).

18 An important list – also considering the authoritativeness of its source – of the positive aspects of SWF activities on international markets comes from the European Central Bank (ECB): *Financial Stability Report*, December 2007.

mere profit maximisation. On the other hand, the legitimacy of host state reactions, that, in order to avoid the risk of investments aimed at pursuing political interest in national enterprises considered as strategic (on account of their activity or of the industry sector they operate in) impose specific quality or quantity constraints to SWF investments.

So far, the debate has been limited to the theory (prominently economic) and was recently added to by international institutions. The IMF has created an international working group (IWG), then evolved in an international forum (IFSWF) composed of a number of sovereign wealth funds among the most important ones, that has developed guidelines (Generally Accepted Principles and Practices, GAPP) for the activities of SWFs (the so-called 'Santiago Principles'[19]). The OECD has started studying guidelines concerning constraints to the application of the national security clause to SWFs.[20] Both these initiatives (aimed at governing activities in home states and host states respectively) led to the development of ethical codes applicable on a voluntary basis. Therefore, the prompt reaction of international institutions has produced a discipline that sets detailed practices which SWFs should abide by.

2.2 Issues Brought by Recent Developments

Until the most recent developments, the investments made by SWFs have not given rise to particular reactions – on the contrary, they were welcomed by international institutions as a market stabilisation factor.[21] According to the economic literature that has studied these funds at empirical level in the face of political reactions, market operators and regulators are

[19] *Sovereign Wealth Funds – Generally Accepted Principles and Practices*, adopted in October 2008 (see in para. 8 an overview of those principles).

[20] OECD Investment Committee report on recipient country policies and SWFs, finalised at the 8th Roundtable on Freedom of Investment (11 October 2008). The works were scheduled for completion, with the publication of detailed guideline, by the second half of 2009. At writing, they are not published yet.

[21] The only exceptions are the attempt by the Chinese sovereign fund to acquire the US oil company Unolocal in 2005 and that of a UAE sovereign fund to acquire certain companies that run several ports in the US. The positive elements for stabilisation purposes were reported by the IMF in the paper entitled *Sovereign Wealth Funds – A Work Agenda*, n 19 above, p. 4: in those countries in which they are established, SWFs do facilitate the cross-generational transfer of non-renewable resources and reduce the risk of export product price fluctuations; moreover, they allow for diversified investments and for higher ROI estimates. On international markets, SWFs facilitate a more efficient allocation of the profits generated by raw material price increases.

reassured by the interventions of SWFs that – as recent researches have shown[22] – have profit maximisation as their main goal,[23] and might act as development drivers in the short term (hence the innovative definition of *Sovereign Development Funds*).[24]

Many observers believe that the problems raised by prospective SWF activities are mostly related to two aspects: lack of transparency and purposes sought, either strategic or political – in any case not purely commercial. These prospective risks may occur if there are no regulations requiring SWFs to disclose to the market the size of their investments, their strategies, goals, purposes, planned instruments and governance rules, as well as the practices implemented to assure proper risk management.

The vagueness that characterises SWF activities increases the diffidence of some observers, who cannot evaluate their action in terms of effectiveness and efficacy, nor check their proper operation and therefore – for instance – their compliance with provisions against corruption.[25] As to purposes, SWFs are generally expected to make long-term investments, on the basis of purely economic and market considerations. However, they may obviously seek other political purposes in making investments decisions.[26] Hence, some observers detected a new form of 'state capitalism'

---

[22] C. Balding, *A portfolio analysis of sovereign wealth funds* (Working paper, University of California, Irvine, 6 June 2008); P. Rose, 'Sovereigns as Shareholders' (2008) *North Carolina Law Review* 83–150 even sees a risk in the fact that sovereign funds are too passive.

[23] See also V. Fotak, B. Bortolotti and W. Megginson, *The financial impact of sovereign wealth fund investments in listed companies* (Working Paper, University of Oklahoma, March 2008).

[24] See for reference J. Santino, *Sovereign Development Funds*, OECD Development Centre, *Policy Insights* no. 58, April 2008, which forecasts an increasingly greater use of SWFs in the economies of less developed countries.

[25] Some authors (E. Truman, *Sovereign Wealth Fund acquisitions and other Foreign Government investments in the United States: assessing the economic and national security implications*, Testimony before the Committee on Banking, Housing and Urban Affairs, United States Senate, 14 November 2007, available at: http://www.iie.com/publications/testimony/testimony.cfm?ResearchID=842 (accessed 3 April 2011)) have tried to classify SWFs according to the principles of transparency and accountability to the market, as well as according to purposes sought, within the limits allowed by the scarce transparency. The result is a variegated one: from transparent funds that pursue typical purposes (e.g. the ones of the Norwegian government, Alaska and Canada) to transparent funds with strategic purposes (e.g. Malaysia, Singapore-Temasek), to non-transparent funds with typical investment purposes (e.g. Chile, Venezuela-NDF, Kuwait, Taiwan, UAE) to non-transparent funds with strategic purposes (Qatar, China).

[26] E. Truman (*Sovereign Wealth Funds: Threat or Salvation?*, n. 9 above, p. 41) admitted that 'the reality is that governments are political organizations, and

where investor governments may use public resources to invest in foreign companies engaged in strategic activities in the telecommunications, energy or financial sectors, so as to secure access to natural resources, or development of their own financial markets, or acquisition of knowledge or technologies.[27] Some of these economic or social purposes are challenged if they imply the participation of SWFs in companies working in sectors that are regarded as strategic.

Other concerns – induced by political rather than economic reactions – derive from the most diverse arguments. It is thought that SWFs might generate diffident and protectionist behaviour in many countries;[28] might jeopardise market stability;[29] might imply uncontrolled reactions by the markets; might lead to money being managed by the public sector in a less efficient manner than it would by the private sector,[30] or to a mismanagement of investments to the economic and financial detriment of the country with the fund;[31] might concentrate equity interests in

---

it is naïve to pretend that they are not', so that 'even if the actions of an SWF are not motivated by noneconomic considerations, noneconomic motives will be read into the SWF's decisions just the same'.

[27] Some observers see SWFs as one of the most critical aspects of interaction between market and state capitalism; see for reference R. Gilson and C. Milhaupt, 'Sovereign wealth funds and corporate governance: a minimalist response to the new mercantilism' [2009] *Stanford Law Review* 1345–69; G. Lions, *State Capitalism: the Rise of Sovereign Wealth Funds* (Standard Chartered Global Research, 2007). Others explain that 'global capitalism does not necessarily translate into a decline of state sovereignty; instead it implies the transformation of the state'. In this scenario, 'SWFs are the institutional expression of the creeping financialization of nation-state policy and its implementation' (A. Monk, *Sovereignty in the era of global capitalism: the rise of Sovereign Wealth Funds*, n. 12 above, p.20).

[28] P. Hildebrand, *The challenge of sovereign wealth funds*, n. 11 above, p. 8. Conversely, many observers do not believe SWFs are a threat to the financial market stability, both at microeconomic and macroeconomic level: see J. O'Neill, E. Nielson and S. Bahay, *In defence of Sovereign Wealth Funds*, Global Economic Paper no. 167, 2008; A. Demarolle, *Report to the Government of France on Sovereign Wealth Funds*, 2008; M. El Arian, 'Toward a better understanding of Sovereign Wealth Funds', in M. Goldstein and N. Lardy (eds.), *Debating China's Exchange Policy* (Peterson Institute for International Economics, 2008); T. Sun and H. Hesse, *Sovereign Wealth and financial stability: an event study analysis* (IMF Working Paper 09/239, 2009).

[29] S. Johnson, *The Rise of Sovereign Wealth Funds* (IMF, 2007).

[30] R. Kimmitt, 'Public footprints in private markets – sovereign wealth funds and the world economy', n. 11 above.

[31] E. Truman (*Sovereign Wealth Funds: Threat or Salvation?*, n 9 above, pp. 35–9), focusing on five areas of concern about SWFs, argues that 'the most serious risk associated with SWFs is related to the economic and financial stability of

Western companies into the hands of non-democratic countries;[32] might allow states to use instruments not available to the private sector and thus gain a competitive edge;[33] might pose risks for competitive processes and for market allocation;[34] might conceal – because of the lack of transparency – market abuse and insider trading practices, to the detriment of private investors and of their confidence in the market;[35] might limit the host government's access to information or move data or records offshore.

Others observed that SWFs could use their influence on investee companies to obtain intellectual and technological skill, to gain access to natural resources or improve competitive positions for domestic markets; or that countries with SWFs may use their investment as leverage for diplomatic purposes,[36] or may pursue non-commercial objectives with regard to their investment activities which could negatively affect portfolio companies, market efficiency and stability.

Others believe that SWFs might simply channel investments from fast developing countries to destinations other than typical ones, removing, for

---

the countries accumulating the huge stocks of assets in the fund – that is, the risk that the wealth will be wasted: because political authorities try to use the assets to promote domestic economic development or social objectives; because SWFs are not subject to the normal market disciplines; because the management of assets via SWFs creates enhanced potential for corruption; because governments do not have strong records as skilled investors.

[32] *Rapport d'information sur les fonds souverains, révélateurs de nos propres faiblesses*, presented at the French *Assemblée Nationale,* 17 June 2008, p.18.

[33] R. Kimmitt, 'Public footprints in private markets – sovereign wealth funds and the world economy', n. 11 above, specifies that 'there is the potential for perceived or actual unfair competitive advantages relative to the private sector. For instance, a government could use its intelligence or security services to gather information that is not available to a commercial investor. With a sovereign guarantee, a SWF could also obtain or extend financing (if needed) at interest rates that a commercial investor could not. It is also possible for a SWF to take an indirect approach by channelling foreign exchange through domestic SOEs, which in turn invest abroad'.

[34] These concerns were discussed at the Ninth OECD Roundtable on Freedom of Investment (see OECD Paper, *Foreign Government-Controlled Investors and Recipient Country Investment Policies: a scoping Paper*, January 2009).

[35] C. Cox, 'The rise of Sovereign Business' *Security Industry News*, December 2007.

[36] R. Gilson and C. Milhaupt, 'Sovereign Wealth Funds and Corporate Governance: a Minimalist Response to the New Mercantilism', n. 27 above; M. Plotkin, 'Foreign Direct Investment by Sovereign Wealth Funds: Using the Market and the Committee on Foreign Investment in the United States Together to Make the United States more Secure' [2008] *Yale Law Journal* pocket 88.

example, one of the supports to the financing of US public debt and thus threatening international stability.[37]

Finally, concerns are that SWFs might threaten national security.[38] This is the most controversial aspect, because while this risk is often implied, each state is free to set the limits of its own national security.[39]

3. RATIONALE AND OBJECTIVES OF THIS WORK

This work plans to analyse the law and regulatory side of the SWF issue, showing its contradictions and viewing it within the broader context of the FGCI 'family'. In fact, what emerges from the current debate on SWFs is very confused. Scholars from time to time focus on definitions, practices and preferred investment areas, on the appropriateness of specific rules for SWFs and for recipient states hosting SWF investments, or carry out statistical examinations. So far, few have investigated the matter as a whole; which means that on one hand the proposals made at various levels (of definitions and of regulations) are often inconsistent with one another, and, on the other, that there is no insight on the consequences that may arise from the fact that foreign investments are made by entities that are not only public, but sovereign, a key qualification factor.

This factor, that qualifies SWFs, is moving the conventional trends. So far, the foreign investments made by states through indirect vehicles like the SOEs have been subject in recipient states to private law. Using a series of instruments, the direct or indirect public ownership of the investor was neutralised. In the case of the SWFs, the 'public' nature of ownership becomes 'sovereign' too. Therefore, SWFs are not just one more vehicle used by states to invest abroad: they 'are' the state. They are identified with the state because they often do not have legal personality of their own, or they have it but lack the appropriate governance devices to guarantee their independence from the state in the decision-making process about investments. Hence, the 'private investor model' hardly fits SWFs, as it is not reasonable (nor actually possible) to neutralise the 'sovereign element'.

---

37 See for reference the CRS (Congressional Research Service) Report for the Congress of 22 January 2008, *China's Sovereign Wealth Fund*, especially pp. 1 and 17.

38 R. Gilson and C. Milhaupt, 'Sovereign Wealth Funds and Corporate Governance: a Minimalist Response to the New Mercantilism', n. 27 above.

39 See ch. 4 for a specific analysis and ch. 5 for an assessment of instrument effectiveness.

The 'sovereign' nature of SWFs makes them different from the other 'genera' in the FGCI 'family' in many respects. For example, it gives a new light on a profile that so far had been relevant both for national or EU regulations and for international law: the conflict of interest of a state that is at the same time a regulator and an operator in the regulated market. The issue was addressed in Europe with the practice of golden shares in the nineties.[40] But now this conflict takes a new face: the regulator/operator state does not exercise its dual role in the domestic market, but regulates internally and makes investments abroad subject to the regulations of another state. Therefore, the (economic, financial, political) conflict of interest[41] changes its perspective, because the competitive edge of the investor state in the foreign market is given by the possibility to change the rules not in the recipient state, but in the state of origin, without the influence of public opinion in the host country. This aspect may impair the effectiveness of host state rules aimed at neutralising the public character of an investor, and calls for new solutions.

Another example of the novelty brought by SWFs in the relationships between host states and 'sovereign' investors is the ability of the sovereign investor to affect home state/host state relationships, for instance by interfering through diplomatic channels or supporting the coming into force of a bilateral investment treaty between the two countries providing adequate guarantees to the investment made (or that the investor plans to make). The conflict of interest that appears here cannot be resolved by the host state downstream, and no-one would expect the home state to settle it upstream. Therefore it must be dealt with in international law.

Our work aims at giving guidelines for a legal environment that consider all the elements highlighted above, starting from the preliminary assumption that the analysis should focus on both the sovereignty and the investment element, and that purposes also play a decisive role. To achieve this result, a definition of SWFs should be provided and an adequate classification pattern should be developed, considering SWFs as belonging to a category (the genus) broad enough to encompass all its (several) 'species', and determining the 'family' which SWFs and other similar 'genera' belong to (Part I).

Part II will deal with the question of whether specific rules are needed for both SWF and host states. This assessment will take the start from the

---

[40] Ch.4, para. 2.2.3.

[41] E. Truman (*Sovereign Wealth Funds: Threat or Salvation*, n. 9 above, p. 56) states that potential conflicts between SWFs and markets, between SWFs and governments, and between governments themselves, because of the activities of SWFs, are indeed real.

assumption that the interest to be protected is that of market freedom, which might be impaired by the 'sovereign' nature of SWFs. Hence, the rules (those applicable to SWFs and those applicable to host states, in Chapters 3 and 4 respectively) should meet the classic requirements of proportionality, transparency and non-discrimination.

Part III will deal with a matter that the literature has so far neglected, i.e. the bilateral relationship between the investment's home state and the host state. SWFs are sovereign entities; in some cases they even lack a separate legal personality, and they often are under the direct control of the government, or of the king or the royal family. Hence, two questions arise: whether the home state can invoke state immunity for its SWFs' operations (avoiding inquiries on or sanctioning of illegal activities carried out by the SWF), and whether a SWF can challenge – on grounds of immunity – the restrictive measures adopted by host states. If state immunity for deeds committed by an SWF might fall within the scope of conventional rules, claiming state immunity to protect a SWF from a restrictive measure of the host state – the most important circumstance for our purposes – would be a totally new case. Therefore all the implications of the case should be reviewed, from the conventional to the more recent ones (Chapter 5).

The second aspect related to the bilateral relationship between the investment's home state and the host state pertains to the subject of Bilateral Investment Treaties (BITs), that might represent in theory a residual form of protection for SWFs, when state immunity cannot be claimed. This part of the work (Chapter 6) will be aimed at assessing whether the protection offered by BITs to foreign investments may be claimed by the SWFs, and in case to what an extent, and whether it may be considered appropriate. The recent practice of BITs, that shows a significant increase in the number of treaties entered into in the last decade but also a (consequent) increase in related controversies, might give useful indications for the purposes of this work.

2. SWFs: definition and classification

The debate about the SWFs seems to lack what should instead be a logical premise of regulating the activities of home states, host states and international organisations: a shared definition of a sovereign wealth fund. A definition is necessary for at least two reasons. First: it is obvious that the decision about whether – and, in case, how – a phenomenon should be regulated cannot be taken regardless of its preliminary qualification. Otherwise, any *ex-post* definition might be applied to just suit a set of rules that were already imposed (and that might not be the best ones). Second: any specific measure that, on one hand, imposes constraints on SWFs activity and, on the other, impairs the freedom of recipient states to protect specific enterprises of industrial sectors from the investments of other states would only be justified if the SWFs' peculiar nature is such as to differentiate them very clearly from other types of investors.

Several qualifications for SWFs are found in literature, especially economic, sometimes incompatible with one another. Those international institutions that have coded best practices for the funds (the IMF in particular) have put together existing definitions in order to broaden as much as possible the concept and consequently the scope of application of the rules they propose. Conversely, the OECD, that has deferred its guidelines for host states, has totally overlooked the issue of definitions. These different approaches have not facilitated the solution of the problem so far; but the question of definitions remains a priority above the regulatory aspect and should therefore be sorted out before questioning about applicable rules.

1. THE DEFINITIONS IN LITERATURE

The initial quantitative growth of SWF investments is currently followed by a qualitative change that deserves attention. The importance of the definition conundrum is then self-evident, in order to give proper qualification to the phenomenon and assess if SWFs can be classified by activity, purpose, or instruments employed. A definition also allows to check whether regulations are appropriate and feasible, assess the efficacy of those already adopted and possibly find the most appropriate ones.

Classification proposals are many, but do not seem to be all equally effective. A recurring solution is the definition by exclusion, i.e. to identify a sovereign fund by first excluding what it is not. However, to consider any organisation of state foreign investment other than reserve management by national banks as a SWF is too general and hardly useful.[1]

Therefore, we will need to review the definitions found in the economic literature and those given by international institutions and verify their appropriateness and efficacy. Then, we will try to define SWFs in a way useful to describe the current scenario and compatible with it.

1.1 Functional Definitions

According to some authors, SWFs are supposed to be a pool of domestic assets owned and managed by governments to achieve a variety of economic and financial objectives, including the accumulation and management of reserve assets, the stabilisation of macroeconomic effects and the transfer of wealth across generations. This first definition underscores both the subjective element (state ownership and management) and the objective one (activity and purposes), but it is too general, as some use it to include government pension funds,[2] while others – based on the same assumption – exclude them.[3]

---

[1] One example is US Undersecretary for International Affairs Clay Lowery, who in 2007 defined sovereign wealth funds as 'a government investment vehicle which is funded by foreign exchange assets, and which manages these assets separately from official reserves'. A definition by elimination is also given by R. Gilson and C. Milhaupt, 'Sovereign wealth funds and corporate governance: a minimalist response to the new mercantilism' [2009] *Stanford Law Review* 1345–69, 1345: according to them 'one way to define sovereign wealth funds is by exclusion: SWFs are sovereign investment vehicles that are not central banks, monetary authorities in charge of foreign reserves, or national pension funds, unless they are financed by commodities exports'. Equally vague for the purpose of classification is the definition given by C. Balding, *A Portfolio Analysis of Sovereign Wealth Funds* (Working paper, University of California, Irvine, 6 June 2008) p. 5, where SWFs are defined as 'a set of assets controlled by one government, that do not correspond to explicit liabilities and that are invested in order to obtain in the long term a yield above the risk free rate. The sources of these assets may be diverse, from income from the sales of natural resources in the case of oil exporting countries to reserves made up of accumulated balance of trade and financial surpluses'. For a critical comment on this approach see: S. Jen, *The definition of a Sovereign Wealth Fund* (Morgan Stanley, Report, March 2007).

[2] E. Truman, *Sovereign Wealth Funds: the Need for Greater Transparency and Accountability* (Peterson Institute for International Economics, 2007), but also S. Kern, *Sovereign Wealth Funds – State Investment on the Rise* (Deutsche Bank Research, 2007).

According to others, sovereign wealth funds can be classified on the basis of their liabilities;[4] a variation from this theory emphasises the relevance of accountability, both private and public, internal and external.[5] Actually, while a relevant element for a definition and a classification, both liability and accountability can hardly be considered in themselves an adequate and useful tool for interpreting the whole SWF phenomenon.

One scholar tries to distinguish, for definition purposes, between international reserves, public pension funds, SOEs and SWFs.[6] In explaining the peculiar features of each of these instruments, the author recognises in some cases they may mix up, compromising the analysis; for instance, pension funds may use sovereign funds (and vice versa) to

---

[3] V. Fotak, B. Bortolotti and W. Megginson, *The financial impact of sovereign wealth fund investments in listed companies* (Working Paper, University of Oklahoma, March 2008) pp. 2 *ff*. The authors note that there is no agreement in literature 'as to whether the SWF category should include stabilization and risk management funds or only funds whose main purpose is generating returns; estimates of total assets under control of SWFs vary greatly according to the accepted definition'. Other purposes, for example, are mentioned in the definition provided by A. Razanov, 'Who holds the wealth of nations?', in (2005) 15 *Central Banking Journal* 4, according to whom SWFs (which he was the first to define this way) 'are neither traditional public-pension funds nor reserve assets supporting national currencies' but rather pursue either one of the following objectives: 'insulate the budget and economy from excess volatility in revenues, help monetary authorities sterilize unwanted liquidity, build up savings for future generations, or use the money for economic and social development'.

[4] A. Razanov, *Sovereign Wealth Funds: defining liabilities* (Working Paper, State Street Global Advisor 2007). He thinks of four different types of profiles: contingent liabilities, typical of stabilisation funds; fixed future liabilities, typical of national pension reserve funds; mixed liabilities (i.e. perpetual capital with interim outflows); open-ended liabilities (i.e. effectively no contractually attached liabilities). But at the end, according to the author liability profiling requires asking two questions: what are the resources of the fund, and what are the intended use of funds, namely the objective and the finalist element respectively.

[5] A. Gelpren ('Sovereignty, accountability, and the wealth fund governance conundrum', in [2011] *Asian Journal of International Law*, forthcoming), differentiates between: public internal accountability (SWFs answer to elected officials or to the monarch); private internal accountability (SWFs answer to shareholders, creditors, stakeholders); public external accountability (a duty to adhere to international norms); and private external accountability (SWFs are subject to host country laws). Actually, this classification does not seem to explain properly the way states and SWFs operate, while it is partially useful for a definition or a classification.

[6] R. Kimmitt, 'Public footprints in private markets – sovereign wealth funds and the world economy' [2008] *Foreign Affairs* n. 1, pp. 119–30.

make investments abroad. There would also be a sub-distinction within the category of SWFs, between those based on raw materials and on cash transfers from official foreign currency reserves.[7] While the former may have various purposes, including stabilisation of tax revenues, cross-generational savings, equilibrium of the balance of payment, the latter are aimed mostly to reducing internal debt.

Another functional classification is given by those[8] who group SWFs into five main categories: (i) stabilising SWFs (to stabilise national income across different periods and reduce the impact of accidental income fluctuations over economy and fiscal budget); (ii) offsetting SWFs (to assist the central bank to channel forex reserve, intervene in the forex market and absorb excessive liquidity); (iii) saving SWFs (to stabilise national wealth across generations and save up for future generations); (iv) preventive SWFs (to prevent national social and economic crisis and promote the smooth socio-economic development); (v) strategic SWFs (to support national development strategy, optimise asset allocation globally, nurture world-class businesses and better serve the national interest in international economic activities).

Other authors merely produce lists: of resources used to set up the funds (commodity/non commodity, raw materials or balance of trade surpluses[9]); of purposes (revenue stabilisation, cross-generational saving, pension system funding, yield optimisation, diversification of investments); of strategies (allocation of different assets); of target investment areas (financial or industrial).[10]

Others do not go beyond recognising that SWFs should meet at least three minimum requirements, taken as the common basis of their various typologies, namely that they: (i) are state-owned; (ii) have no significant liabilities; and (iii) are managed separately from the rest of the central

---

[7] This distinction is also used by D. Siniscalco, 'Governi alle porte – crisi del credito e fondi sovrani' in *Mercato, Concorrenza, Regole* (2008) pp. 75–86, at p. 81.

[8] C. Chao, *The rise of Global Sovereign Wealth Fund*, in *Modern Bankers* (2006) v. 10.

[9] These are two general categories of 'commodity' and 'non commodity' SWFs. Among the former are SWFs of Norway, UAE, Qatar, Bahrain, Chile; among the latter: China and Singapore.

[10] C.B. Delacour, *Les Fonds Souverains – Ces nouveax acteurs de l'économie mondiale* (Paris, 2009); S. Cehajic, *Sovereign Wealth Funds: Contingent Risks and a Laissez-Faire Approach Complemented with a 'Just in Case' Reactive Regulatory Framework* (available at: http://papers.ssrn.com/sol3/papers.cfm?abstract_id=1494291 (accessed 3 April 2011)). SWFs invest in long-term government bonds, corporate bonds, equities real estate, private equity and hedge funds.

bank's reserves.[11] According to others the three common requirements should instead be: ownership, source of funding, purpose and style of investment.[12] These latter three requirements are thought to be sufficient to distinguish SWFs from government pension funds (GPFs), monetary authorities and state-owned enterprises (SOEs).[13]

Others again suggest a classification of hybrid forms of state investments, which are assumed to include SWFs in one or more (broad) categories, such as: (i) central banks, (ii) stabilisation funds, (iii) public pension funds, (iv) government investment corporations, and (v) state-owned enterprises.[14]

1.2 The Differences Between SOEs and SWFs

Others focus on the distinction between SWFs and SOEs.[15] According to most of the observers, the main characteristics that differentiate the former from the latter are the source of their funding, their function, the form of their respective investments: SWFs by portfolio investments, SOEs by Foreign Direct Investments (FDIs, implying the control of the company).[16] Conversely, one author concludes that in spite of the

---

[11] R. Beck and M. Fidora, *The Impact of Sovereign Wealth Funds on Global Financial Markets* (Occasional Paper, European Central Bank, 2008) at p. 6.

[12] X. Ping – C. Chao, *The Theoretical Logic of Sovereign Wealth Funds*, China Investment Corporation paper, 2009. According to them, an SWF is 'a market-oriented and professional investment body owned and managed by a state's central government, which uses mainly foreign exchange reserves and export revenues to make overseas investment and seeks to maximize long term return. The management of such a body should be independent from the passive forex reserve management as exercised by monetary authorities to stabilize the currency'.

[13] However, it is clear that these requirements are not enough to outline a differentiation. For example, the authors distinguish SWFs from SOEs on the basis that 'the former is held by the central government and is funded by forex reserve and export revenues; the latter is held by the central or local government and is funded by the government grants and corporate profits. In terms of legal structure, SOEs are corporations regulated by the general company law while SWFs may take three forms: a pool of assets, a legal entity under a specific public law, or a legal entity under the general company law'. Obviously, none of these differences is structural or necessary and might therefore change any time.

[14] E.F. Greene and B.A. Yeager, 'Sovereign Wealth Funds – A Measured Assessment' [2008] *Capital Markets Law Journal* 247–74.

[15] L. Catà Backer, 'Sovereign Investing in Times of Crisis: Global Regulation of Sovereign Wealth Funds, State Owned Enterprises and the Chinese Experience' [2009] *Transnational Law and Contemporary Problems* 101–228.

[16] L. Catà Backer, Ibid. on page 109, the author explains that '[L]ike SWFs, SOEs have begun to invest in economic markets abroad. More importantly,

differences,[17] a regulatory standard should be reached that may neutralise the choice by the states to use a vehicle rather than another.[18] He suggests to replace the traditional distinction between public and private with that of regulation and participation, applying the same rules to SOEs and SWFs abroad, where states are only operators and can not regulate.[19]

Actually, while one can agree on the need to overcome the 'private investor model' tailor-made to public entities, one cannot deny that there are many substantial differences between SWFs and SOEs. As for the subjective element (the ownership), both SWFs and SOEs are controlled by governments, but while the former is totally owned by the state, the latter can be partially controlled, by central or local governments. Furthermore, SOEs are separate entities with legal personality, while this is not necessarily true for SWFs. Moreover, SOEs are accountable to their shareholders, SWFs also to their stakeholders and the public opinion (even differently according both to their purposes and the level of democracy of their home state). Finally, only SOEs (not also SWFs) must

---

unlike sovereign wealth funds, whose activities do not generally seek controlling interests in investment targets, SOE investments may more often have as their object the acquisition of control of a private economic entity operating or based abroad. That has raised some significant concerns that have flowed from SOE interventions in foreign economies to the activities of SWFs'.

17 In particular, as for funding sources, the difference would be in that 'the former is held by the central government and is funded by forex reserves and export revenues; the latter is held by the central or local government and is funded by the government grants and corporate profits . . . on a superficial level, the difference between SWFs and SOEs is obvious: it is the same that between any type of investment fund and any type of company. But in reality the difference is not that obvious . . . Yet, SOEs can invest, and SWFs can acquire controlling interests in operating entities, and thus become, at least indirectly, SOEs'. (L. Catà Backer, n. 15 above, pp. 155 *ff*).

18 On p. 118 the author says that 'it may not make sense to segregate SWF regulation from other investment vehicles, and that it may be possible for a state to employ a policy of politically motivated interventions in foreign markets and markets for control that is, simultaneously, financially motivated'. On p. 140 he clarifies that '[T]his might suggest a regulatory framework based on the regulatory or commercial objectives of investment irrespective of the ownership of the investment vehicle'.

19 L. Catà Backer, 'Sovereign Investing in Times of Crisis: Global Regulation of Sovereign Wealth Funds, State Owned Enterprises and the Chinese Experience', n. 15 above, pp. 101–228; L. Catà Backer, 'The Norwegian Sovereign Wealth Fund: between private and public' [2009] *Georgetown Journal of International Law* 1271–80; L. Catà Backer, 'Sovereign Wealth Funds as regulatory chameleons: the Norwegian Sovereign Wealth Funds and public global governance through private global investment' [2010] *Georgetown Journal of International Law* 425–500.

comply with home and host state company rules as well as consolidated international standards.

As for the objective element (investments) SWFs make financial investments, while SOEs industrial ones. This circumstance has three consequences. First, an SWF will probably have a more passive role than a corporation in the participated company. Second, SOEs aim at controlling the participated company, while SWFs investments hardly exceed the 10 per cent of company shares, and few SWFs admit that their investment strategies involve the acquisition of a controlling interest in foreign companies. Third, SOEs, unlike SWFs, do not invest necessarily on a long-term horizon.

Finally, as for the finalistic element (purposes), SOEs pursue a private (company) interest, while SWFs a public welfare (saving fund for future generations, stabilising national income, prevent social and economic crisis, etc).

The above-mentioned differences between SWFs and SOEs are important in our work's perspective because they make it impossible to simply apply to SWFs both home or host national company law and international standards. Indeed, all those rules aim at neutralising the 'public' factor, pursuing the so-called 'private investor model', while SWFs are not 'public' but 'sovereign', and their investment cannot be treated as a private one. Moreover, SWFs often do not have a separate legal personality, and anyway they are not companies. Furthermore, SWFs aim at public objects, not only at maximising profits (as a private investor is supposed to do). Hence, one should admit that company laws are not applicable to SWFs. Two questions then arise: if a specific regulation for SWFs is necessary or even useful, and how to deal with a more sophisticated scenario in which SWFs and SOEs are connected and states use equally either instruments to reach their goals. In such a case, a different regulatory environment for SWFs and SOEs could have a significant impact.

1.3 The 'Five Pillars' Definition

Some scholars[20] give a more exhaustive definition based on the five main elements that are supposed to characterise a SWF, identified as sovereign – i.e. totally owned by a government, with high foreign currency exposure, no explicit liabilities, high risk tolerance, long investment horizon. These elements may distinguish SWFs from official foreign currency reserves, government pension funds, or hedge funds. In fact, forex reserves are

---

20 S. Jen, *The Definition of a Sovereign Wealth Fund*, n. 1 above.

only in foreign currency and are characterised by low risk tolerance, short time horizon, a certain degree of government accountability in funding exchange interventions. Government pension funds have instead an express or implicit system of accountability related to pension constraints, and a low propensity to risk. Lastly, hedge funds have a very short time horizon and are not necessarily associated with a government (on the contrary, usually they are not). As far as literature is concerned, at the moment this definition appears to be the most accurate.

According to one variant of the 'five pillars definition', SWFs are investment funds or other investment vehicles expressly created and owned by governments for macroeconomic purposes. They hold, manage and run their activities to achieve financial targets, adopting investment strategies (also) in foreign activities. They are characterised by five distinctive features: they are owned by a sovereign state, their investment portfolio is in foreign currency, they have a low level of indebtedness, are separated from the central bank's official reserves and operated according to different criteria, and aim at obtaining yields above the risk-free rate.[21]

1.4 The Definitions Misconception (Definition by Classification)

The misunderstanding arising from a review of the definitions found in literature originates from two factors. First, definition overlaps classification. There are those who define and those who classify. There are also those who classify and then define. Instead, a correct methodology approach would be to give a definition and then classify consistently, according to the purposes of the analysis. Second, definitions emphasise the subjective or the objective element respectively: ownership or activity.[22] All in all, SWFs are 'private sovereign entities' (entities with sovereign owners operating in private sectors). The discussion in literature is all about this dilemma. On the subjective side, ownership, and hence the sovereign character of the fund, is taken as reference.[23] On the objective

---

21 A. Quadrio Curzio and V. Miceli, *I fondi sovrani – I nuovi attori della finanza mondiale: opportunità o rischi?* (Bologna, 2009).

22 According to L. Catà Backer (*Sovereign Investing in Times of Crisis*, n. 15 above), those who focus on the subjective elements are formalists, while the others are functionalist. This classification is not fully convincing, as ownership, accountability and governance are crucial elements, not saying that for jurists form is substance.

23 Again L. Catà Backer, n. 15 above, p. 123: '[t]he focus of the character of the ownership of these investment vehicles produces an identity between the sovereign and the investment vehicle. Because the state is the owner, the fund *is* the state'.

side, prominence is given to the commercial nature of the activity, pointing out that where operating a private economic activity, all the players in the market should be treated as private, irrespective of their ownership.

The many and variegated solutions proposed in literature pay toll to their ideological premises and lead to contradictory results. The fact is, we are facing a sovereign entity engaged in typically private activities. This is a conundrum we may clash with many times during our research, as it is relevant from the standpoint: of regulating fund activity; of constraints to the measures that host states may implement; of state immunity and of the other forms of investment protection provided for in bilateral international treaties. If this dual characteristic is overlooked, by giving relevance to one factor rather than the other we run the risk of losing sight of the innovative aspect of this phenomenon. Furthermore, this (conflicting) perspective (subjective–objective, private–public, regulatory–participatory) hides some errors, that we can see as a syllogism. The major premise is that the two elements we should consider in giving a definition are not ownership and activity, but ownership and purposes. As shown above, purposes influence investment activity, not the opposite.[24] The minor premise is that there is not a conflict between the two, subjective, cornerstone elements of SWFs; they all contribute to a definition. The corollary is that it is not reasonable to apply a 'private investor model' to SWFs, as both the decisive elements are on a subjective side: states pursuing public welfare are not supposed to operate as a private company.

Hence, no dualistic (subjective–objective, private–public, participation–regulation) distinction can be correct. The peculiarity of SWFs is exactly their duality of sovereign ownership and public welfare objects. We purposely refer here to the sovereign rather than to the public nature of the fund, because it is what is relevant for the purpose both of active and passive regulation and for protecting investments. This will also help to overcome the distinction private-public that today does not make much sense in absolute terms, and it is only likely to generate misunderstanding.

Therefore, a correct methodology should consider the ownership and purpose components equally, and admit that SWFs are a new instrument under many respects. They should then be defined and classified without leaving out either of their subjective or objective aspects only to have

24 Once the proper purposes are specified, identifying investments is nothing but a consequence. A. Popova ('Sovereign Wealth Funds: To Be or Not to Be Is Not the Question; Which One to Choose, Is' [2009] *Georgetown Journal of International Law* 1191–1206) explained with details the errors made in Russia when SWFs were used to make investments non complying with funds stated purposes.

them fall under one of the existing classification. The purpose aspect, currently almost neglected by scholars, should also be given the appropriate importance.

2. THE DEFINITION IN THE INTERNATIONAL ORGANISATIONS' PRACTICE

International organisations have so far followed a different approach: the International Monetary Fund (IMF) has worked, among other things, at finding a definition for SWFs both publishing papers and participating in a working group that has developed specific guidelines for state funds (International Working Group – IWG). The OECD instead has not provided a clear definition yet. This is no minor want, as the discipline that host states are supposed to adopt legitimately, regardless of a definition of the regulated subject, might grant to the states themselves an uncontrolled discretionary power.[25]

2.1 The IMF and OECD Definitions

The IMF provides a definition and a functional or purpose-based classification according to which SWFs are investment funds operated by governments to achieve various objectives, created by allocating funds intended for long-term investments.[26]

---

[25] The final report of the investments committee on sovereign wealth funds and host state policies was expected to be issued in the Spring of 2009 (a preliminary report was presented in June 2008) but at the moment of writing this book was not published yet. The working group was formed by 30 OECD member states, 10 non-member states that have however adopted OECD instruments in the investments area (Argentina, Brazil, Chile, Egypt, Israel, Romania, Slovenia, Lithuania, Latvia, Estonia) and four other non-member countries involved in the project (South Africa, China, India and Indonesia).

[26] See the Paper published by the International Monetary Fund *Sovereign Wealth Funds – A work agenda*, of 29 February 2008, where the following definition is proposed: 'SWFs are special purpose public investment funds, or arrangements. These funds are owned or controlled by the government, and hold, manage, or administer assets primarily for medium- to long-term macroeconomic and financial objectives (these in principle include: (i) fiscal stabilisation funds; (ii) saving funds; (iii) reserve investment corporations; (iv) development funds; and (v) pension reserve funds – those without explicit pension liabilities – while they exclude inter alia: (a) government-employee pension funds; (b) social security funds; (c) government lending funds; and (d) government-owned banks). The Funds are commonly established out of official foreign currency operations, the

This definition is not entirely satisfactory, for at least two reasons. First, SWFs are not only operated but (totally) owned by governments. Second, this classification would not distinguish SWFs from other similar forms of state investment and would not remove the doubts about the most controversial questions. And, as the IMF has stated, a classification based on investment strategies is equally inadmissible, as they may be extremely diverse and can change over time.[27] Another limit lies in the fact that the definition is founded on an assumption (i.e. the difference between pension funds and sovereign funds) which is still a matter of discussion.[28]

Based on the above definition, the IMF classification provides for only three categories of sovereign wealth funds: stabilisation funds, savings funds and reserve investment companies. Stabilisation funds have an anti-cyclical function and are used by the government of countries with economies based on natural resources and agricultural produce to neutralise price fluctuations in the international market and hence stabilise taxation revenues. Due to their function, these funds keep a conservative behaviour on the markets. Examples of sovereign funds with these characteristics and functions are the Russia Stabilization Fund and the Kazakhstan National Oil Fund.

Savings funds have instead long-term objectives that consist mainly of converting the resources from non-renewable sources into a broader set of assets in order to minimise risks and be a guarantee for future generation. So their investments are more variegated, from bonds to equities, from real estate to hedge funds, from commodities to agricultural

---

proceeds of privatisations, fiscal surpluses, and/or receipts resulting from commodity exports. These funds employ a set of investment strategies which include investments in foreign financial assets'.

[27] Again in the Paper *Sovereign Wealth Funds – A work agenda*, n. 26 above, p. 9, we read that 'SWFs are a heterogeneous group of investors that apply a wide range of investment strategies reflecting their different objectives. When executing their strategic asset allocation (SAA), some SWFs invest solely in publicly-listed financial assets (e.g. bonds and equities), while others invest across all major asset classes, including alternative investments. Some SWFs invest relative to market indices and sometimes put additional caps on the maximum holding of each company's shares with a view to ensuring diversification. Other SWFs that aim at maximizing absolute returns over longer time horizons may shift between different asset classes and acquire larger stakes in specific companies that they see as profitable investments'.

[28] About the reasons for the differentiation see IMF, *Sovereign Wealth Funds – A work agenda*, n. 26 above, p. 27, and also A. Blundell-Wignall, Y. Hu, J. Yermo, *Sovereign wealth and pension fund issues* (OECD Working Papers on insurance and private pensions, 2008) n. 14.

produce. Examples of these are the Abu Dhabi Investment Authority, the Kuwait Investment Authority, the Singapore Government Investment Corporation, the China Investment Corporation.

Reserve investment corporations are funds used to reduce the opportunity costs of maintaining foreign reserve surpluses or of implementing high-yield investment policies; these are characterised by more aggressive strategies and more lack of transparency (examples of these are Singapore Temasek, Qatar Investment Authority, Abu Dhabi Mudabala).

While, on one hand, the categories identified by the IMF are clear, as each one – if the classification proposed in literature as above is applied – has different risk propensity, investment horizon, reserve allocation, tools and constraints, it is actually hard to distinguish them when it comes to reality: a fund may be created as a stabilisation fund and then change its function (and strategy) when it reaches an endowment far greater than needed to stabilise the market.[29] Therefore, the classification proposed in IMF studies may be a good starting point, especially for the relevance it gives to the purpose element, but not the conclusion of the review.[30]

In 2008 the IMF created a working group (IWG – International Working Group on Sovereign Wealth Funds, then evolved in a lasting International Forum) composed of high officials of the IMF and representatives of some leading sovereign wealth funds, that has adopted guidelines (the so-called 'Santiago principles') and formulated an accurate definition. The definition is theoretical,[31] and emphasises the following aspects to qualify a fund

---

[29] M. Weiss, Congressional Research Service – Report for Congress: *Sovereign Wealth Funds: Background and policy issues for Congress*, January 2008, p. 7. Besides, sovereign wealth funds are derived from funds established for other purposes. V. Fotak, B. Bortolotti and W. Megginson, in *The financial impact of sovereign wealth fund investments in listed companies*, n. 3 above, pp. 4–5, admit that 'in the majority of cases, SWFs are an evolution of funds whose primary purpose was revenue stabilization. That is, governments whose revenue streams are heavily dependent on the value of one single underlying commodity have engaged in diversification of investments with the goal of stabilizing revenues'.

[30] It should also be noted that it is still difficult to take the various forms of fund management individually: certain funds are run by politicians, others by components of executive families (for instance in Persian Gulf countries), by ministries of finances or directly by central banks. This further classification criterion is therefore of relative usefulness.

[31] The first part of the definition (Appendix I to 'Santiago Principles') identifies sovereign funds as 'special purpose investment funds or arrangements, owned by the general government. Created by the general government for macroeconomic purposes, SWFs hold, manage, or administer assets to achieve financial objectives, and employ a set of investment strategies which include investing in foreign financial assets'.

as sovereign: subjective aspect (owned by a government), objective aspect (activity consisting of the management and administration of equity investments including abroad) and purpose aspect (aiming at developing macro-economic policies).[32] The IWG lists, by way of example, certain patterns followed for fund creation[33] and certain cases that do not fall within the category.[34] The IWG definition excludes, directly or implicitly, funds operating in domestic markets, central banks and monetary authorities with excess foreign exchange reserves, and funds owned by sovereign rulers.[35]

2.2 The Limits of IMF Definition and Classification

The definition given by the International Working Group (IWG) gives a clarification and raises perplexities. The clarification lies in that the rules (general accepted principles and practices) do not apply to those funds that do meet the definition but only invest in domestic enterprises or activities and not abroad. This principle gives a clearer picture and allows for a further distinction; in fact, according to recent analyses, there are several state funds that invest mostly in domestic businesses.[36] The costs of obtaining compliance in terms of transparency and governance

---

[32] The appendix to the 'Santiago Principles' specifies for definition purposes that 'established by the general government for macroeconomic purposes, SWFs are created to invest government funds to achieve financial objectives, and (may) have liabilities that are only broadly defined, thus allowing SWFs to employ a wide range of investment strategies with a medium- to long-term timescale. SWFs are created to serve a different objective than, for example, reserve portfolios held only for traditional balance of payments purposes. While SWFs may include reserve assets, the intention is not to regard all reserve assets as SWFs'.

[33] In the second part of the definition it is said that 'the SWFs are commonly established out of balance of payments surpluses, official foreign currency operations, the proceeds of privatizations, fiscal surpluses, and/or receipts resulting from commodity exports'.

[34] In particular, the working group states that 'this definition excludes, *inter alia*, foreign currency reserve assets held by monetary authorities for the traditional balance of payments or monetary policy purposes, operations of state-owned enterprises in the traditional sense, government-employee pension funds, or assets managed for the benefit of individuals'.

[35] According to A. Rozanov, *What is 'Sovereign Wealth' Anyway?* (AsianSIL Working Paper 2009/45), the exclusion of funds operating primarily on domestic markets looks artificial, the excess portion of reserves could easily be managed as sovereign wealth, and the line between sovereign and private wealth is quite blurry in certain countries.

[36] C. Balding, *A portfolio analysis of sovereign wealth funds,* n. 1 above; P. Rose, 'Sovereigns as Shareholders' (2008) *North Carolina Law Review* 83–150.

with international guidelines might lead these funds, or a few of them, to keep on focusing on investments in their country of origin or, at most, in a reference region, playing a more powerful role as development drivers (so much so that the new category of Sovereign Development Funds is starting to be recognised).[37]

The perplexities lie in the fact that the definition is maybe too descriptive; while it does provide useful elements for classification, there still is confusion about conclusions. For example, at subjective level, considering the guidelines as applicable to state-owned funds would leave the public audit issue entirely open, as it would exclude those forms of resource gathering and management operated by states that are, under many respects, very similar to sovereign wealth funds (from foreign currency reserves used to manage monetary or trade policies to public company activities, to government pension funds). The subjective limits that derive from a functional definition focused on activities and purposes might narrow the scope of the provisions. The compromise reached in terms of definition is therefore only partially satisfactory.

2.3 The Consequences of the Lack of a Shared Notion

The lack of a single, clear and specific definition of sovereign wealth funds, in the economic literature and in the practice of international institutions, that can differentiate these funds from other similar ones (it is still unclear whether state pension funds belong or not to this category) prevents any specific regulation from being applied. The reason why it is important to provide a definition – considering the proposals of economists and also developing a relevant definition for legal purposes – is that, for the time being, the literature has not proposed any suggestion for a regulation of sovereign wealth funds, different from the rules applied, for instance, to government pension funds or foreign currency reserves managed by central banks, or hedge funds. These specific rules, if any, should be based on the significant subjective and objective differences that may arise from a legal analysis of these funds. This would also allow to overcome the limits of a 'purely economic' definition arising (among other things) from the inefficacy of 'static' solutions that do not take into account the possibility

[37] J. Santino, *Sovereign Development Funds*, OECD Development Centre, *Policy Insights* no. 58, April 2008; E. Truman (*Sovereign Wealth Funds: Threat or Salvation?*, Peterson Institute for International Economics, 2010, pp. 12–14) lists SWFs investing exclusively in domestic assets: Strategic Investment Fund in France; SWF of Brazil; Public Investment Fund in Saudi Arabia; Executive Yuan Development Fund in Taiwan.

that SWFs invest massively in speculative or private equity funds, using different vehicles to achieve the same goal, or convert themselves (as it already occurred in the past, as many sovereign wealth funds are a development of stabilisation funds).

According to the definitions suggested by the economic literature and international institutions, these funds may be classified by subjective factor (how they are created, where do resources come from, who controls them), objective factor (what they do, what investment strategies they follow[38]), or *raison d'être* (what their purpose is). The variety of classifications shows that there is no common standing, and that each definition depends on its intended purpose.

In order to provide a definition that may have relevance also in the legal framework, the purpose of and the need for such definition should be investigated. The common – and usually implicit – answer to this question is that a shared definition of SWFs is required in order to identify specific rules applicable to them. And specific rules are in turn required because general rules are considered inappropriate or insufficient, or only partially applicable, because the case presents specific issues.

3. THE DEFINITION AND CLASSIFICATION SUGGESTED

3.1 Our Proposed Definition

The analysis carried out so far allows for a more accurate definition. In fact, we have understood that SWFs are state investment vehicles that differ significantly from one another, so that there cannot be one all-inclusive definition. We should choose among the various options the one that suits best the goal we want to pursue. In our case, the definition is needed to meet the growing demand for regulation that derives from host state concerns. We may select true concerns among these, as distinguished from unjustified or generic ones. The main concern for host states is that sovereign funds may invest in companies operating in strategic sectors of the economy, in order not only to optimise the investment but also to take over those companies, affect their policies, obtain know-how. We concluded in previous paragraphs that to meet such a demand of regulation,

---

38 On the basis of this the IMF (see *Sovereign Wealth Funds – A Work Agenda*, n. 26 above, p. 26) distinguishes sovereign funds from public enterprises, pension funds and hedge funds.

both ownership (i.e. legal personality, governance, accountability) and purposes (connected to source of funding) elements should be taken in consideration.

Hence, an appropriate definition for SWFs may be the following:

> 'funds established, owned and operated by local or central governments, which investment strategies include the acquisition of equity interest in companies listed in international markets operating in sectors considered strategic by their countries of incorporation'.

Under a subjective profile, the definition proposed has, on one hand, the advantage of being a very broad one, which therefore does not exclude any of the funds reviewed in the first part of this work, and, on the other hand, is very specific in terms of attribution of a fund to a government. This way, no state fund may be excluded *per se*, in abstract terms, from the category of SWFs; the funds may be excluded from the SWF regulation (to which the definition is ancillary), if any, if they are not settled and owned by governments, or if they do not invest (even by statute) in companies considered strategic by host states. The legal structure and governance of the SWF will be meaningful for a subsequent classification.

Under an objective profile, the definition proposed is both accurate (it embodies both activity carried out and purpose sought by the operators), and flexible in its application. State funds not tied to similar strategies, with different purposes and that actually do not make this kind of investments, have no risk profile and need not be regulated. State funds (including those indirectly controlled by a government) will be subject to the rules applicable to SWFs only if and to the extent they make investments as described, showing those purposes and strategies. Finally, it also helps in settling measures host states can adopt, as they only should be applicable to funds investing in strategic sectors, that national laws should clearly list *a priori*.

Hence, we can submit a classification consistent with the definition proposed and then consider whether a specific regulation is required at all, or whether the existing ones (both at national and international level) can be considered sufficient or should be integrated.

3.2 The Resulting Classification

The classification we propose according to the definition provided is based on ownership and purposes, crucial distinctive elements that substitute the subjective/objective, public/private, regulatory/participatory ones.

As to the ownership profile, legal personality, governance and accountability appear to be adequate classification criteria. As to legal structure, a SWF may be independent or identify with the state; its legal personality may be either of civil or public law. Using this classification principle, we may include in one category all those SWFs that do not have a separate legal personality from their state of origin, i.e. the funds of Norway, Saudi Arabia, Canada (Alberta), Russia, Chile, Mexico. These funds are identified with the government. Other funds are separate legal entities: certain under public law (KIC in the Republic of Korea, KIA in Kuwait, QIA in Qatar, ADIA in United Arab Emirates) others under civil law (CIC in China, Temasek and GIC in Singapore).

As to governance, it depends on the legal structure: if the SWF is not a separate legal entity, the governing body may comprise only government officials, and operational independence is sought through the delegation of responsibility for the SWF's operational management to the central bank or a statutory management agency.[39] The governance of those funds that are independent entities should be explored to assess their actual degree of independence from the government. Indeed, all SWFs have a board, but while some are entirely government-controlled, others have mixed representations from the government and private experts and a few are even independent from the government and account to the Parliament.[40]

As to accountability, that is a consequence of both legal status and governance, funds can be accountable to elected officials, to the monarch, to stakeholders (public accountability), to shareholders and creditors (private accountability). Governance and legal structure influence private accountability, with reference to both shareholders and creditors, while public laws affect public accountability to stakeholders, citizens, taxpayers. Of course, transparency and, more generally, the level of democracy of the home state also influence SWFs' public accountability.[41]

---

39 C. Hummer, P. Kunzel and I. Petrova, *Sovereign Wealth Funds: Current Institutional and Operational Practices* (2008), available at: www.iwg-swf.org.

40 See JPMorgan Research, *Sovereign Wealth Funds: a bottom-up primer* (2008).

41 Interesting data have appeared about the answers given by the main SWFs in a survey. Most of the SWFs with a separate legal entity centralise investment policies, managerial and operational decisions through a board of directors or a steering committee. Where the SWF is not a separate legal entity, the Minister of Finance takes the responsibility of investments. SWFs' institutional framework often guarantees operational independence, ensuring their accountability both to the government and the public by requiring disclosure of audited financial reports and regular reporting to the Ministry of Finance and Parliament. For a detailed analysis of the survey, see: C. Hummer, P. Kunzel and I. Petrova, *Sovereign Wealth Funds: Current Institutional and Operational Practices*, n. 39 above.

With regard to the purposes profile, some investments are typically sovereign, i.e. aimed at providing specific guarantees to the community, while others are more general and aimed at diversifying and/or increasing the return on the investments. There may also be a correlation between purpose of the investment and sector chosen (financial institutions or industrial sectors). This form of classification is particularly useful if we consider that so far only the latter have given rise to concerns and to the demand for protectionist measures. The purpose element is also relevant to immunity protection issues. As we will see in Chapter 5, 'sovereign' purposes can, at certain circumstances, be considered a decisive factor in the application of direct and indirect immunity protection according to national rules and international treaties. Hence, we may distinguish between SWFs with stabilisation purposes (KIA in Kuwait, Reserve Fund in Russia, Libyan Investment Authority in Libya, the State General Stabilization Fund in Oman, the Oil Income Stabilization Fund in Mexico, the Economic and Social Stabilization Fund in Chile); those that pursue cross-generational savings (ADIA in United Arab Emirates, QIA in Qatar, the Norwegian Fund); those intended for financing pension programmes (the Russian National Wealth Fund, the Australian Future Fund, the Chilean Pension Reserves Fund). Then there are the SWFs with return-optimisation purposes (CIC in China, GIC in Singapore, KIC in Republic of Korea), diversification purposes (Temasek in Singapore, Khazanah in Malaysia, Public Investment Fund in Saudi Arabia, Mubadala in Abu Dhabi, ICD in Dubai, QIA in Qatar).

That said, the following classification may be outlined. One first category (a 'species' in the SWF genus) includes SWFs with separate legal entity and with an appropriate legal structure and governance, and a consequent clear private and public accountability. A second 'species' includes SWFs with separate legal personality but with legal structure and governance inadequate to guarantee their independence from the government in investment decision-making. A third 'species' includes SWFs without separate legal entity but with legal structure and governance adequate to guarantee decision-making autonomy. A fourth 'species' includes SWFs without separate legal entity and without adequate legal structure and governance. Each 'species' shows different degrees of compliance with international standards according to the purposes pursued.

Any SWF would fall in one of the four 'species' described above. The value of this classification is that it points at criteria that will in any case be functional to our research: (i) legal structure, formal separation – hence the importance of governance – from the government (which is relevant for the purpose of the immunity and the protection of the investment by means of BITs; see Chapters 5 and 6 respectively); and (ii) objective sought (important for the purposes of immunity because of the relevance of the commercial or non-commercial nature of the activities but also, in certain cases and under certain conditions, of the purpose). On the basis of the definition and classification provided, we can start researching 'active' and 'passive' SWF regulation.

PART II

SWFs' national and international regulation

3. Sovereign wealth funds' regulation

The economic literature suggests various forms of SWF activity regulation. International organisations have tried to identify the most appropriate one, because neutral for the market. However, there are three underlying misunderstandings that should be removed to begin with.

First, the proposal of a regulation for SWFs cannot avoid taking in consideration their qualification, and should be consistent with it. SWFs must be defined and then classified within basic categories. Thereafter, they can be regulated, where required. And the proposed regulation cannot be in conflict with the definition and classification suggested. While this assumption should be taken for granted, it is often ignored by scholars and analysts.

Second, as we saw in Chapter 1, the traditional conflict of interest between states both regulating (domestically) and investing (abroad) operates here in a very original way, applying to home states, SWFs and host states. Two consequences originate from this assumption. First, regulating SWFs requests rules not only in host states but also in home states: stand alone (home, or host) state measures run the risk of being ineffective. Second, absent an adequate multilateral system, home and host state measures should be consistent and coordinated.

Third, regulation is necessary where the market falls short. In the case of SWFs, market failure is still unproven – it might occur in the future. In spite of that, an SWF's regulation is often justified by host states' concerns that SWFs might make 'political' investments, try to acquire know-how, or aim at taking over, even indirectly, of companies working in strategic industries. According to the mainstream, these concerns exist insofar as the 'sovereign' nature, anomaly and peculiarity of these funds, exists: SWFs are sovereign funds acting as a private entity. Sovereigns in terms of ownership, privates in terms of activity. The 'sovereign' factor set aside, these concerns would by no means be justified in international markets. Hence, the only specific regulation one should need is the one required to 'neutralise' sovereign ownership.

The error in perspective is evident, for all that we have assumed in the previous chapters. The key factors for definition and classification are not sovereignty and investment, but sovereignty and purposes: the latter influences investments, that are nothing but a logic consequence. Hence, as ownership is sovereign and purposes are sovereign, it is not reasonable to demand regulation to neutralise SWFs' sovereign constitutive elements. It is also unreasonable to expect that SWFs act as private investors or even as private companies, because – as we have seen in section 1.2 of Chapter 2 – they differ both from private and public enterprises (SOEs). Therefore, if the application of the 'private investor model' is the final goal of SWF regulation, it is based on a mistake and doomed to fail.

The path we traced in Chapter 2 leads us to a different perspective. A regulation for SWFs could only be appropriate to address host states' concerns about SWFs' purposes. The fear is that states can control or influence a state company operating in strategic sectors. This is the main point, although not the only one. This is where we should start from.

At the end of Chapter 2 we suggested a way to interpret the current scenario. As not all SWFs are equal – on the contrary, they differ from one another – a classification consistent with our definition and functional to a possible regulation should originate a scale of values both for sovereignty and purposes. A regulation should apply only to those SWFs which are at the lower level of the scale, because they do not have (i) a legal personality, (ii) an adequate governance structure, or (iii) a sufficient level of accountability, and if (iv) they have speculative purposes. Such a regulation should aim at strengthening one or more of those elements, should be gradual, based on the principle of proportionality, and should deal only with really critical areas, which may vary according to the category each SWF falls in.

We will now review the proposals for a SWF's regulation formulated in economic and legal literature, and so far adopted by international organisations, to verify if and how these do match our framework. Finally, we will propose our solutions.

1. THE PROPOSALS FOUND IN LITERATURE

Some observers believe that the existing laws and regulations (competition policies included) can control foreign government investments on a national treatment basis, or applying the regulation on foreign investments in force.[1] Others suggest a policy response based on a reciprocal

[1] E. Greene, B. Yeager, 'Sovereign Wealth Funds: a measured assessment' [2008] *Capital Markets Law Journal* 247–74. *Contra*, E. Truman (*Sovereign Wealth Funds: Threat or Salvation?* (Peterson Institute for International Economics, 2010)), according to whom such regulation (i) would have to be broadly applied internationally, and (ii) would be difficult to apply because of the amorphic nature

treatment that seems to be impossible to define and apply, not considering that is it contrary to most of the multilateral and bilateral investment treaties in force (see Chapter 6 below).[2] Others suggest applying to SWFs one of the multilateral measures currently available, rather than adopting new guidelines and codes of ethics, or unilateral measures. Indeed, soft regulation is not binding, while unilateral solutions have evident limits, as they: (i) are likely to engender protectionist reactions, (ii) force investor states to bear high costs to comply with the required standards and reduce the efficiency of their actions, (iii) require host states to perform complex, expensive and often ineffective monitoring. However, there are many multilateral solutions offered by the economic literature and international institutions.

1.1 The 'Book of Rules' Model

One trend is based on developing models that impose constraints on all the critical aspects of SWFs. A minority considers that certain rules in the GATT treaties could already be applicable to foreign state investment funds.[3] According to most scholars, international regulation is lacking

---

of SWFs. Even if the author admits that a 'broad, comprehensive approach to government-controlled investments is an appropriate long-term goal', he concludes that 'it does not appear to be in the cards and, in any case, would only address one or two of the concerns about them – the potential pursuit of national, political or economic power objectives and, perhaps indirectly, concerns about market turmoil and uncertainty'.

[2] G. Lyons, *State capitalism: the rise of Sovereign Wealth Funds*, Standard Chartered Global research, 2007.

[3] A. Mattoo and A. Subramanian, *Currency undervaluation and sovereign wealth funds: a new role for the World Trade Organization*, Working Paper (WP 08-2), Peterson Institute, January 2008. In particular, according to the authors, obligations of home states are apparently set forth in Art. XVII GATT and in government procurement agreement (GPA). Art. XVII GATT prohibits to public companies to bring alterations to international markets, and particularly makes them subject to private investor, non-discrimination, transparency obligations. The government procurement agreement (GPA) adds to the non-discrimination obligation the requirement for a high level of transparency and makes all exceptions conditional on the commercial purpose of the investment. Neither of the solutions proposed appears to be completely efficacious. Art. XVII GATT imposes obligations to the host state and not the investor state, as it concerns regulatory or administrative measures on imports or exports made by private entities. The GPA has a dual limitation, *ratione materiae* (public contracts) and *ratione loci* (national territory of the host state). Therefore, in general, it is really difficult to apply GATT rules to direct state investments made through sovereign wealth funds, as the scope of application of these rules is limited to goods.

and specific multilateral guidelines should regulate SWFs. According to the mainstream, the rules should be based on four essential factors: investment goals and strategies, governance, transparency and behaviour of fund administrators.[4]

As regards goals and strategies, the standards should guarantee that fund activities are based on transparent objectives that allow to understand how the fund is established and administered by the investor; how the returns, if any, arc spent or re-invested; what kind of assets are included in the portfolio; how these are to be administered; what is the managers' accountability; what investment and risk management strategies are implemented; how can procedures and objectives be changed.

As for governance, the standards should make clear the role of the public entity and of its managers, state who establishes the strategies and who implements them, what is each one responsible for. There should also be rules on corporate governance, sanctions in case of breach of internal rules and, in certain cases, specific ethical constraints.

Transparency should result from reports issued (at least) every year, and rules should define horizontal and vertical responsibilities through regular and public information on investment strategies, results, nature and allocation of the investments made.

As regards behaviour, according to the size of the fund or of its objectives, there should be rules governing the practices and timeline of acquisitions and the internal discipline fund managers should comply with. This would be required in order to balance the legitimate intention of governments to protect their foreign investments and the interest of host countries to protect strategic industries, so as to prevent protectionist reactions.

Others believe that there should be multilateral constraints imposed on both host states and investor states making use of SWFs.[5] The

---

4 E. Truman, *Sovereign wealth funds: the need for greater transparency and accountability*, (Peterson Institute for International Economics, 2007); E. Truman, *Sovereign Wealth Fund acquisitions and other Foreign Government investments in the United States: assessing the economic and national security implications*, Testimony before the Committee on Banking, Housing and Urban Affairs, United States Senate, 14 November 2007 (available at: http://www.iie.com/publications/testimony/testimony.cfm?ResearchID=842 (accessed 4 April 2011)), and in particular – for more details on the guidelines proposed and an analytic review of the criteria presently followed by funds: E. Truman, 'A blueprint for sovereign wealth fund best practices', in *Policy Brief* (Peterson Institute, April 2008) pp. 1–21; E. Truman, *Sovereign Wealth Funds: Threat or Salvation?* n. 1 above, pp. 69–120.

5 R. Kimmitt, 'Public footprints in private markets – sovereign wealth funds and the world economy' [2008] *Foreign Affairs* 119–30.

former should avoid protectionist attitudes and refrain from barring investments; guarantee to investors certain and transparent environments; accept the free decisions of funds and act in a non-discriminating manner. The book of rules does not include the principle of reciprocity, which is not considered essential as investment policy decisions are taken in a broader political scenario that implicitly takes into account reciprocity and intellectual property protection. As for SWFs home states, they should: (i) invest according to market (and not political) logics; (ii) guarantee transparency of behaviour[6] and (iii) adopt adequate internal risk and governance auditing systems; (iv) compete fairly with private funds without taking advantage of opportunities available on the public side; (v) promote financial stability; (vi) comply with the rules dictated by the host state.

1.2 The 'Double Constraint' Theory

Under a different approach, some assert that such a detailed set of rules might turn out to be counter-productive, if the demand for rules is too vague or conceals protectionist intentions.[7] Two obligations would be sufficient to solve this problem. The first one should call for fund governance rules guaranteeing that investment decisions are based on non-political objectives and therefore – based on this assumption – basically tend to maximising profits. A virtuous example of this are central banks: like SWFs, these are exposed to the risk of being attracted by the governments' political objectives, but this risk may be overcome by assigning a specific mandate – e.g. obtaining price stabilisation – and, to this end, by making them independent from the government. The second obligation should

---

[6] The author specifies that 'it is also worth addressing the frequently made comparison between the transparency of hedge funds and the transparency of SWFs. Transparency is very important in both cases, but each requires a different approach. Unlike SWFs, hedge funds are private-sector entities. Disclosure is important to foster market discipline, which helps to mitigate systemic risk. . . . This framework for market discipline to mitigate systemic risk does not apply to SWFs. SWFs are public-sector entities managing public funds, and profit maximization may not be considered the primary objective. Investor discipline depends on citizens and the government, rather than savvy of institutional investors. SWFs' counterparties thus may not exercise market discipline, by limiting exposures or tightening financial terms, because they assume a sovereign guarantee will assure full payment'.

[7] P. Hildebrand, *The challenge of sovereign wealth funds*, report presented to the International Center for Monetary and Banking Studies, Geneva, 18 December 2007. pp. 8 *ff*.

consist of a cap on the shares in foreign companies made available to SWFs, e.g. below the dominant influence. Here the purpose would be of course to guarantee that SWFs will only make portfolio investments and not foreign direct investments (FDI), which presuppose taking majority control. No obligations in terms of transparency or accountability would be required.

1.3 The Temporary Suspension of Voting Rights and Other Related Measures

Others note that most states have already passed unilaterally regulations to prevent the taking over of national strategic companies by funds controlled – even indirectly – by other states.[8] So when the investments of these funds do not imply a take-over and are aimed at fulfilling purely financial interests of the investor state, there would be no measure available at multilateral level.

Hence, the fear that the regulatory action is expected to address is that SWFs may not have a merely financial interest (alternative purposes might be the acquisition of know-how and technologies, the access to natural resources, the acquisition of competitive advantage by national companies, etc.).[9] The solution some scholars proposed to prevent the consequences of investments that are not purely financial is the suspension of voting rights in the shares purchased by a governmental entity, *latu senso*; the right would be exercised again entirely when the fund re-sells the shares to non-governmental entities.[10] The value of this solution would be that it may apply to all state-controlled entities, including those indirectly controlled, and not only to SWFs, thus overcoming the subjective limit

---

[8] R. Gilson and C. Milhaupt, 'Sovereign wealth funds and corporate governance: a minimalist response to the new mercantilism' [2009] *Stanford Law Review* 1345–69, pp. 5 *ff*.

[9] In these terms, according to the authors fund action transparency would lose relevance, as they often have the same transparency as many hedge funds. Transparency obligations might actually be circumvented, as long as government control may also be exercised by informal ways.

[10] R. Gilson and C. Milhaupt, *Sovereign wealth funds and corporate governance: a minimalist response to the new mercantilism*, n. 8 above, p 13. The authors acknowledge that 'the key characteristic is government ownership of the fund, but this characteristic is shared by a host of other entities, sovereign wealth funds belong to a *continuum* of sovereign investment vehicles. At one end of the spectrum are central banks. At the other end are state-owned enterprises . . . In between these poles are sovereign stabilization funds, sovereign saving funds, and government investment corporations'.

and the consequent possible lack of effectiveness of this measure. And merely suspending voting rights in function of share ownership would avoid conflicts between the state enforcing the measure and the investor fund, as the shares would maintain their value unaltered.

According to the authors, the limits of this proposal in terms both of subjects and of contents will not impair its results. However, on one hand, the instruments that can be used to influence company managers are many and not all of them are related to voting rights; on the other hand, the measure might also involve entities (pension funds for example) that do not give rise to the concerns it is supposed to address. Besides, this constraint would represent an exceptional rule in states corporate law, affecting one of the fundamental ownership rights of shareholders. Actually, these limits show that the suspending vote measure is, in one respect, ineffective (as it does not apply to all irregular situations), and harmful in another (it affects situations not at risk). Not to mention that in the European Union it would probably be illegitimate if it implies a discrimination based on the public or private nature of the investor. If, on the other hand, it applies only to funds owned by non-EU countries, it might bring an unreasonable discrimination and would therefore be in conflict with the general principles of international economy law (first and foremost, the non-discrimination principle).

Others consider as an adequate measure against non-commercially motivated SWFs the disclosure of voting records,[11] or the delegation of the investment mandate to external, independent managers or intermediaries,[12] or a well-diversified investment index.[13] Most of these proposals appear to create more problems than they are meant to resolve.

---

[11] See A.D. Keller, 'Sovereign Wealth Funds: Trustworthy Investors or Vehicles of Strategic Ambition?' [2009] *Georgetown Journal of Law and Public Policy* 333–72; S. Mezzacapo, *The so-called 'Sovereign Wealth Funds': regulatory issues, financial stability, and prudential supervision* (available at: http://ec.europa.eu/economy_finance/publications/publication_summary15062_en.htm, (accessed 4 April 2011)). C. Lowery (*The role of Sovereign Wealth Funds in the global economy*, Remarks at the Barclays Capital's 12th Annual Global Inflation-Linked Conference, 2008) proposes that either an SWF should choose voluntarily not to vote its shares or it should disclose how it votes (as required by SEC for US mutual funds).

[12] See C. Cox, 'The Rise of Sovereign Business', *Security Industry News*, December 2007; A.D. Keller, 'Sovereign Wealth Funds: Trustworthy Investors or Vehicles of Strategic Ambition?', n. 11 above.

[13] J. Aizenman and R. Glick, *Sovereign Wealth Funds: Stumbling blocks or stepping stones to financial globalization?*, FRBSF Economic Letter 2007-38.

2. THE IMF GUIDELINES ('SANTIAGO GAPPS')

The IMF, by request of the G7, has developed an original and efficient procedure, setting up an international working group (IWG) which includes a number of major state investment funds – that in a few months has adopted 'virtuous' behaviour guidelines (the Santiago Principles) SWFs should comply with if they voluntarily decide to accept them. The IWG evolved in 2009 in a lasting International Forum (IFSWF), that is not a supranational binding authority but a network of SWFs endorsing the Santiago Principles and supporting the four guiding GAPPs objectives[14]: an *agorà* where SWFs can share ideas and views, coordinating their activity.

The innovative and peculiar feature of both the procedure and the international body, that have obtained a recognition of the main recipient of the guidelines, produced in the short term a result that should not be viewed as the conclusion, but rather as the starting point for a self-regulation of sovereign wealth funds.

2.1 GAPP Assumptions and Their Limits

The so-called 'Santiago principles' are made up of 24 rules that code down generally accepted principles and practices (GAPPs) – some of which divided in two or more sub-principles – covering specific topics and purposes. The principles are preceded by an introduction and broken down into three categories.

The introduction warns that the principles are to be applied by state funds on a voluntary basis, in compliance with the rules and obligations of their home state. This apparently obvious statement might narrow the scope of application of the principles – especially those dealing with transparency – if they are incompatible with the regulations in force in their home states.[15] Therefore, the introduction has at least five weak points. The first one is represented by the scope of application of the measures.

---

[14] I.e.: to help maintain a stable global financial system and free flow of capital and investment; to comply with all applicable regulatory and disclosure requirements in the countries in which they invest; to invest on the basis of economic and financial risk and return-related considerations; to have into place a transparent and sound governance structure that provides for adequate operational controls, risk management, and accountability.

[15] *Pendant* of the introduction is an encouragement to comply with the rules of the country where the fund makes an investment (GAPP Principle 15).

The definition of SWFs provided by the working group[16] excludes a wide series of entities and funding purposes, which might compromise the trustworthiness of the entire code. It may well happen that excluded forms of resource funding (e.g. forex reserves held by monetary authorities to manage typical monetary or balance of payments policies, or government pension funds) carry out functions similar to those of state funds, or are used by them, and are submitted to a different (home state) regulation.

The second weak point is represented by the state's voluntary acceptance: codes of ethics, being non-binding regulatory measures – or, in other approaches, non-regulatory measures at all – do not provide for sanctions in case of violation. The lack of rules and of corresponding sanctions highly reduces the code actual deterrent efficacy.[17]

The third weak point lies in the lack of a single auditing body to monitor the compliance with the principles even by those state's that declared their intention to adopt them. The International Standing Group (and now the International Forum replacing it) will only have coordination duties, and will not oversee the compliance with the guidelines by the state funds. Actually a third-party, impartial monitoring entrusted to an international institution (rather than to a single SWF) would be decisive, especially in the absence of adequate sanctions, because it would allow host states to verify from time to time the type and seriousness of each violation committed and (consequently) to tailor the application of restrictive measures as appropriate. Otherwise one will leave to the discretionary power of host states the assessment about the full compliance of funds with the GAPPs, with the obvious inherent risks.

The fourth weak point relates to the reference to home state regulations that SWFs must comply with. Many countries not only do not provide for

---

[16] In Chapter 2 we commented the IWG definition of SWFs: 'special purpose investment funds or arrangements, owned by the general government. Created by the general government for macroeconomic purposes, SWFs hold, manage, or administer assets to achieve financial objectives, and employ a set of investment strategies which include investing in foreign financial assets'.

[17] D. Shelton, 'Normative Hierarchy in International Law' (2006) 100 AJIL 291–323, 319 *ff*) specified that while 'soft law usually refers to any international instrument other than a treaty that contains principles, norms, standards, or other statements of expected behaviour', from a more careful analysis we see that 'from the perspective of state practice, resolutions, codes of conduct, conference declarations and similar instruments are apparently not viewed as law, soft or hard, albeit they may be related to or lead to law in one manner or another . . . there is not a continuum of instruments from soft to hard, but a binary system in which an instrument is entered into as law or not-law'. In the case at issue, according to this classification, the applicable discipline would qualify as non-regulatory measures.

public disclosure of the rules followed by funds in the administration of public assets, they may even hold it as being against the law. The reference to ethical principles made in certain GAPPs might also be misinterpreted and lead to different enforcement patterns at national or regional level. The conflict might appear right from the first enforcement, or (in absence of a monitoring action as described above) it might remain underlying and arise when fund activity is actually challenged.

The fifth weakness of the introduction lies in that no exceptional case, nor any possible procedure is provided to justify a temporary suspension of principles enforcement. If there are no waivers applicable in exceptional circumstances, it may well happen that certain states refuse to accept the constraints implied by the principles on grounds that they are unbreakable, while others, may comply with certain principles but fail to do so in particular circumstances. All this, in the absence of institutional oversight: control is left to the market or to host states.

2.2 The Classification by Regulatory/Institutional Framework and by Investment Activity

GAPPs may be classified by regulatory/institutional framework and by investment activity. The former classification can be divided in three main categories. The first one (principles 1–5) defines a clear regulatory framework and specifies investment objectives and the coordination of fund activities with the macro-economic policies of the home state. This category encompasses principles relating to clarity of objectives and connections with macro-economic policies, rules for the establishment and withdrawal of funds and for the drafting of statistics and questionnaires. The provisions use verbs in conditional tense – which is typical of non-binding measures – very general terms[18] and an unspecified form of activity disclosure.[19]

---

[18] For example, the Code (GAPP 1) rules that the regulatory framework should be 'fair' and that there should be public disclosure of 'the legal foundation and structure of the funds', their relationships with other public agencies, their operating strategies (GAPP 2), their use or withdrawal of funds.

[19] The principle states that there should be a form of disclosure but do not specify how. Apparently, also on the basis of the contents of the introduction, the level of guaranteed disclosure will vary in each country according to the laws in force on the matter. It is unclear whether there are supposed to be 'minimum thresholds' below which the form of disclosure chosen will not be considered acceptable. It is also true that, without a coordinated monitoring, the judgment will be left to host states, which will evidently imply risks of abuse or, in any case, of uneven judgment.

The second category of principles (6–17) defines the institutional framework and the governance structure SWFs are expected to comply with. The principles about governance,[20] however general, focus on a division of roles and responsibilities of the managers (principle 6),[21] provide guidance about the authorities of the owner state (principle 7)[22] and the criteria management activities should abide by (managers are required to operate according to a clear mandate with specific responsibilities and should guarantee adequate expertise: principles 8 and 9). Minimum governance requirements provide for a distribution of the roles and responsibilities of managers, who should be appointed with adequate procedures (GAPP 7 and 9) and receive a clear mandate (GAPP 6 and 8). A clear regulatory framework is also called for with respect to accountability (principle 10) and internal audit (with auditing procedures and adoption of ethical and professional codes – principles 12 and 13).

The third category (principles 18–24) defines investment and risk management rules (consistent with the objectives stated and the level of risk allowed – principles 18, 19, 21 and 22) also providing for specific performance measurement methods (principle 23). States are generally required not to take advantage of privileged information and not to exercise 'inappropriate' pressure in competition with private investors (principle 20).[23] This latter provision is meaningful, if we consider that it is aimed at overcoming one of the main objections brought against sovereign wealth funds. The general character of the principle, far from removing concerns,

---

[20] An example in this sense is GAPP 1: 'The legal framework for the SWF should be sound and support its effective operation and the achievement of its stated objective(s)'. The sub-principles are no more specific: '*GAPP 1.1 Subprinciple* The legal framework for the SWF should ensure the legal soundness of the SWF and its transactions; *GAPP 1.2 Subprinciple* The key features of the SWF's legal basis and structure, as well as the legal relationship between the SWF and the other state bodies, should be publicly disclosed'. And the same goes for principle no. 2, concerning the disclosure of investment policies, or no. 3, concerning the coordination of fund activities with the macro-economic policies of the state.

[21] GAPP 6. The governance framework for the SWF should be sound and establish a clear and effective division of roles and responsibilities in order to facilitate accountability and operational independence in the management of the SWF to pursue its objectives.

[22] GAPP 7. The owner should set the objectives of the SWF, appoint the members of its governing body(ies) in accordance with clearly defined procedures, and exercise oversight over the SWF's operations.

[23] GAPP 20. The SWF should not seek or take advantage of privileged information or inappropriate influence by the broader government in competing with private entities.

risks, on the contrary, to raise further troubles as it shows that the funds participating in the IWG did not agree to one of the factors that were supposed to qualify their code of ethics.

Another level of principle classification relates to fund investment activities. We find three main categories across all GAPPs, based on: (i) transparency of actions and activities, (ii) activities control and (iii) definition of actual operating pattern.

Transparency is guaranteed essentially in two ways: through the disclosure of the main aspects of the legal framework and structure of the fund (GAPP 1.2), of the investment policy (GAPP 2 and 18.3), of the policies, rules and procedures relating to the general approach followed by the fund to collect, withdraw and spend resources (GAPP 4), of the regime and objectives of governance rules (GAPP 16), of the relevant financial information about the fund (GAPP 17), of investment objectives, when guided by other than economic or financial considerations (GAPP 18.3), of the rules for the exercise of voting rights (GAPP 21). The other form of disclosure is represented by regular reports to the owners (GAPP 5 and 23) and to the market (GAPP 11).

The control of fund activities is ensured by an annual audit and by the compliance with ethical and professional principles (GAPP 12 and 13). However, again no external and independent control is required.

Lastly, the specific discipline of fund operations provides for: clarity and consistency of investment policies (GAPP 18 and 19); agreement to refrain from using privileged information or exercising inappropriate influence on the market (GAPP 20), and a structure capable of identifying and dealing adequately with risks (GAPP 22).

2.3 The Limits of Santiago GAPPs' Classification

The adoption of 'principles considered as shared' (and not of the 'best current practices': a signal of prudence and compromise) by the leading state funds certainly represents a significant step forward in the regulation of SWFs activity, as for both methods and results achieved. However, contents do give rise to some doubts.

First, the definition of funds, as mentioned earlier, could be reductive, and might limit the efficacy of some principles. At the same time, it shows how difficult it is to bunch together heterogeneous funds that can hardly be submitted to codes of conduct or to rules based on one common denominator that maybe has not been identified yet.

Second, most principles requiring general disclosure of information fail to give hints about the how and when. The vagueness of the principles becomes even more radical when disclosure obligations relate to the compliance with codes of ethics (that are obviously different in the various geographical regions) or (GAPP 19.1), to submitting investment decisions to other than purely economic or financial considerations (i.e. political considerations: we wonder which fund who actually has such intentions will state them beforehand, and how can a purpose be proved *ex-post*). Even if we agree that transparency principles are not critical in such an environment (see Chapter 2), more precise disclosure obligations could be appropriate.

Third, the vagueness of the principles makes it evident that they are a mere compromise, and limits the efficacy of many provisions relating to the objectives and goals of the funds (including GAPP 18 and its three sub-principles). For instance, there is no provision about the specific public disclosure of the fund's interest to take control (or dominant influence) of the companies it invests in. An explanation on this would remove many concerns of those host states that now limit in various forms SWF activities. Nor is there any provision about the regular public disclosure of fund size, or of the specific investments made, which would be general and detailed information, respectively, useful to determine the matters addressed, in different forms, by code provisions.

Fourth, as to accountability, the rules seem to mistake, in part, the various aspects of the matter, at domestic and external level (for investments within the state territory or abroad).[24] According to the introduction, GAPPs rules do not apply to domestic investments. The code does set forth the behaviour that funds should have in compliance with international rules, but the trouble comes when these need to be qualified (e.g. determine when the behaviour of a fund becomes 'too' aggressive, or when its purpose is not economic but political, etc.). In fact, the applicable multilateral rules (first and foremost, WTO rules[25]) are addressed to host states rather than to home states, as the scenario assumed by multilateral agreements (one-way investment flows) is quite different from the current practice, which is being changed mostly by SWFs activity.

---

[24] On the partition of the matter with respect to sovereign wealth funds see A. Gelpren, *A Sovereign Wealth Turn*, Rutgers School of Law-Newark, Research Paper Series, paper no. 25. As an example of the existing confusion the author explains that 'the final product contains elements of several established species: best practices produced by and for the public sector (for example, IMF on fiscal transparency), corporate codes of conduct produced by the private sector to regulate itself, and principles jointly produced by public and private actors to regulate private conduct (for example, the Equator Principles, a collaboration between private banks and the International Finance Corporation). GAPP would be unusual because the principles are produced by and for public entities'.

[25] Chapter 4 below, ss. 1.1.1 and 2.2.1.

Fifth, on the governance side, the code establishes the SWFs' accountability towards their owners, in compliance with home state and host state laws. The fact that funds are public might in fact induce its managers to behave improperly based on the idea that they are not responsible due to the sovereign nature (i.e., state ownership) of the fund. This is one of the most delicate issues of the entire code, because it is unclear who should be responsible for what and to whom. Furthermore, the essential issue of the responsibility of states for fund behaviour is not dealt with, either. If responsibility is charged to the state, a fund that has infringed the code might invoke immunity protection, insofar as its activity is attributable to a function of the state; in this case purpose becomes relevant.[26] Otherwise, the fund should be considered directly liable for having infringed the code (or any other provision of international law). Of course, it also depends on the SWF's legal structure and on the fact that the fund can be identified with the state.

3. A PROPOSAL TO TRANSFORM CONDUCT CODES INTO MEASURES BINDING ON HOST AND HOME STATES

The rules that currently govern SWFs activities globally are the IWG GAPPs guidelines, that have the limits described above. The voluntary nature of the code of ethics; the open-endedness of certain principles and practices; the vagueness of the obligations and the way they should be fulfilled; the lack of an independent body in charge of verifying the compliance of the funds that have stated their intention to abide by the principles: all these factors contribute to the limited enforceability of the code.

Our goal is to suggest a form of regulation where and to the extent it is necessary. The principle of proportionality in the enforcement of measures implies the need to plan a gradual intervention based on certain variables according to the classification proposed in the previous chapter. In this view, the code of ethics becomes a benchmark to measure the need for intervention in each specific case. As assessed in the previous chapter, we can imagine a scale of values, on the top of which we find SWFs with legal personality, adequate corporate governance structure and a sufficient level of accountability, pursuing typical public welfare purposes (i.e. saving generations goals) through portfolio investments. At the lower level of the scale we find SWFs with neither legal personality nor governance

26 On this matter see also Chapters 5 and 6.

rules, not accountable to any controlling body, pursuing mere political strategic goals, aiming at controlling participated companies. A regulation for SWFs activity should be requested for the latter, not also for the former, and it should be proportionate, gradually applying to each scale-step, aiming at providing the minimum requirements sufficient to prevent host state restrictive measures. Indeed, in this perspective, state measures should be residual, applying only if SWFs regulation does not apply or is disrespected.

Therefore, we may already identify, in the absence of further international developments – or however until such developments occur – two instruments to implement SWFs regulation, tied to the intention of using GAPPs as international benchmark, and the possibility for state funds to resort to international measures to settle possible controversies arising from host state protectionist reactions, conditional on GAPPs compliance. The compliance with the international code should allow SWFs to prevent host states from taking specific actions to bar or however influence SWF investments, and to seek appropriate relief against such restrictive measures from international authorities.

3.1 At Domestic Level: Host States' Restrictive Measures Applicable Only to SWFs Not Complying With GAPPs

The first instrument we recommend using to convert (indirectly) Santiago GAPPs into a binding or at least deterring rule, is host state assessment that the investments in national companies of funds complying with GAPPs are legal. In particular, it should be sufficient that SWFs respect governance and accountability principles, and that pursue only public welfare purposes. Restrictive host state rules (from the prohibition to take controlling interest in companies operating in certain strategic sectors, to the functional suspension of voting rights, to the approval and *ex-post* evaluation of the strategic decisions of companies in which SWFs have invested[27]), should only apply to those funds that disregard the code of ethics. Such an attitude by host states would induce most SWFs interested in investing abroad to comply with GAPPs and, at the same time, encourage all those funds not willing to comply with GAPPs to invest mainly in their respective domestic territories or reference regions, if these have less stringent rules. This would generate a systematic distinction between SWFs based on their commitment to compliance.

[27] On this matter see also Chapter 4.

3.2 At International Level: The Guidelines as a Benchmark in Bilateral Investment Treaties

The second instrument – complementary to the first one – that we suggest to make GAPP guidelines binding, is converting them into a benchmark in bilateral treaties on investments (BITs). As we will see in Chapter 4, multilateral rules on investments can be applied only to host states, not also to SWFs. As for now, SWFs activity can be ruled only by BITs binding clauses. While we will deeply handle the issue in Chapter 6, we can say here that new versions of BITs provide for rules guaranteeing host states exemptions to the general freedom of investments to protect national security interest. We propose on one hand, to limit the application of those BITs clauses to SWFs that disregard Santiago GAPPs, and on the other hand to make in BITs explicit reference to such investment obligations in order to make them binding SWFs' activity.

4. Host states' laws and SWFs

We saw in Chapter 3 the current regulation governing SWFs activity. We will deal now with the rules applicable to recipient states, hosting SWFs investments. We will assess which obligations they have, according to international multilateral investment rules, and which exceptions they can invoke to waive such obligations in particular circumstances. We will also verify whether and to what extent states can self apply safeguard clauses to the case at issue. We will start the analysis keeping in mind the conclusions we arrived at in the previous chapters: the SWFs definition we propose; the two SWFs qualifying elements (sovereignty and purposes); a regulation of SWFs activity that should aim not at neutralising the sovereign element but at guaranteeing a correct use of sovereignty. With these assumptions, host states should apply all the relevant international investment rules, and adopt restrictive measures in domestic strategic sectors only towards SWFs that do not endorse GAPPs regulations suitably.

1. THE GOVERNING LAW: OBLIGATIONS OF HOST STATES

The review of the discipline applicable to host state obligations should start from the multilateral regulations in force, analysing both the relevant GATT (for trade) and GATS (for services) rules, and the OECD regulations. It would have been logical to start with a review of the multilateral rules of TRIMs agreements concerning trade-affecting investments that might, in theory, apply to the case. However, investments are still regulated by bilateral or, at most, regional agreements governing their access, treatment and protection, while TRIMs only deal with trade issues and are aimed at guaranteeing that foreign investments are not subject to trade restricting measures. Notwithstanding the many attempts to change TRIMs agreements by: (i) broadening the notion of investment to include not only productive but also speculative investments, and (ii) extending the scope of dispute settlement rules so that they may apply to disputes between not only states but also states and private individuals, a solution has not been reached yet. A positive conclusion of the negotiations is certainly desirable; however, for the time being, TRIMs rules do not seem to provide appropriate tools.

1.1 In WTO Treaties

As we mentioned above, TRIMs provisions can not be helpful; we should therefore focus on GATT and GATS rules.

1.1.1 GATT

GATT rules may hardly be used to regulate the behaviour of states hosting SWFs investments. In theory, some general GATT principles might apply, such as the principle of mandatory national treatment on internal taxation and regulation (Art. III[1]) and of non-discrimination, external (Art. I and most favoured nation clause[2]) and internal (Arts XIII and XIV[3]). The same is true for the principle of reciprocity (preamble and Art. XXVIII *bis*) intended in both formal (reciprocity of obligations taken) and substantial terms (actual balance of economic interests and guarantee of equal trade opportunities). Also the principle stated in Article X on transparency[4] may be relevant to the case, as it is supposed to guarantee the publication of the measures that a state may take to restrict foreign SWF activities in its territory.[5] Finally, rules relating to state trading enterprises (Art. XVII) could apply.[6]

---

[1] Art. III states that: internal taxes and other internal charges, and laws, regulations and requirements should not be applied to imported or domestic products so as to afford protection to domestic production (para. 1); imported products shall not be subject, directly or indirectly, to internal taxes or other internal charges of any kind in excess of those applied, directly or indirectly, to like domestic products (para. 2); imported products shall be accorded treatment no less favourable than that accorded to like products of national origin (para. 4); no quantitative regulation relating to the mix, processing or use of products is allowed (para. 5). Of course, Art. III para. 8(a) states that the provision of that article 'shall not apply to laws, regulations or requirements governing the procurement by governmental agencies of products purchased for governmental purposes and not with a view to commercial resale or with a view to use in the production of goods for commercial sale'.

[2] According to the most-favoured-nation treatment, any advantage, favour, privilege or immunity granted by any contracting party to any product originating in or destined for any other country shall be accorded immediately and unconditionally to the like product originating in or destined for the territories of all other contracting parties (Art. I).

[3] Respectively, 'non discriminatory administration of quantitative restriction' and 'exceptions to the rule of non-discrimination'.

[4] Art. X requires a prompt publication and administration of trade regulations.

[5] For a first attempt to apply certain WTO treaty rules to the SWF see A. Subramanian and A. Mattoo, *Currency undervaluation and Sovereign Wealth*

The application of GATT principles to protect SWFs investments is however limited in many ways. First, these are general principles that can hardly regulate specific investment cases. Second, the lack of specific rules protecting foreign investments in the reference treaty (TRIMs) makes it difficult to refer to the general treaty, as it should have a residual relevance from an interpretation standpoint. Third, GATT agreement relates to the trading of goods and therefore GATT rules – including those that provide for general principles – would apply only indirectly to investments (i.e., GATT rules on SOEs only apply to import or export of goods). So, applying GATT rules to regulate host states' activity towards SWFs appears controversial.

1.1.2 GATS

The GATS agreement should lend itself more to the regulation of foreign direct investments, in all those cases (many, according to recent studies[7]) where the target is a service company. Therefore, however indirectly and within a narrow scope, the GATS might simplify the access to and favour the circulation of investments. GATS is based on general rules, special provisions for specific sectors, and lists that include states obligations and exemptions; it also provides for restrictions for both the recipient state and the investor. Hence, it is flexible enough to meet the needs of each case, and it is effective, being bound by the general WTO dispute settlement provisions.

In general terms, unless included in the list of exceptions, or falling under general exceptions (Arts. XIV and XIV *bis*) or reserves for regional integration agreements (Art. V), we can apply the general GATS principles of transparency and of most favoured nation treatment,[8] and – only if subject matter of a specific obligation – the principles of market access

Funds: A new Role for the World Trade Organization, Centre for Global Development, Working Paper no. 142, February 2008.

[6] Art. XVII states that if a state 'establishes or maintains a state enterprise wherever located, or grants to any enterprise, formally or in effect, exclusive or special privileges, such enterprise shall, in its purchases or sales involving either exports or imports, act in a manner consistent with the general principles of non-discriminatory treatment prescribed in this agreement for governmental measures affecting imports or exports by private traders' (para. 1). Para. 2 states that those enterprises should make any such purchases or sales 'solely in accordance with commercial considerations'.

[7] According to the results from the survey *Assessing the risk. The behaviours of Sovereign Wealth Funds in the Global Economy*, Monitor Company Group, June 2008, p. 40.

[8] Arts III and II respectively.

(Art. XVI)[9] and of national treatment (Art. XVII).[10] The latter two are obligations taken by the states when establishing each its own terms and conditions for service deregulation. Among the prohibitions implemented to guarantee market access there is also (Art. XVI, § 2.*f*) the establishment of a cap to foreign shareholding in service companies or however measures aimed at (or that have the effect to) reduce opportunities for foreign investments.[11]

As regards rules for specific business sectors, while telecommunications are now in a fully competitive environment (after the IV Protocol, effective from 1998), the GATS still does not apply, in the financial business sector, to the activities provided in the exercise of government authority and hence to the activities of central banks or other public entities in enforcement of monetary or exchange policies, nor to the activities related to pension or social security schemes (Art. 1, § 3.*b*, first attachment on financial services). SWFs' activity could often fall in those exemptions.

GATS rules, more than GATT rules, might therefore apply – however indirectly – to the case at issue, but again with significant restrictions that would apparently affect their efficacy. Indeed, GATS rules may be the basis for a discipline governing the access and circulation of investments, but not the way in which these are treated. Furthermore, investments may be relevant for GATS purposes only if they imply taking control of the target company.[12] Therefore, GATS rules may apply to FDI and not to portfolio investments, the typical SWFs investment (that do not request

---

[9] Market access should be guaranteed, for example, through the prohibition of quotas, quantitative restrictions, monopolies and exclusive service suppliers.

[10] Art. XVII states that 'each Member shall accord to services and service suppliers of any other Member, in respect of all measures affecting the supply of services, treatment no less favourable than that it accords to its own like services and service suppliers'.

[11] Art. XVI.2 states that '[I]n sectors where market-access commitments are undertaken, the measures which a Member shall not maintain or adopt either on the basis of a regional subdivision or on the basis of its entire territory, unless otherwise specified in its Schedule, are defined as: . . . (f) limitations on the participation of foreign capital in terms of maximum percentage limit on foreign shareholding or the total value of individual or aggregate foreign investment'.

[12] According to Arts I.2(c) and XXVIII(d)(i), GATS rules may apply to service provision 'by a service supplier of one Member, through commercial presence in the territory of another Member'. A 'commercial presence' is 'any type of business or professional establishment'. Article XXVIII(m)(ii) states that a 'commercial presence' by a 'juridical person of another Member' is a juridical person that is 'owned or controlled by' (natural or legal) person of that Member. Art. XXVIII(n)(i) states that a juridical person is 'controlled' 'if such persons have the power to name the majority of its directors or otherwise to legally direct its actions'.

for taking control of a company). Moreover, the GATS lists system actually reduces the efficacy of the rules, that are applied differently in each state. Hence, the degree of efficacy of the rules may be evaluated only on a case by case basis, for the lists filed by the host state and home state as part of a controversy. Besides – as we will see – GATS rules may be waived in certain circumstances, as GATS state exemptions can be often applied to SWFs investments. Finally, we should remind that many SWFs home states are not yet parties to the GATS agreement, so they can not invoke its protection.[13]

1.2 In OECD Regulations

Many rules applicable within the OECD may be relevant to SWFs. As was stated in a preliminary and tentative survey report on the promotion of freedom of SWFs' investment,[14] the 1961 OECD Code of Liberalisation, the principle of national treatment provided for in the 1976 Declaration on International Investments and Multinational Companies (amended in 2000) and the guidelines on corporate governance for state-owned enterprises (SOE Guidelines) would apparently apply to SWFs.[15] According to these rules, the principles of non-discrimination of foreign investments, transparency obligations (on any restrictions adopted) and the commitment to a gradual, one-sided deregulation (with standstill clauses preventing any reversion to more restrictive measures) may be regarded as applicable to OECD member states, beyond the principle of reciprocity.

The OECD has recently dealt specifically with the issue. Indeed, the Provisional Report by the OECD Investment Committee on SWFs and recipient country policies describes the investment policy principles that bind recipient state behaviour. These (generally accepted) principles are: (i) non-discrimination (foreign investors are not to be treated less favourably than domestic investors in comparable situations); (ii) transparency (information of restrictions on foreign investment should be comprehensive and accessible to everyone); (iii) progressive liberalisation (gradual elimination of restrictions on capital movements across their countries); (iv) 'standstill' (no introduction of new restrictions) and (v) unilateral liberalisation (to allow all other state members to benefit from the liberalisation measures they take and not to condition them on measures taken

13 We are referring to Russia, Iran, Libya, Kazakhstan, Azerbaijan, Taiwan.

14 *Sovereign wealth funds and recipient country policies*, Report by the OECD Investment Committee, April 2008.

15 OECD *Guidelines on corporate governance for state-owned enterprises*, OECD Publishing, 2005.

by other countries). The OECD Committee announced in 2008 a more detailed set of rules that at the time of writing this document has not been published yet.

1.3 In EU Laws

The European Commission and the European Council[16] have called for the development of and compliance with ethical codes for the SWF, but did not consider providing for rules binding on host states, as they considered the fundamental principles of the European treaties as fully applicable and adequate. According to a 'eurocentric' vision, while the Commission has deemed it appropriate to increase the set of rules applicable to SWFs and their home states, it recognised the existing rules governing host state obligations as sufficient. These rules are classified at both EU and member-state level and concern system restrictions and specific waivers justified by public order and public security reasons, adopted by member states within the framework of the general and specific safeguard clauses provided for by the treaties.

The EC stance will probably change in the next years, considering the new competence on foreign direct investments provided for by the Lisbon Treaty.[17] Indeed, the Lisbon Treaty grants the EU the exclusive competence only to the progressive abolition of restriction on foreign direct investments. And the difference between FDI and portfolio investments is clear in EU law and practice.[18] Nevertheless, the recent EC

---

[16] We are referring to the conclusions by the Council of Europe of 13–14 March 2008, and to the Communication from the European Commission on sovereign wealth funds of July 2008 (COM115).

[17] Art. 206 of the Treaty on the functioning of the European Union (TFEU) provides that by establishing a custom union in accordance with article 28 to 32, the Union shall contribute, in the common interest, to the progressive abolition of restrictions on international trade and foreign direct investment, and to the lowering of customs and other barriers. Article 207 includes foreign direct investments as one of the areas covered by the common commercial policy of the Union. The common commercial policy is an area of EU exclusive competence pursuant to Art. 3(1)(e) of the TFEU.

[18] When foreign direct investments take the form of a shareholding, the shares enable the shareholder to participate effectively in the management of that company or in its control (see e.g. judgments of: 12 December 2006 in Case C-446/04 *Test Claimants in the FII Group Litigation* [2006] ECR I-11753, para. 182; 24 May 2007 in Case C-157/05 *Holböck* [2007] ECR I-8995, para. 18; 20 May 2008 in Case C-194/06 *Orange European Smallcap Fund* [2008] ECR I-3747, para.101; and 26 March 2009 in Case C-326/07 *Commission v. Italy* [2009] ECR I-2291, para. 35). Conversely, 'portfolio investments' are 'the acquisition of shares on the

Communication and the regulation proposed clearly show that EU external competence will cover all investment areas.[19]

2. EXEMPTIONS FROM HOST STATES' OBLIGATIONS

Once described the applicable international rules that set forth obligations for states hosting SWFs investments, we can search for the exemptions that recipient states may invoke to justify restrictive measures to SWFs investments.

2.1 In WTO Treaties

In section 4.1 we explained how the WTO rules can hardly apply and cannot therefore be invoked by states hosting SWFs investments. Similarly, host states can hardly implement the WTO exceptions to the ordinary regime of trade. In fact, the general safeguard clauses provided for in Articles XX and XXI of the GATT[20] (and in the corresponding GATS articles XIV and XIV *bis*[21]) seem not to apply to host state actions towards SWFs. Article XX, which was, besides, included in Article 3 of TRIMs, apparently does

capital market solely with the intention of making a financial investment without any intention to influence the management and control of the undertaking' (Judgment of 26 September 2008 in joined Cases C-282/4 and C-283/4 *Commission v. Netherlands* [2008] ECR I-9141, para.19).

[19] Communication 'Towards a comprehensive European international investment policy' (COM(2010)343 final), and Regulation 'establishing transitional arrangements for bilateral investment agreements between member states and third countries' (COM(10) 344 final).

[20] Art. XX (General exceptions) allows measures necessary to protect public morals; human, animal or plant life or health; national treasures of artistic, historic or archaeological value; exhaustible natural resources, etc. Art. XXI (Security exceptions) allows actions that the state considers necessary for the protection of their essential security interests only in very specific areas (fissionable materials, arms ammunitions), moments (time of war) or purposes (the maintenance of international peace and security).

[21] GATS Article XIV *bis* states that 'nothing in this Agreement shall be construed . . . to prevent any Member from taking action which it considers necessary for the protection of its essential security interests': (i) relating to the supply of services as carried out directly or indirectly for the purpose of provisioning a military establishment; (ii) relating to fissionable and fusionable materials or the materials from which they are derived; (iii) taken in time of war or other emergency in international relations.

not apply because none of the (ten) specific points of the rule suit the case at issue.[22] On the other hand, GATT Article XXI (and the corresponding GATS Article XIV *bis*), provides for certain restrictions based on activities (trade of fissionable materials or of materials used in their manufacturing; supplies of weapons or of materials even indirectly intended for the armed forces) or on circumstances (time of war or of major international friction) that in principle are unrelated to the ordinary activities of SWFs.[23]

The GATS Annex on financial services, that allows host states to adopt 'prudential measures', *inter alia* 'for protecting investors, depositors, policy holders or persons to whom a fiduciary duty is owed by a financial service supplier, or to ensure the integrity and stability of the financial system', is even more ambiguous.[24] These are preventive measures that require a preliminary survey but that actually guarantee discretionary action and must not undergo the necessity test. In this case too, however, the discipline cannot be applied easily to any specific SWF's financial or industrial activity, be it a portfolio investment or a FDI.

2.2 In OECD Regulations

The rules considered as relevant to SWFs' activity within the OECD include, as we have seen, the Code of Liberalisation, that in Article 3 sets a national security exemption clause. Notwithstanding the seriously limiting lack of a shared definition of 'national security' that would justify the exemption,[25] which remains entrusted to individual states,[26] the notion

[22] The only possible application of Art. XX (and above all of GATS Art. XIV) might refer to the general clause of public order. However, as GATS note 5 specifies, this clause should be interpreted in a particularly restrictive form, because '[t]he public order exception may be invoked only where a genuine and sufficiently serious threat is posed to one of the fundamental interests of society'.

[23] The developments of the Argentina crisis have shown how difficult it is to provide an exhaustive interpretation of GATT Art. XXI; see on this J. Kurtz, *Adjudging the exceptional at International law: security, public order and financial crisis*, paper presented to the Annual Meeting of the Society of International Economic Law (SIEL), 15–17 July 2008.

[24] Para. 2(b) of the GATS Annex on Financial Services.

[25] Threats to national security may be, from time to time: terrorist or criminal infiltration into the national economy; losing control of essential resources for national defence; losing control of borders or of places geographically relevant for security; energy security; water supply; accidents involving the outspill of radioactive materials; terrorism; military threat; economic or industrial espionage; natural or environmental disasters; economic or financial crises; threat to national security or to the public defence, health or order, etc.

[26] The OECD has tried to provide an explanation of the notions of 'public

finds a (restrictive) application within the OECD in compliance with the principles of proportionality, transparency of intervention, regulation predictability, accountability of regulatory authorities.[27]

On these issues the OECD has reviewed the behaviour of a number of states in the practice, and commented it in summary surveys[28] that were used as the basis for the first provisional report by the OECD Investment Committee on Sovereign Wealth Funds and Recipient Country policies (October 2008). The report has developed a preliminary set of guidelines as the best practices that host states should follow. In particular, the 'investment policy guidance from the freedom of investment project' states that 'in general, governments should rely on measures of general application which treat similarly situated investors in a similar fashion'. Where such measures are deemed inadequate to protect national security, 'specific measures taken with respect to individual investments should be based on the specific circumstances of the individual investment which pose a risk to national security'. As for transparency and predictability, the guidelines provide for a procedure of codification and publication, prior notification to and consultation with interest parties, according to procedural fairness and predictability and allowing a full disclosure of investment policy actions. As regards regulatory proportionality, the guidelines state

---

order and essential security interests under the OECD National treatment instrument', with the 'Investment Committee's clarification reproduced in national treatment of foreign-controlled enterprises' (OECD, 2005). The examples provided in the declaration, however, are purely indicative. The literature is now starting to deal systematically with energy security – intended as energy supply security – and proposes, according to a certain practice, to include it in the exemption for national security; see on this W. Shih, *Energy security, GATT/WTO and regional agreements*, paper presented at the annual convention of SIEL, 15–17 July 2008. The author reports various different cases of energy security, from that of an industrialised country to that of a developing country without any energy resource or of a country rich in resources.

27 These OECD countries discussed with third countries the application of this safeguard clause, within the framework of the *OECD Investment Committee's project on 'Freedom of investment, national security and strategic industries'*.

28 See in particular, *Protection of 'critical infrastructure' and the role of investment policies relating to national security* (May 2008); *Transparency and predictability for investment policies addressing national security concerns: a survey of practices* (May 2008); *Proportionality of security-related investment instruments: a survey of practices* (May 2008); *Accountability for security-related investment policies* (November 2008). See also 'Freedom of investment, National Security and "Strategic" Industries: An Interim Report', in *International Investment Perspectives: Freedom of Investment in a Changing World* (OECD, 2007) ch 3, pp. 53–63, and 'Essential Security Interest under International Investment Law', Ibid ch. 5, pp. 93–133.

that restriction on investment or conditions on transaction should not be greater than needed to protect national security and should be avoided when other existing measures are adequate and appropriate to address a national security concern.[29] As far as accountability is concerned, the guidance requests procedures for parliamentary oversight, judicial review, periodic regulatory impact assessments, and requires that decisions to block an investment should be taken at high government levels.

If they resulted in a mere statement of general principles, the OECD guidelines would be insufficient and inadequate, if not useless as a reference, as these principles are already found in the practice. This would not induce – as it occurred for instance with the GAPP published by the IMF, any effort to improve the current obligations of the states, but would only represent a list of the existing ones.

2.3 In EU Law and Practice

2.3.1 In the case law

Many EU member states have recently intervened helping in several ways national companies operating in strategic sectors or that provide services of general economic interest. These state interventions to protect 'national champions' – important precedent cases for possible restrictive measures against third-country SWFs investments – are aimed essentially at preventing foreign companies from entering in strategic activities and have reserved a privileged role to public shareholders, giving to them special authorities (internal audit) or alternatively, a preventive veto power (by means of discretional authorisation) or a control *ex post* (external monitoring).

These forms of state intervention have been the subject of recent EU case law – where they are generally referred to as '*golden share*' – that has clearly defined the scope of a legitimate government intervention.[30] In

---

[29] In accordance with the principle of 'regulatory proportionality', the interim guidelines set a number of tenets: (i) essential security concerns are self judging (each country has a right to determine what is necessary to protect its national security); (ii) investment restrictions should be narrowly focused on concerns related to national security; (iii) appropriate expertise; (iv) tailored responses (restrictive investment measures should be tailored to the specific risks posed by specific investment proposals); and (v) last resort (restrictive measures should be used as a last resort when other policies cannot be used to eliminate security-related concerns).

[30] For comments about the EU case law on golden shares, see S. De Vido, 'La recente giurisprudenza comunitaria in materia di golden shares: violazione delle norme sulla libera circolazione dei capitali o sul diritto di stabilimento?', in

particular, restrictive measures were interpreted pursuant to Art. 58.1 of the EC Treaty (now 65.1 TFEU) and hence in accordance with the limits to the free circulation of capital. Specifically, the limits invoked on grounds of public order and public security were considered legitimate in cases of real and serious threats to an essential interest of the community,[31] or of imperative reasons of public interest,[32] or for energy services security.[33] These state measures may apply only whether and to the extent to they are proportionate; hence, any preventive authorisation to the purchase of shares or quotas in a company would hardly be allowed,[34] while an *ex-post* intervention to neutralise corporate decisions or protect strategic interests will be more easily accepted,[35] regardless of the contents of the

---

[2007] *Diritto del commercio internazionale* 861–91. For an attempt to consider how past case law decisions may affect sovereign wealth funds see L. Catà Backer, 'The private law of public law: public authorities as shareholders, golden shares, sovereign wealth funds and the public law element in private choice of law' [2008] *Tulane Law Review* 1–67.

[31] See on this the judgment of 13 May 2003 in case C-463-00 *The Commission v. Spain*, Rec. p. 4581, item 72.

[32] See on this the judgment of 2 June 2005 in the case C-174-04 *The Commission v. Italy*, Rec. p. 4933, item 35. Similarly, and again about golden shares, see also: judgment of 4 June 2002, Case C-367-98 *The Commission v. Portugal*, Rec. p. 473, item 49; of 4 June 2002, Case C-483-99 *The Commission v. France*, Rec. p. 4781, item 45; of 4 June 2002, Case C-503-99 *The Commission v. Belgium*, Rec. p. 4809, item 45; of 13 May 2003, Case C-463/00 *The Commission v. Spain*, item 68; of 28 September 2006, Cases C-282-04 and 283-04 *The Commission v. The Netherlands*, Rec. p. 9327, item 32.

[33] Case C-503-99 *The Commission v. Belgium*, Rec. p. 4809, item 48; Case C-483-99 *The Commission v. France*, Rec. p. 4781, item 47, and Case C-463/00 *The Commission v. Spain*, item 71. The so-called 'Belgian scheme' provides for: (i) *ex-post* intervention; (ii) objective and non discriminatory criteria; (iii) procedural rules: time limits, duty of disclosure and motivation, judicial scrutiny; (iv) a strong link between golden shares and pursuance of the general interest declared.

[34] For instance, in *The Commission v. France*, Rec. p. 4781, the preventive authorisation to purchases of securities corresponding to only one-tenth of the capital was rejected; similarly in Case C-463/00 *The Commission v. Spain*, even though the measure was in that case made conditional on a subjective, objective and time basis.

[35] In particular, in *The Commission v. Belgium*, Rec. p. 4809, items 48–52, the measure was considered compatible with the treaty because it: (i) was subsequent and not preventive to the resolution; (ii) was to be enforced only in case of strategic decisions of the company; (iii) required adequate justification; (iv) was subject to an effective jurisdictional control. Italian lawmakers have also moved in this direction with Law no. 350 of 24 December 2003, Art. 4, §§ 227–31, enacted by Prime Minister's Decree of 10 June 2004. However, the Commission has filed a new proceeding against Italy, and the Court of Justice recently confirmed the condemnation of Italy (Case C-326/07 *Commission v. Italy* [2009] ECR I-2291, 26

measure, that may either set limits to direct investments in the capital of a company or provide exemptions from the general principles of company law (e.g. on voting rights). Furthermore, these measures may be exercised by the states subject to the control of European institutions, that will verify their legitimacy, also with respect to the principle of free circulation of capital.

A possible step towards a less restrictive approach to rules potentially discriminating SWFs might consist in assessing the violation of the rules not on free circulation of capital, but on freedom of establishment. For instance, a more restrictive definition of 'capital' than the one now provided by Directive 88/361/CEE, to include only portfolio investments leaving direct investments out, would allow to apply the rules on the right to establishment.[36] In this case, a procedure of the EU Commission against national restrictive rules would only be justified if it were proven that those rules would not only discourage foreign investors from purchasing shares in a company, but also set significant restrictions to their managing power. In fact, the restrictions to the free circulation of capital might be in any case justified by the right of establishment pursuant to Article 58.2[37] of the EC Treaty (now 65.2 TFEU). However, neither the European Commission nor the Court of Justice seem to have accepted this interpretation internally, and are unlikely to accept it externally for certain specific applications (i.e. when SWFs are the purchasers).

March 2009). See on this subject: A. Sacco Ginepri, 'La nuova *golden share*: l'amministrazione senza diritto di voto e gli altri poteri speciali' [2005] *Giur. Comm.* 707 *et seq.*

[36] The Directive applies to both portfolio investments, indicated as transactions on generally traded securities, and direct investments, that allow shareholders to take part in the management or control of a company. There would obviously be problems if the discipline was applied to the former alone and not to the latter, as it is clearly to be seen if we try to apply the rules to the case at hand.

[37] This line was supported by Advocate General Tesauro in Case C-148/91 *Veronica Omroep Organisatie v. Commissariaat voordeMedia* and by Advocate General Colomer in the general conclusions presented on 3 July 2001 concerning the Portuguese, Belgian and French cases, and on 6 February 2003 concerning the Spanish and British cases. The theory is based on two reasonable assumptions, i.e. that the free circulation of capital is functional (*inter alia*) to the freedom of establishment, and that in the cases tried what is relevant is the limit imposed by the measures to the actual management of a business, and hence to the formation of its corporate will, rather than to the free circulation of capital. According to this assumption, Advocate General Colomer has determined that golden shares and similar measures should be considered as legitimate unless they imply actual discrimination.

2.3.2 In a specific Communication

In a Communication entitled 'A common European approach to Sovereign Wealth Funds',[38] the European Commission does underline the need – in order to obtain results in terms of governance and transparency – for a common EU action founded on certain essential principles such as: (i) the commitment to an environment open to foreign investments, (ii) EU support to multilateral activities, (iii) compliance with EU and international obligations, (iv) enforcement of the principles of proportionality and transparency – but it also underlines the opportunity to apply the existing rules at both European and member state level.[39] As far as EU treaties and legislation are concerned, reference is made to Article 56 of the EC Treaty (now Art. 63 TFEU), and the exceptions that may be invoked, in the Commission's view, refer expressly to Article 57.2[40] ECT (now Art. 64.2 TFEU).

The Commission considered applicable the EU framework in order to control SWFs investments under various respects. First, by making reference to Article 57.2 of the EC Treaty (now Art. 64.2 TFEU), the Commission expressly evokes measures – adopted by qualified majority – on the movements of third-country capitals, and measures – adopted unanimously – that provide for restrictions to third-country investments in EU enterprises. Second, the Commission refers to the applicability of the merger regulation to protect not only competition but also other legitimate interests (e.g. public security, plurality of mass media, principles of

---

38 COM(08) 115 provisional.

39 The Council of Europe too, in its meeting of 13–14 March 2008, has joined the Commission's intention to reach a 'common approach' taking into account member state prerogatives. The prudent statements of the EU have so far dealt with a 'participating observation' of the development of multilateral regulations on the matter. This attitude is now being challenged by those who call for a more specific EU framework (see on this the report 'les fonds souverains, révélateurs de nos propres faiblesses' of the French Parliament, presented by MP D. Garrigue to the delegation of the National Assembly for the European Union, pp. 29 *et seq.*).

40 In particular the Commission has specified that 'with regard to the EU legal framework, investments by SWFs in the EU are subject to the same rules and controls as any other form of investment, either foreign or domestic, where the principles of free movement of capital between Member States, and between Member States and third countries stipulated in Article 56 apply. The free movement of capital is not absolute. As a fundamental principle of the Treaty, it may be regulated in two respects at the European level under article 64.2 TFEU: first, the Community may adopt by qualified majority measures on the movement of capital from third countries involving direct investment. Second, it is not excluded that the Community can introduce – by a unanimous decision – measures that restrict direct investment'.

prudence) or other public interests (considered on a case by case basis), as long as they comply with the principles of proportionality and non-discrimination. Last, the Commission reminds that EU Treaties already consider public security and plurality of information as legitimate interests *per se* – and as such worthy of protection – while other interests may be evaluated as such by the Commission on a case by case basis.

As for member-state regulation, the Commission notes that states do have rules that can apply, conforming to the principles of proportionality and non-discrimination, and others that can be adopted (with express reference to strategic network service providers) conforming to international and EU obligations. All measures requiring prior approval to the purchase (inclusive by sovereign wealth funds) of relevant shares of companies working in strategic businesses must be proportionate. In particular, such measures are allowed only if they actually protect general legitimate interests and provide for tight deadlines for the exercise of veto powers on strategic decisions identified beforehand, and if they are subject to jurisdictional review.

2.4 Exemptions Applied by Host States: Preventive and Repressive Measures

In recent years, many European states have restricted the freedom of foreign (not only sovereign) investments in the defence industry or in other sectors considered essential for national security.[41] New definitions were introduced (e.g. 'critical infrastructures', 'economic security') to reflect the progress of recent member-state policies; other definitions (public order, national security, national defence) have taken different meanings and earned wider, in certain cases more specific, scopes of application than in the past. Each member state has developed an independent system of preventive and repressive measures. Therefore, the general picture is far from being homogeneous. This section will describe the recent developments that are considered as most significant.

2.4.1 In EU member states

Any containment to the freedom of SWFs' action as shareholders of EU member states national companies is allowed only on the conditions

---

[41] For preliminary considerations on this see: B. Cohen, *Sovereign Wealth Funds and National Security: the great tradeoff*, working paper, University of California, August 2008; D. Marchick and M. Slaughter, *Global FDI Policy: correcting a Protectionist Drift*, Council Special Report 34 (US Council on Foreign Relations).

stated above, consolidated by the Court of Justice in a solid case law and resumed by the Commission in its recent communication. This approach admits a restrictive regime where the competent Ministry may challenge – within a short deadline – a shareholders resolution if 'the state's vital interest' is threatened. Such interest has been defined in many ways.

In Italy, Article 1 § 2 of Prime Minister's decree of 10 June 2004 – which enforced Law no. 350 of 24 December 2003 (Art. 4, paras 227–31) – identifies the vital interest in the actual and serious danger: (a) of a shortage of minimum national supplies of oil and energy products; (b) to the continuity of a public service obligation to the community; (c) to the safety of essential public service infrastructures and networks; (d) to national defence, military security, public order and security; and (e) of health emergencies.

Other EU member states, adopting a different approach, specify the areas where such limits may apply and the reasons why such interest is vital. For example, in France limits are provided for the protection of public order, public safety, national defence, whenever these are threatened in any of the eleven areas identified as critical.[42] Therefore, exemptions may apply on two conditions, i.e. if the matter affects one of the areas considered critical, and if the interest to be protected is considered relevant. The Ministry of Economy must release its prior authorisation to a transaction within thirty days from the relevant request.[43]

In Germany – after the 2004 reform[44] – restrictions on the shareholding

---

[42] These eleven areas include gambling, public security, research, development, production of hazardous substances capable of being used as pathogenic or toxic agents, wiretapping systems, IT security, dual use (civil and military) tools and technologies, encryption products and services, national defence and security, research, manufacturing and trade of weapons and ammunitions for military action or of warfare materials.

[43] The rule (Law 2004-1343, and its enforcement decree no. 1739 of 2005) is now being reviewed by the European Commission to verify its asserted incompatibility with the circulation of capital and freedom of establishment. In fact, while the Commission recognises the validity of the purposes of the law in terms of public security and defence, it has deemed that the prior authorisation procedure is disproportionate with respect to its end. After the reply from France, the procedure is for the time being still open but 'frozen'. In fact, the French Government has stated that: (a) if the company concerned is one that performs only part of its business in sensitive areas, the inquiry will be limited to its activities in these areas, and (b) the Government is free to take adequate measure that do not prevent the investment but require the investor to commit to specific behavioural or structural obligations, only for the part concerning sensitive materials and areas.

[44] The reform was approved in Germany with an amendment to the 1961 law on foreign trade.

by foreign investors are admitted in companies engaged in defence-related activities: a foreign entity may not purchase more than 25 per cent of voting rights in companies that produce weapons, ammunitions, encryption systems, warfare systems. The interests protected are national and international public security. Preventive monitoring duties are entrusted to the Ministry of Economy and Technology, that is required to give its opinion within thirty days from receiving notice of a transaction.[45] A reform that the German Parliament passed in 2009 provides for specific and more stringent restrictions, applicable to all investors and not only to SWFs.[46] The law does no longer provide for a list of strategic sectors, that was waived in favour of a 'case by case' approach within the framework of protecting public order and security as defined by Article 58 § 1 of the EC Treaty (now Art. 65 TFEU) and related case law (areas such as energy supplies, telecommunication networks security and certain particularly strategic public services are supposed to be included). The law requires a foreign investor wishing to purchase more than 25 per cent in a German company to give notice thereof, on a voluntary basis. If no prior notice is given, the Government – specifically, a committee composed by the four Ministers of Economy, Finance, Foreign Affairs and Interior – will in any case be free to start an inquiry that will last no more than three months, and then the Government will be entitled to approve, cancel or submit the transaction to certain conditions. Applicable conditions may include: (i) a prohibition or limitation of the exercise of voting rights in the acquired company, or (ii) the appointment of a trustee to reverse the transaction.

The United Kingdom has set less stringent restrictions to purchases by foreign entities, aimed at protecting the public interest or securing the control of proprietary technologies, and these are based on the prior clearance by the Office of Fair Trading granted within 30 days from the relevant request. Few specific sectors are listed as being of particular interest: defence, press, water distribution.[47] One restrictive rule provides as the only form of general protection the intervention of the Ministry of Industry with an action justified by reasons of public interest (the notion of which is however undefined). The action must be validated

[45] The proposal is only available in German (see *Bundesgesetzblatt*, I, 2009, 770).

[46] Entwurf eines Dreizehnten Gesetzes zur Änderung des Außenwirtschaftsgesetzes und der Außenwirtschaftsverordnung, Government draft published on 20 August 2008.

[47] While the Enterprise Act 2002 provides for the possibility to make additions to the list, it is extremely libertarian and takes care not to tie market supervision to politics.

by the Parliament within 24 weeks: in this case only the Commission on Competition may consider public interest in evaluating the transaction.[48]

2.4.2 In the United States

The reactions to the increase in the number of SWFs and the assets they manage have spurred a hot debate in the United States. On one hand, the investments of these funds reduced, at least at an early stage, the adverse effects of the subprime loan crisis and ensured market stabilisation. On the other hand, SWFs' investments raised concern that certain strategic sectors of the national economy might fall under the control of foreign states driven by political, and not merely economic goals. Therefore, in July 2007 the Congress of the United States passed the Foreign Investment and National Security Act – FINSA – to supplement US regulations governing foreign investments in the USA.[49] Before this act, foreign investments were subject to the control of the U.S. Government's Committee on Foreign Investment in the United States (CFIUS) whenever there were national security implications. However, the test used to verify whether the investment could be allowed (denominated Exon-Florio National Security Test) was applied only to transactions involving the purchase of at least 10 per cent of the stock in a company, or however of a controlling share thereof (in the case of a public company). This procedure did not apply to SWFs because in most cases they invest in shares without voting rights, or purchase non-controlling interest, below 10 per cent of the capital stock. The amendment passed in 2007, aimed at avoiding that these transactions may escape the Commission's monitoring, has added two more cumulative conditions to the evaluation criteria[50] according to which

---

48 So far the procedure has not been applied, but its possible implementation was maybe one of the factors that in 2008 barred Gazprom's offer for Centrica. Another never applied procedure is the one provided for by the 1975 Industry Act, where the transfer of control of any 'important manufacturing undertaking' that 'appears to the Secretary of State to be of special importance to the United Kingdom or to any substantial part of the United Kingdom' to a foreign entity is allowed only on condition that it does not compromise the 'national interest'. Also in this case the veto by the Secretary of State must be confirmed by the Congress.

49 The Foreign Investment and National Security Act of 2007 (P.L. 110-49, 121 Stat. 246) contains a further amendment to the 'Omnibus Trade and Competitiveness Act', already amended in 1988 with the 'Exxon Florio' amendment that had established the Committee on Foreign Investment in the United States (CFIUS).

50 The conditions for the exercise of the authority by the President, amended by the Exxon-Florio Amendment of 1988 to the Defense Production Act, were two: credible evidence that the transaction might threaten the national security, and lack of rules allowing to cope with the threat adequately and appropriately.

a transaction may be prohibited: if the infrastructures are strategic and if the transactions are made by parties controlled, even if only indirectly, by foreign states.[51]

Under the new rule, the President of the United States is authorised to bar foreign investments that might threaten national security, which is not however defined specifically. There being no accurate definition, a list of criteria is used to identify a threat to security;[52] but they are general, and the list is not exhaustive. The 2007 reform has added two new circumstances to the set of criteria by which a transaction may be authorised, which has the advantage of not providing a list of sectors strategic *per se*: (i) the case of an investment concerning a 'critical' infrastructure or technology or, if the transaction involves foreign states, (ii) the case that any of the latter is not a party to a non-proliferation treaty.

The CFIUS Committee, chaired by the Secretary of the Treasury, will then review the investment proposal within 30 days from the notice thereof (notice is still voluntary). An inquiry may follow the preliminary review, and is mandatory if the prospective investor is a foreign government or a state-owned company of a foreign state.[53] The inquiry must be completed within 45 days with a recommendation by the CFIUS to the President of the United States, who in turn will take a decision and disclose it to

---

[51] Under the amendment, the CFIUS is now authorised to monitor all transactions (mergers, acquisitions, hostile takeovers, etc.) that may give rise to 'foreign control of any person engaged in interstate commerce in the United States', or where the transaction translates into foreign control of a 'critical infrastructure that could impair the national security', or simply when the transaction is a 'foreign government-controlled transaction', defined as 'any covered transaction that could result in the control of any person engaged in interstate commerce in the United States by a foreign government or an entity controlled by or acting on behalf of a foreign government'. Foreign control is defined (the list being without limitation) as the transfer of main assets, the dissolution, shutdown or reallocation of production or R&D sites, decisions about termination or breach of agreements, relevant by-law amendments relating to the transactions at issue. In any case, the authority to suspend or bar *tout court* a transaction remains entrusted to the President of the United States.

[52] Factors to be considered are, among others: domestic production needed for projected national defence requirements, capability and capacity of domestic industries to meet national defence requirements, control of domestic industries and commercial activity by foreign citizens as long as it affects the capability and capacity of the United States to meet national security requirements.

[53] The percentage of inquiries started compared to notices of proposed transactions received is very low. Between 1988 and 2007 the CFIUS received 1500 notices and started only 25 inquiries, of which only one led to the rejection of the proposal (acquisition of a Boeing supplier by a Chinese company in 1990).

the Congress within 15 days. The procedure has proved to have a major deterrent effect: the 2007 reform improved its transparency (a notice to the Congress must be released at the end of each stage, but the Congress has no decision-making authority) and specified which criteria are to be verified.[54]

Notwithstanding this very restrictive measure that secures preventive control on any transaction made by an investment fund including those indirectly controlled by a foreign state, the amendment was considered insufficient, as it would allow an intervention only to protect the national security risk and not the economic security risks as well.[55] Therefore, in September 2007 the House of Representatives approved (H. Res. 552 – 110th Congress) by very large majority (401 votes for, 4 against) a resolution in favour of reciprocity in the investments with China,[56] and the Congressional Research Service suggested additional specific restrictive measures in respect of sovereign wealth funds.[57]

---

54 For a preliminary review see G. Georgiev, 'The reformed CFIUS regulatory framework: mediating between continued openness to foreign investment and national security' (2008) 25 *Yale Journal of Regulation* 125–34, and A. Guaccero, E. Pan and M. Chester, 'Investimenti stranieri e fondi sovrani: forme di controllo nella prospettiva comparata USA–Europa' [2008] *Rivista delle società* 1359–94.

55 E. Truman, in a US Senate hearing on 14 November 2007 (for its transcript see *Sovereign Wealth Fund Acquisitions and other foreign government investments in the United States: assessing the economic and national security implications*, Testimony before the Committee on Banking, Housing and Urban Affairs, available at: http://www.iie.com/publications/testimony/testimony.cfm?ResearchID=842 (accessed 4 April 2011)), reported the concerns of many observers about the implications for the stability of US economy and financial systems of SWF dealings in 'private equity firms, hedge funds and regulated financial institutions'.

56 According to the Resolution, 'United States financial service regulators, in assessing whether applications from Chinese financial institutions meet comprehensive consolidated supervision standards, should consider whether the applications are for operations and activities in the United States that are currently prohibited for United States institutions in China'.

57 The CRS Report for the Congress of 22 January 2008, *China's Sovereign Wealth Fund*, p. 19, suggests: '1) requirements that any SWF interested in investing in the United States publicly release audited financial statements, that follow international accounting standards on a regular basis; 2) restrictions on the percentage of a U.S. company a SWF may own; 3) restrictions on the type of investment SWF may make in U.S. companies – alternatives include restricting SWFs from negotiating a seat on the company's board of directors or representation in the company's senior management'.

2.4.3 In other states of special interest

The growth of SWFs has recently led other states to consider the need to adopt measures to control the phenomenon. The requirements, and the consequent forms of protection, differ according to the context and may be hardly classified.

In Australia, the pending debate on SWFs reflects the concerns about the growing Chinese investments in raw materials (extraction of ores) and in infrastructures (for the transportation of natural resources). These investments are more 'aggressive' today than in the past. Acquisitions by foreign entities are submitted to the procedure established by the Foreign Acquisition and Takeover Act of 1975, according to which mandatory notice must be given to the Foreign Investment Review Board (FIRB). The Board has a consultative role; investment proposals are regarded as approved if the Ministry of Finance does not reject them (or make them subject to conditions) within 30 days from notice.

In February 2008, the Australian Government published six main guidelines to improve the transparency of the assessment of foreign investments in Australia.[58] These guidelines require the FIRB to evaluate whether the initiative of the prospective investor 'is independent from the foreign government' of the country in which the investor is based. The FIRB must then evaluate to what an extent the investor's initiative is of a commercial nature and compliant with governance best practices; in the case of a SWF the FIRB will also evaluate the fund's investment policy and the form in which the fund intends to exercise its voting right in the Australian company. Finally, the FIRB must guarantee the compliance with fair competition rules and assess whether the investment may affect the national security and the strategic interest of the country.

In Russia, the Duma passed in April 2008 a law on foreign investments based on a classification by business sectors, with as many as 42 sectors considered as strategic, where the acquisition by a foreign investor of more than 50 per cent of the quotas or shares in a Russian company (more than 25 per cent if the foreign investor is a state-owned company) is made conditional on a special clearance by a commission chaired by the Prime Minister, that must be released or denied within a term ranging between 90 to 180 days according to the circumstances.[59] Among the sectors considered as critical and hence subject to evaluation

---

[58] Principles Guiding Consideration of Foreign Government Related Investment in Australia, 17 February 2008.

[59] Federal Law of the Russian Federation on Foreign Investments in Companies Having Strategic Importance for State Security and Defence, n. 57-FZ, signed by the President on 29 April 2008, and effective from 7 May 2008.

(which have been brought from 33 to 42 during the parliamentary debate) are: nuclear power, weapons, aeronautics, space sector, extraction of natural resources, fishery, publishing industry, mass-media and telecommunications.

In Canada, the Government passed, in December 2007, guidelines for the application of rules on the foreign investments of state-owned enterprises (SOEs) under the Investment Canada Act. The guidelines, on the basis of which a foreign investment proposal has been recently blocked, state that the Canadian Government, when reviewing investments by state-owned enterprises, will consider whether the SOEs adhere to Canadian standards of corporate governance. Another bill that is now being discussed plans to introduce a further restriction to foreign investments according to a 'national security test', the qualification and application of which are however still unclear.

China too is restricting the criteria for the admission of foreign direct investments in certain areas of its economy. For instance, in December 2006 the State-owned Assets Supervision and Administration Commission (SASAC) published a list of 'critical economic sectors' in which China should maintain strong state control and restrict foreign participation.[60] Further, the Ministry of Commerce can review foreign acquisitions for their impact on 'national economic security'. Finally, the new anti-monopoly law of 2008 provides regulators with additional discretion in applying competition rules to state-owned companies that are 'relied upon by the national economy and national security'.[61]

Japan has recently considered for the first time the decision to block an investment proposal, based on paragraph 5 of Japan's Foreign Exchange and Foreign Trade Act. The reason for the restrictive measure was said to be 'the possibility that the maintenance of public order is disturbed'.[62]

---

[60] Among others: automotive, chemical, construction, electronic information, equipment manufacturing, iron and steel, non-ferrous metal, science and technology, survey and design.

[61] D. Marchick and M. Slaughter, *Global FDI Policy: correcting a Protectionist Drift*, n. 41 above, p. 9.

[62] As reported by the Japanese representative at the OECD eighth roundtable on 'freedom of investment, National security and strategic industries' (held in Paris, 8 October 2008), the decision concerned the investment proposal by a foreign investor in the Japanese electrical power industry. Japan noted that the sector was a critical infrastructure and that the target company played a key role in the 'nuclear fuel cycle in Japan'. The Japanese authorities feared that, under pressure to meet its new owners' high demand for annual returns, the target company would under-invest in long-term projects for new sources of energy production, and that as a result the 'stable supply of electric power' would not be assured.

3. LITTLE EFFICACY OF THE MEASURES ADOPTED AT MULTILATERAL AND NATIONAL LEVEL

The measures adopted both at international and national level appear to be hardly effective, for reasons that can be summarised as follows.

3.1 Soft Law and International Protection of SWFs Investment

The review of the existing legal framework governing the rights and obligations of host states as recipients of SWF investments has shown articulated forms of protection, at multilateral, regional and bilateral level, that have their main weaknesses in the excessive fragmentation and in the vagueness of safeguard clauses. A short summary to describe these general limits will therefore be appropriate.

The protection of SWF foreign investments and of the host states' vital interests are the two faces of the same coin. However, the reconciliation of all these interests may take different forms, contents and balances depending on the context, that may be multilateral, regional or bilateral.

At multilateral level, the treaties in force give limited guarantees to SWF investments. Due to the lack of a specific treaty on investments, the forms of protection are indirect, conditional, fragmented, if not occasional. The GATS discipline recognises to SWFs some kind of investment protection – as for services supply only – in the host states' obligation to ensure transparency and non discrimination, as well as access to the market and national treatment. Nevertheless, these obligations are subject to general exceptions (Arts. XIV and XIV *bis*) and to the reserves for regional integration agreements (Art. V), while market access and national treatment are also subject to the liberalisation practices and conditions listed by each state. Moreover, many SWFs home states are not yet participating in GATS. Finally, GATS safeguard clauses do not apply to portfolio investments but only to foreign direct investments (FDI), so that they can hardly protect SWFs, that do not seek a controlling interest. Considering also that GATS exemptions are allowed in the practice with a restrictive interpretation, the GATS general principles do not appear to be an adequate tool SWFs can use to protect their investments abroad.

OECD rules help in interpreting host state measures and in assessing their legitimacy. However, OECD rules are also characterised by a very high fragmentation; they are not binding, in the absence of an adequate dispute settlement system; they are vague in their definition of principles protected, exemptions allowed and procedures applied.[63] An attempt of monitoring these practices did not lead to the development of an ethical code, nor may we predict it will in the near future. In fact, due to the variety of tools adopted by host states (from list of industries considered as 'critical' to lists of critical infrastructures, to the broadening of essential security notions to include an economic profile) the identification of a common denominator for the protection of interests considered essential by host states appears to be particularly complicated. Also, to expect host states to accept unilaterally to impair their freedom of action for the protection of interests they consider essential would be unrealistic.

At regional level, EU regulations show continuity with both international law and bilateral treaties. The restrictions to the free circulation of capital (on grounds of public order and security) are well defined in the TFEU, and the case law (especially referring to the 'golden share') provides decisive elements for the interpretation of rules and exemptions, allowed under very restrictive criteria. In particular, repressive, precautionary measures must comply with the principle of proportionality, while preventive measures are screened with greater diffidence by courts. As for SWF investments, these rules and practices are relevant insofar as they apply to state measures regardless whether the investments they are supposed to restrict are made by companies or funds, within or outside the EU.[64]

At bilateral level, SWFs are entitled to take action to protect their investments by resorting to the BIT dispute settlement procedure; of course, absent a treaty, SWFs can support the negotiation of a new bilateral treaty between their home state and the state they would be interested in investing in. However, these protection measures may not be appropriate to prevent or repress a wrongful restrictive measure taken by the host state. As to the BITs, the current trend towards broadening safeguard clauses to cover a not (or vaguely) defined essential security interest, qualified at the host state's discretion, reduces the margin of action for SWFs in a dispute.

---

63 These limits are clearly to be seen in the activities of the two OECD commissions relevant for the case at hand: the Investment Committee on Sovereign Wealth Funds and Recipient Country policies and the Investment Committee's Project on Freedom of Investment, National security and strategic industries.

64 At best, it might be more difficult, in case of an illegitimate restrictive measure that restricts an investment or of a preventive decree against the SWF, to implement protection measures.

3.2 Host State Measures, Law and Practice

Coming to a national level, the recent reactions of those states that have adopted measures on SWF activities appear to have two main forms. The first one qualifies the interest that the measure aims at protecting; however, this interest is seldom identified with accuracy: for example, the notion of national security is always very vague and gives a wide discretionary margin to thc host state. The second form (i.e. a negative list of sectors) leaves the interest protected undetermined and rather qualifies the areas (from natural resources to energy, from aerospace to electronic communications, from automotive to chemical industry) or even the company activity (holding or operating 'critical infrastructures' or providing essential services) to protect.[65]

In both these forms, the measure taken by a host state facing a SWF investment – which indeed is always defined accurately – may be exercised autonomously: state laws do not provide for external circumstances which the adoption of the measure should abide by. The only exception is that of EU member states, that are required to comply with EU rules on the movement of capital.

It is interesting to verify, in defining either the interest or the business sectors protected, as well as the forms in which host state measures are adopted, whether national laws comply with international law and practices. Compliance is a benchmark for effectiveness: the more the notion of security interest is consistent with international rules, ethical codes and practices, the less controversial should appear the host state action.

The effectiveness of national measures adopted applying safeguard clauses depends on the extension of the notion of essential security interest and on the alleged self-judging character of essential security provisions. Hence, we should qualify this principle and analyse ways and methods for its evaluation.

3.2.1 The uncertain qualification of essential security interest

The safeguard clause which the exemptions introduced by the states seem to focus on is based on a new and wider notion of essential security interest. As seen in section 2.4, there are many measures that states can adopt to justify waivers to the general principle of freedom of investment. Some states would adopt a system of lists, classifying the business sectors in

[65] See a focus on the prevailing negative effects of such measures in D. Marchick and M. Slaughter, *Global FDI policy correcting a protectionist drift*, Council of Foreign Relations Special Report 34 (June).

which there might be an essential security interest;[66] others would invoke a broad notion of security interest that can be qualified only on a case by case basis;[67] others would extend the notion to include economic interest or even the protection of certain lifestyles.[68]

The significant uncertainties that these national practices produce on the definitions side, so much so that the notion of essential security interest is often unclear, are reflected in the international law: in fact, there is no shared notion of essential security interest in international treaties, customary law or case law.[69]

As regard to treaties, a comprehensive but vague notion of essential security interest is found in the OECD Code of Liberalisation of Capital Movements, where Article 3 states that the provisions 'shall not prevent a member from taking action which it considers necessary for the essential security interest'. While, according to the Investment Committee's commentaries of the Codes, this safeguard provision is 'deemed to address exceptional situations', a restrictive definition of the notion was never established.[70] Recently, the OECD published Guidelines for Recipient Country Investment Policies Relating to National Security,[71] recommending that investment policies and measures to safeguard national security should be guided by the principles of non-discrimination, transparency of policies and predictability of results, proportionality of measures and accountability of implementing authorities. As for essential security

---

[66] See on this the French law, but also the Chinese, German and Japanese law.

[67] Section 2.4.2 above.

[68] See on this *International Investment Perspectives: Freedom of Investment in a Changing World* (OECD, 2007) and particularly Ch. 3, 'Freedom of Investment, National Security and "Strategic" Industries: An Interim Report' 53–63, 59.

[69] For a preliminary, general review of the issue, see *International Investment Perspectives: Freedom of Investment in a Changing World* (OECD, 2007) and particularly Ch. 5, *Essential Security Interests under International Investment Law*.

[70] The Recommendation of the OECD Council on 'Member country measures concerning National Treatment of foreign-controlled enterprises in OECD member countries and based on considerations of public order and essential security interest', adopted at its 646th meeting on 16 July 1986, provided for general provisions and recommended to member states, inter alia, to 'practice restraint in their use of the limitation to accord National Treatment for . . . essential security interests, aiming at circumscribing their measures related to . . . essential security interests to areas where such concerns are predominant'. The Recommendation also provided that 'the member states study the possibility of alternative regulations which would allow them to fulfil their objectives concerning . . . essential security interests and also permit foreign-controlled enterprises to operate in the countries concerned'.

[71] Recommendation adopted by the OECD Council on 25 May 2009.

concerns, the Recommendation recognises that each country has the right to determine what is necessary to protect its national security, the only limit being that such determination should be made using rigorous risk assessment techniques, and that there should be a clear relationship between investment restrictions and the national security risks identified.

The draft MAI also provided for essential security as a general exception;[72] so did other regional and multilateral agreements, such as NAFTA[73] and the Energy Charter Treaty.[74] The practicc of Bilatcral Investment Treaties (BITs) shows that essential security interest provisions are not always included, and that even when provided for, they differ in their content and scope.[75]

In international customary law, the essential security safeguard clause is generally viewed as a state of necessity, as defined in Article 25 of the International Law Commission's (ILC) Draft Articles on State

---

72 The Multilateral Agreement on Investments, Draft consolidated text of 1998, Chapter 'Exceptions and safeguards'. The essential security interests' exception was limited to periods of war, armed conflict or other emergency, or to the implementation of national policies or international agreements respecting the non-proliferation of weapons of mass destruction, or related to arms production. However a specific clause aimed at preventing a disguised protection of economic interests or actions that are disproportionate in relation to the protected interests.

73 NAFTA Ch. XXI does not prevent any Party from taking any actions that it considers necessary for the protection of essential security interests: (i) relating to the traffic in arms, ammunition and implements of war and to such traffic and transaction in other goods, materials, services and technology undertaken directly or indirectly for the purpose of supplying a military or other security establishment; (ii) taken in time of war or other emergency in international relations, or (iii) relating to the implementation of national policies or international agreements respecting the non proliferation of nuclear weapons or other nuclear explosive devices. These essential security provisions have an explicitly self judging character.

74 The Energy Charter Treaty Art. 24 states that 'the provisions of this Treaty . . . shall not be construed to prevent any Contracting party from taking any measure which it considers necessary: (a) for the protection of its essential security interests including those (i) relating to the supply of Energy Materials and products to a military establishment, or (ii) taken in time of war, armed conflict or other emergency in International relations'. These provisions have an explicitly self-judging character.

75 A specific provision on the protection of essential security interest is in the new model BITs of Canada (2004), Germany (2005), India (2003) and United States (2004), but not in the new model of France and United Kingdom. Some states have never included an essential security interest clause in their BITs: Brazil, Denmark, Greece, Iceland, Ireland, Italy, Norway, Slovenia and South Africa. Other states have included such provision most of the time: Germany, India, Mexico, Belgium and Luxembourg.

Responsibility. The scope of application of necessity to justify an exemption from a state's international obligations is narrowed, both by its definition 'in negative terms'[76] and by the conditions that must be met in order to invoke it. Firstly, even though the law does not provide a specific definition of it,[77] according to Article 25 necessity may only be invoked to safeguard an essential interest from a serious and imminent danger. Secondly, the action taken must be the 'only way' available to safeguard that interest of the state (so, implementing the proportionality and last resort principles). Thirdly, the action must not seriously impair an essential interest of the other state or states concerned, or of the international community as a whole. Fourthly, necessity cannot be invoked to exclude wrongfulness of a non-conforming measure where the international obligation explicitly or implicitly excludes the plea of necessity. In case of implicit exclusion of necessity, the unavailability of such a plea emerges from the object and the purpose of the agreement. Finally, necessity may not be invoked as an excuse if the responsible state has contributed to the event. Although the Draft Articles on State Responsibility have not yet led to the execution of an international convention, they are a specific reference often used in recent international judgments and practices.

The notion of necessity narrowed in the international customary law is therefore far more accurate than the definition of essential security interest in national statutes – although the latter is often assimilated to the former; moreover, its application is subject to the existence of specific requirements. Hence, the notion of essential security interest will be very difficult to ascertain and actually apply – for state of necessity reasons – in a ICSID controversy arising from the breach of a BIT by a state that has prohibited or conditioned an SWF's investment in a company incorporated in

---

[76] Art. 25 of the International Law Commission's Draft Articles on State Responsibility states that '[N]ecessity may not be invoked by the State as a ground for precluding the wrongfulness of an act not in conformity with an international obligation of the State unless. . .'.

[77] The last Special Rapporteur Prof. Crawford, in his Second Report on State Responsibility (Addendum, International Law Commission, 51st Session, at 30, U.N. Doc. A/CN.4/498/Add.2 (1999)) noted that 'essential' cannot be defined and must depend on the specific facts of each case. On the contrary, the first Special Rapporteur Prof. Ago, stated in 1980 (Documents of the Thirty-Second Session (1980) 2 Y.B. Int'l L. Comm'n 14, U.N. Doc. A/CN.4/SER.A/1980/Add.1 (Pt 1)) that the 'essential state interest' that would allow the state to breach its obligation must be a vital interest, such as 'political or economic survival, the continued functioning of its essential services, the maintenance of internal peace, the survival of a sector of its population, the preservation of the environment of its territory or a part thereof, etc.'

the same state, if the assessment is not (or not only) based on the specific provision of a BIT but (also) on international customary law.[78]

In other words, the freedom claimed by the states in stating the national interest they need to protect, conflicts with the freedom that states mutually recognise each other internationally. It remains to be seen whether a similar conflict also arises between recent national rules and established international rules and practices regarding how a host state may adopt restrictive measures to protect its national security interest.

3.2.2 The alleged self-judging character of essential security provisions

The second factor that contributes to the uncertain application of the essential security interest is the alleged self-judging character of essential security provisions.

With reference to EU law, according to the 'golden share case law', state action is subject to EU control, both in the actual enforcement of the proportionality principle, and in assessing whether there is or not an essential interest of the state that, if violated, would justify a state measure against the SWF.

In other cases, the plea of necessity is expressly provided for and its self-judging character is determined clearly. For example, the OECD Codes of Liberalisation of Capital Movements allow OECD members to take all the measures they 'consider necessary', which means that this provision is explicitly self-judging. In other cases, action in circumstances of necessity is allowed, but it is not said whether a state may or not implement it on the basis of self-judgement. In this case, the object and the purpose of the agreement must be reviewed. In the only cases where the matter was

---

[78] A conspicuous example of this uncertainty are the ICSID awards related to the Argentina economic crisis. While in the cases of CMS (*CMS Gas Transmission Company v. Argentine Republic*, ICSID case no. ARB/01/8, Award 12 May 2005) and Enron (*Enron Corporation Ponderosa Assets, L.P. v. Argentine Republic*, ICSID case no. ARB/01/3, Award 22 May 2007) the Court decided that there were no presuppositions for an action by the Argentine government justified by an essential security interest: (i) because the crisis was not so serious as to justify such an action; (ii) because the Government could still use less invasive instruments (under the principles of proportionality and of last resort); and (iii) because Argentina had materially contributed to the worsening of the crisis, in the case of *LG&E* (*LG&E Energy Corp., LG&E International Inc. v. Argentine Republic*, ICSID case no. ARB/02/1, Decision on liability, 3 October 2006) the Court decided that the crisis was serious enough to threaten 'total collapse of the Government and the Argentine State', and stated that 'from 1 December 2001 until 26 April 2003, Argentina was in a period of crisis during which it was necessary to enact measures to maintain public order and protect its essential security interests'.

discussed in Court, in connection with the economic crisis that Argentina faced in 2000 with the 'pesification' of its economy, the courts resolved, in the absence of relevant provisions in the bilateral treaty, that Argentina was not entitled to self judge the existence of circumstances of necessity.[79] Therefore, the legitimacy of a measure taken by a host state in respect of a SWF investment in a state-owned company on grounds of essential security reasons would be uncertain. At the same time, the international practice calls for a greater accuracy in the BITs, that should deal with the matter explicitly and clearly in order to ensure certainty of right. We will deal with this in Chapter 6.

4. THE CHALLENGING TASK SWFS MUST CARRY OUT, AND SOME PROPOSALS TO SIMPLIFY IT

The limits of the existing international multilateral system, not providing for any real form of investment protection, force those SWFs that want to invest abroad consciously in a particularly complex activity that involves: (i) reviewing all national regulations (or at least those adopted by the states of higher interest) governing the forms of protection for foreign investments (many of which are being or will soon be amended in a restrictive direction); (ii) inducing the home state to negotiate, sign and ratify BITs with certain host states (where there are no such agreements); (iii) supporting the review of the BITs in force between the home state and the state where the SWF wants to invest in, and request from the home state, as the case may be, the renegotiation of existing BITs that do not provide suitable guarantee under the profile of access to the market and security of the investment made; and (iv) securing sophisticated (law) risk analysis tools, by country and industry sector, adopting specific risk-minimisation

[79] In particular, in the *CMS* case (*CMS Gas Transmission Company v. Argentine Republic*, ICSID case no. ARB/01/8, Award 12 May 2005), the Court stated that 'when States intend to create for themselves a right to determine unilaterally the legitimacy of extraordinary measures importing non-compliance with obligations assumed in a treaty, they do so expressly'. The Enron Court (*Enron Corporation Ponderosa Assets, L.P. v. Argentine Republic*, n. 78 above) stated that 'truly exceptional and extraordinary clauses such as a self-judging provision normally must be expressly drafted to reflect that intent, as otherwise there can well be a presumption about not having that meaning in view of its exceptional nature'. In both cases the Courts referred to the judgments of the International Court of Justice, and particularly to the cases *Nicaragua* (1986), *Gabcikovo-Nagymaros* (1997) and *Oil Platforms* (2003). A similar decision was taken by the court in the *LG&E* case.

procedures when the investment is made in critical countries or sectors. These assessments are particularly complex due to the absence, both at (host state) domestic and at international (bilateral and multilateral) level, of tools capable of ensuring the transparency of the procedures adopted by host states, but also of the contents of exemptions, the predictability of timeframes and results.

All these difficulties taken together imply, on one hand, a greater caution in SWF investments and, on the other, a sort of competition between the legal systems of host states which, in the absence of a multilateral regulation, risks to lead to greater uncertainty.

We propose to go back and start from the assumptions we made in previous chapters: host states regulation should be: (i) residual, applying only if and to the extent to which SWFs do not endorse or comply with GAPPs;[80] (ii) predictable (as for timeframes and outcome of the investment assessment); (iii) transparent (regarding the exemptions and the risk assessments justifying them, specifying which factors – and how – should be taken into account[81]); (iv) confidential (as regards aspects of the investment that SWF deems should not be disclosed); and (v) proportionate, aiming at meeting the real host state needs. The proportionality test should include: (a) as for the time factor, a temporary measure, adopted *ex post* for a short time period, (b) as for contents, a clear definition of the scope of the measure (i.e. clarifying what essential security interest consist in, or what are essential defence interest, critical infrastructures, public order, public security, public interest, strategic industries).

Our research also highlights that host state regulation differs from

---

80 The assessment of SWFs' GAPPs compliance could be entrusted to an independent body (which may also belong to the IMF); in this way the decision about allowing a SWF investment potentially threatening national interest will not be subject to the sole discretion of the host state. A third-party impartial institution assessing SWFs' compliance with the GAPPs would be in the interest of both the host and home state, as on one hand it would allow the former to apply a different treatment to SWFs without incurring in the non-discrimination obligations provided for by international treaties (differences would be justified by the SWFs' different degree of GAPPs acceptance). On the other hand, the assessment of the compliance with (all or the most important) GAPPs obligations would allow SWFs' home states to invest freely in all those states where the application of specific barring rules to protect national interest is only limited to those funds that refuse to comply with the code.

81 The risk assessment criteria used in national-security review processes when screening specific investments should be formalised. As was noted by B. Cohen (*Sovereign Wealth Funds and National Security: the great tradeoff*, n. 41 above), risk analysis procedures are not completely transparent: which factors are assessed, and how, is still unclear.

(international, multilateral) SWFs regulation in an important aspect: national company law can be applied also to sovereign investors, as it does not make any difference between public/private company/investor; on the contrary, active SOEs multilateral regulations cannot apply to SWFs, for the reasons listed in section 2.1.2. Hence, there would be a rather minor need for host state specific rules governing SWFs investments than for SWFs' operations.

A few examples might help to understand the importance of this point. Let's take the case of Unicredit, the Italian bank. Unicredit's articles of association state that shareholders cannot exceed 5 per cent of the assembly voting shares. The Central Bank of Libya owned 4.99 per cent of voting shares, when (July 2010) a Libyan SWF (Libyan Investment Authority – LIA) acquired 2 per cent of shares. Both the Italian Central Bank and the Italian Securities Commission opened a file; if the two Libyan institutions hold as one investor, LIA voting rights will be suspended. Hence, the importance of the ultimate control and the relevance of a separate legal personality and of an adequate corporate governance regulation.

National company law, securities regulations, but also antitrust law apply irrespectively of investor ownership. What if a SWF acquires the control of a company even in the form of dominant influence (presumed by antitrust law when an investor owns 20 per cent of voting shares)? It would have to submit a file to the national antitrust authority or to the European Commission, depending on the size of the operation of concentration. A similar case will occur when two or more SWFs, even from different states, operate joint ventures (this appears to be the most recent trend). Also in this case, antitrust rules – together with their safeguard clauses – will apply.

Some measures could however be taken to strengthen the legal environment. Enforcement patterns should be guaranteed at multilateral, regional and bilateral level; obviously by means of different tools. At multilateral level, considering that negotiations are very unlikely to be resumed and a multilateral treaty on investments to be finalised soon, a restrictive interpretation of safeguard clauses in the GATS practice would be a benchmark for the development of best practices (or of general accepted principles and practices – GAPPs) for investments recipient states. The best practices (or the GAPPs) could be defined within the OECD (that could publish more detailed rules and practices) or even within the IMF: this would enable reciprocity in the obligations of home and host states and increase the effectiveness of both. Best practices should be reflected in a code; the limit of such code being voluntary might be overcome at least in part by connecting it to the other code (the so-called 'Santiago principles') already in force and binding on SWFs (e.g. the compliance with the respective constraints could be mutually binding). As to contents, the code should provide an accurate definition of host state obligations and of the ways available to SWFs to obtain compliance with them, and also set the limits and enforcement practices of the exemptions host states may invoke.

Finally, at bilateral level, considering the high degree of BIT standardisation,[82] SWFs should make sure that home states obtain (by maintaining the existing BITs into force or renegotiating them as required) a restriction (and possibly its specification) to the application of the general security clause and the definition of a sound and adequate controversy settlement system (ideally at ICSID level). Also (and above all) at bilateral level, the differentiation of the requirements for investment legitimacy and of the procedures to verify such requirements on grounds of the compliance by the SWFs with the ethical code developed together with the IMF ('Santiago principles') would make the inquiry easier. Therefore, the BITs would need to be amended, during the course of negotiations, in this direction as well.

[82] Standardisation has reached such a level that some experts have hypothesised a form of indirect multilateralisation: see A. Shill, *The multilateralization of International investment law: the emergence of a multilateral system of investment protection on the basis of bilateral treaties*, paper presented at the annual SIEL convention, 15–17 July 2008, where the author explains the multilateralisation drive also on the basis of the fact that the most favoured nation clause is now generally adopted in multilateral treaties. For a detailed analysis see G. Sacerdoti, 'Bilateral treaties and multilateral investments on investment protection' (1997) 269 ADI, RC 251–490.

PART III

SWFs' protection in bilateral relations

5. SWFs and state immunity

1. IN SEARCH OF A DIRECT RELATIONSHIP

One issue that observers did not delve into is whether or not, and in case to what extent, SWFs can invoke state immunity, protecting their action or challenging the enforcement of host state measures. At a first glance, the question may be answered negatively. In fact, according to a general principle variably used in international law, when a state invests as a private entity it should be treated as such. However, more insight should be required here. As we saw in previous chapters, SWFs lie in the 'middle ground' between SOEs (that do not enjoy immunity) and central banks (whose state immunity is generally recognised). They share some instruments with the former, sometimes share purposes with the latter. Also on structural and governance terms, SWFs can hardly be ascribed entirely to either category (public companies or central banks). And, historically, SWFs are a development of the typical forms of public resource management operated by states. The 'sovereign' origin of these funds is an important legacy that still leaves traces.

Hence, even for 'immunity purposes', we need to understand if SWFs should be treated like private investors (that of course do not enjoy immunity) or like central banks (that enjoy almost unquestioned immunity); or whether it is appropriate to assume that there is a new category, independent from the other two, where SWFs belong due to their peculiar characteristics, and in case, which of the two opposite poles should attract it; or if this new category finds its place in the middle. We should also assess the relevance of the transaction nature (i.e. the investment, the exercise of shareholders' power) and the purpose it seeks.

Therefore, the issue is more problematic than it may appear and should be studied thoroughly, both in theory and practice. The conclusions we reached about definition and classification may help. Sovereignty (legal structure, governance and accountability) and purposes are decisive elements to verify if the fund identifies itself or not with the state; this is also useful for starting a research on a possible SWFs immunity. The FGCI classification (Chapter 1, section 1) and the differences we found between SWFs and SOEs (Chapter 2, section 1.2) may help too.

The classification by sovereignty and purposes proposed in the previous chapters allows for an independent examination aimed at classifying properly these new entities that express the will of the state and through which states exercise part of their economic sovereignty.

We propose conducting the research along the path described as follows. Firstly, we will focus on which host state measures might be challenged by a SWF invoking state immunity (Chapter 5, section 2.1). The analysis in Chapter 4 of the measures proposed in literature and actually adopted by the host states so far will be useful here. We can call it 'passive immunity'. This is a new approach, as immunity has always represented a guarantee of non-punishability condition for illicit acts committed by sovereign entities; on the contrary, we will here assess if SWFs can invoke immunity protection against restrictive measures adopted by states where they invested in and that they consider prejudicial.[1] Then we will investigate which SWF actions in host state territories might be covered by immunity; this might concern a more traditional case which we will call here 'active immunity', as opposite to the passive one (Chapter 5, section 2.2).

Secondly, we will try to understand if the immunity invoked is from jurisdiction or from execution, as the discipline applicable to either case is different, in theory and in practice. In fact, as we will see, according to the dominant pattern, the scope of application of immunity from execution is broader, as immunity from jurisdiction necessarily implies that from execution, and not vice-versa. However, this assumption too should be verified in theory and tested on a case by case basis (Chapter 5, section 3).

Thirdly, we should consider whether SWFs may be treated as a state for the purpose of immunity, even acting as agency or body, in order to develop theoretical solutions applicable to a variety of cases (Chapter 5, section 4). In fact, as we have seen, as there is no single basic SWFs type defined, we may assume that the rules of immunity may apply or not, or may apply in many different forms according to the type of fund, its structure, its governance, etc. Chapter 2 about definitions and classifications will be useful here.

Fourthly, and this part will lead us on to next chapter, we will assess if and how the issue of state immunity becomes relevant for SWFs according to bilateral investment agreements (BITs), and if and how the international practice in investment treaties affects the matter[2] (Chapter 6).

---

[1] Logically (and not procedurally) the same question arises when a state opposes to an injunctive order against assets considered sovereign: it is in any case a judicial action brought by a state to protect a sovereign interest (or asset).

[2] In fact, an arbitration finalised between a state and a foreign individual or legal person in order to settle a controversy about a commercial transaction

2 'PASSIVE' AND 'ACTIVE' IMMUNITY: HOST STATE AND SWF ACTIONS RELEVANT FOR APPLYING STATE IMMUNITY

Chapters 3 and 4 focused on two main profiles regarding the active and passive rules applicable to SWFs, i.e. the regulation of fund activities and the restrictive measures host states may adopt to limit SWFs investments. We will test both these aspects for immunity. However, while the former profile falls easily within the traditional debate about state immunity, a few arguments should be added to support an innovative approach to the latter profile.

2.1 Host State Actions That Might be Challenged by an SWF Under the Profile of State Immunity

We have seen in Chapter 3 that international organisations (OECD) and states have adopted or are discussing the adoption of specific national rules aimed at regulating SWFs investments. These measures are instrumental and operate according to the nature of the fund; they apply to state funds by reason of their public and 'sovereign' nature and are aimed at both inhibiting fund actions (e.g. purchasing shares) and limiting their rights (e.g. 'neutralisation' of voting rights). In many cases these measures may be exercised at preventive level.

Our proposal to verify the operation of state immunity with respect to host state measures might seem peculiar. In fact, immunity applies at judicial level, state measures apply at law-making or government level. However, there is an important point of contact. In fact, the measures should be enforced on specific assets. In the case at hand, as the main activity of the funds consists in making investments, the assets subject to host states' restrictive measures will embed mostly stock or interest in companies, the purchase or use of which may be barred or restricted in many ways. Therefore, immunity may be relevant – with respect to host state measures – in terms of immunity from execution.

After all, the very fact that restrictive measures are adopted by states – as explained in Chapter 4 – on the terms and within the limits in which

---

(including investments) excludes immunity from a proceeding concerning not only the validity, interpretation or enforcement of the arbitration, but also the arbitration procedure or the appeal against the arbitration award. It then appears that submitting these controversies to jurisdiction does not exclude the possibility for a state to claim immunity in the enforcement of the award, unless this is expressly excluded by an arbitration clause (Art. 17 UN Convention).

an SWF exercises its sovereign function poses a question about the actual enforceability of those measures. If the public purpose, and hence the sovereign function of the investment fund is what the host state measure intends to challenge, it may be reasonably assumed that such measure will clash with the principle of immunity protected by the sovereign function itself. The discussion appears even more relevant with respect to preventive, precautionary measures. While, on one hand, these are the main tools used to enforce host state measures, on the other hand – as we will explain – they probably find a limit in immunity from execution, as they are prohibited by the most recent international convention and rarely admitted by national courts.

2.2 SWF Actions and Assets that Might be Protected by State Immunity

Another – more conventional – profile of state immunity, concerns SWF investments. The issue relates to a profile which we might define as 'active', as opposed to the former ('passive'). Here we look at immunity as an instrument to protect the fund not from host state measures but from jurisdiction or enforcement in the host state with respect to illicit acts committed by the SWF and otherwise punishable (i.e. abuses of authority, insider trading cases, market manipulation, irregularities with respect to large block trading, violation of securities laws or of company laws).

Immunity is not a cause for exclusion of illegality but rather the waiver by a state of its jurisdiction or of the enforcement by reason of the sovereign nature of the other party. It may then happen that certain SWF actions enjoy state immunity: it remains to be seen whether and to what extent immunity from execution or immunity from jurisdiction may be invoked.

3. IMMUNITY FROM JURISDICTION AND IMMUNITY FROM EXECUTION

The state immunity issue is relevant at international level but originates and develops at national level. National laws and practice recognise – first in absolute and then in relative terms – the impossibility to judge the actions (due to immunity from jurisdiction) or dispose of the assets (due to immunity from execution) of a foreign sovereign state.[3] This origin

[3] The rationale of immunity consisted originally in a corollary of sovereignty, protected in all its forms of expression, with the consequent prohibition for other

explains the fragmentation of the discipline and the absence of specific rules in many states where the matter has evolved mostly in the case law, and also the absence, until recent times, of international agreements and the consequent difficulty in recognising to such principles an autonomous and broader value in international law.[4]

It is on this sloping and sometimes slippery ground that the specific issue of SWFs fits in, adding other peculiarities. Hence, we will start attempting to make a simplified analysis following the typical differentiation between immunity from jurisdiction and from execution.

3.1 Immunity from Jurisdiction

The traditional notion of the absolute immunity of a state from the jurisdiction of another state founded on the brocard *par in parem non habet imperium* was left behind in the past century.[5] Originally, the case law of national Courts (especially in Italy and Belgium),[6] and later the laws of

---

states to interfere in internal and external state affairs carried out in the exercise of sovereign functions. This justified sovereign immunity. Today, the rationale of immunity is to allow a state to carry out in autonomy and independence the functions related with publicity and institutional purposes; therefore, immunity is limited to the relationship where such functions are expressed.

[4] For a review of the developments of State immunity law and practice see: J. Crawford, 'Execution of Judgements and Foreign Sovereign Immunity' (1981) 75 AJIL 820; C. Schreuer, *State Immunity: Some Recent Developments* (1988); H. Fox, 'International Law and Restraints on the Exercise of Jurisdiction by National Courts of States', in M.D. Evans (ed.), *International Law* (2003) 357; A. Dickinson *et al.* (eds.), *State Immunity: Selected Materials and Commentary* (2004) 326; H. Fox, *The Law of State Immunity* (2nd edn., 2008); N. Ronzitti and G. Venturini, *Le immunità giurisdizionali degli Stati e degli altri enti internazionali* (2008).

[5] Nevertheless, the path is not completed yet, for some countries (i.e. Bulgaria, Czech Republic, Poland, Romania, Russia) still apply the doctrine of absolute immunity.

[6] In particular, the Italian case law has considered *iure imperii* actions of nationalisation (Cass. 5 December 1966, n. 2830), or of attachment (Cass. 26 May 1979, n. 3062), judicial and police actions (Cass. 12 June 1999, n. 328), and *iure privatorum* – hence not enjoying immunity – the purchase and sale and the supply of goods and services (Cass. 25 November 1983, n. 7076), the execution of lease agreements and the sale of real property (Cass. 29 April 1961, n. 1001; Cass. 18 October 1982, n. 5399; Cass. 15 July 1987, n. 6171; Cass. 30 May 1990, n. 5091; Cass. 18 May 1992, n. 5937; Cass. 18 October 1993, n. 10294) and, above all, for the purposes of this work, the stipulation of mortgage loans and other financial transactions (Cass. 5 December 1966, n. 2830; Cass. 19 October 1984, n. 5275). The *Empire of Iran* case is also relevant (German Federal Constitutional Court (1963) 45 ILR 57).

certain countries (especially the United States and the United Kingdom)[7] defined a narrower scope of immunity for the activities carried out by a state in the exercise of its public prerogatives, and did not recognise immunity to the activities going beyond such prerogatives. The typical classification of activities *iure imperii* (where immunity is recognised) and *iure gestionis* (where immunity is denied) is grounded on the different *nature* of the action. In the case law of the states, the purpose of the action is irrelevant.[8]

The first international codification of state immunity, the 2005 UN Convention on Jurisdictional Immunities of States and their Property, partly disrupts this one-way development of case law and will probably affect its future developments.[9] Indeed, the Convention does not represent a codification of international customary law as it introduces new categories of state property immune from enforcement and contains a connection requirement of property serving commercial purposes with the entity against which the claim was directed, that is novelty in international law.

Article 10 of the Convention establishes that a state cannot invoke immunity from jurisdiction in a proceeding arising from a commercial

---

[7] Reference is made to the US Foreign Sovereign Immunity Act of 1976, and to the UK State Immunity Act of 1978, which influenced immunity-related laws in other states, such as Canada, Australia, Malaysia, Pakistan, South Africa, and Singapore.

[8] For example, an Italian Court of Cassation ruling established that, 'by giving prominent relevance to the end purpose of the entity, the distinction between deeds committed in the exercise of sovereign powers and transactions of private law is deprived of all practical effect, . . . as it should be assumed that any activity of a public entity is somehow connected with the institutional purpose of that entity and aimed at its achievement' (Cass. 5 Dec. 1966, n. 2830).

[9] The UN Convention will enter into force once thirty states have submitted their ratification, acceptance, approval or accession with the Secretary-General of the United Nations. At present, 28 states signed the Treaty during the period open for signature, and another 8 had ratified or acceded to the Convention, that is still not in force. For specific comments on the 2005 UN Convention see, apart from the monographs mentioned in n. 4: G. Hafner and L. Lange, *La Convention des Nations Unies sur les immunités jurisdictionnelles des Etats et de leurs biens*, in [2004] AFDI, 45 ss.; G. Hafner and U. Kohler, 'The United Nations Convention on Jurisdictional Immunities of States and their Property' [2004] *Netherlands Yearbook of International Law* 3–49; E. Denza, 'The 2005 UN Convention on State Immunity in Perspective' [2006] ICLQ 395–8; H. Fox, 'In Defence of State Immunity: Why the UN Convention on State Immunity is Important' [2006] ICLQ 399–406; R. Gardiner, 'UN Convention on State Immunity: Form and Function' [2006] ICLQ 407–10, L. McGregor, 'State Immunity and *Jus Cogens*' [2006] ICLQ 437–46.

transaction. Commercial transaction means (according to Art. 2.1(c) of the Convention): '(i) any commercial contract or transaction for the sale of goods or supply of services, (ii) any contract for a loan or other transaction of a financial nature, including any obligation of guarantee or of indemnity in respect of any such loan or transaction, (iii) any other contract or transaction of a commercial, industrial, trading or professional nature, but not including a contract of employment of persons'. The immunity exemption does not apply to cases of a commercial transaction between states or if the parties to the commercial transaction have expressly agreed otherwise.

The list of cases where a transaction is commercial, as an exception to the general rule of immunity, is exhaustive. This interpretation is confirmed in the broad meaning of the term 'commercial transaction' (Art. 10) compared to the term used ('contractual obligations') in the 1972 European Convention on State Immunity.[10] For what is relevant here, investments are 'commercial transactions', and could not be considered as 'contractual obligations'. Therefore, the broader definition provided by the UN Convention implies a meaningful shift for SWF, whose activity was originally excluded from the definition and is instead now included within 'commercial activities'.

The most controversial part of the definition, and maybe of the entire Convention, subtracts clarity to this classification by establishing (Art. 1.2) that:

> '[I]n determining whether a contract or transaction is a "commercial transaction" under paragraph 1(c), reference should be made primarily to the nature of the contract or transaction, but its purpose should also be taken into account if the parties to the contract or transaction have so agreed, or if, in the practice of the State of the forum, that purpose is relevant to determining the non-commercial character of the contract or transaction'.

Therefore, the activity must be considered first according to the nature of the transaction and then – only in case of an agreement or the practice of the forum state allows to do so, according to the purpose of the contract or transaction. Unlike what arises from the practice of national Courts,[11]

---

[10] Convention stipulated in Basel on 16 May 1972.

[11] For a review of Italian case law in the sense that the distinction between immune actions and non-immune actions should be based on the objective nature of a transaction and not also on its purpose, see: Cass. 5 December 1966, n. 2830; Cass. 19 October 1984, n. 5275; Cass. 15 July 1987, n. 6171; Cass. 18 October 1993, n. 10294. According to the Federal Constitutional Court of Germany (*Empire of Iran*, 30 April 1963, (1963) 45 ILR 57), 'the distinction between sovereign and not

here purpose takes a clear role, albeit secondary and possible (it is not relevant if there is no agreement or if the practice of the state of the forum does not allow it). This role changes according to the practice of states and cannot therefore be defined *ex ante*. The consequent risk of fragmentation of state practice was apparently considered by the UN Convention an acceptable compromise, that will in any case drive a proliferation of both bilateral relationships – including bilateral treaties on investments – and national laws. In fact, we may reasonably assume that many states will pass laws governing mutual guarantees concerning the relevance of purpose as for immunity from execution. Be it as it may, the relevance of purposes widens the scope of application of immunity in the Convention and will probably affect national laws.[12]

3.2 Immunity from Execution

When recognised, immunity from jurisdiction excludes the enforcement of immunity from execution, which is not implied: it merely does not apply. It only applies if immunity from jurisdiction is not admitted. The applicability of enforcement measures indeed can be discussed only when a state acts commercially and is therefore deprived of its immunity from jurisdiction. In this perspective, immunity from jurisdiction and from execution

---

sovereign cannot be drawn according to the purpose of the state transaction . . . For, ultimately, activities of the state . . . serve sovereign purposes and duties'. Conversely, in *I Congreso de Partido* case (UK House of Lords [1983] 1 AC 244, 64 ILR 307) the 'whole context' of the transaction was taken in consideration; also French courts evaluated both the nature and the purposes of the acts. Again, the Italian Court of Cassation found that a bond issue was a commercial matter, but the subsequent default of Argentina's public debt obligations was motivated by the sovereign purpose of managing a serious economic crisis, that justified the application of state immunity from jurisdiction (*Borri Loca v. Republic of Argentina*, Cass. Civ. sez. un., decision no. 11225 of 27 May 2005).

[12] In this sense the Italian Court of Cassation on 27 May 2005 (no.11225) recognised the immunity of Argentina with respect to the bonds issued in the State of New York in 1998, listed in Luxembourg and re-sold in secondary markets. US courts instead did not consider bond issuing as an immune activity, but held that there was no 'direct effect in the United States' of the commercial activity (Supreme Court of the United States, 12 June 1992, *Republic of Argentina and Banco central de la Republica Argentina v. Weltover Inc. et al.*, 504 U.S. 697; United District Court for the Southern District of New York, 21 March 2007, *Morris Jr. v. The People's Republic of China, Bolanos Pons et al. v. the People's Republic of China*, 478 F. Supp. 2d 571). See on this: C. Schmerler, 'Restructuring Sovereign Debt', in Schmerler and Silkenat (eds.), *The Law of Insolvencies and Debt Restructuring* (2006), pp. 431 *ff.*; M. Bordoni, Default nel debito pubblico e immunità dello Stato estero dalla giurisdizione civile, [2006] RDI, 1031 ff.

are alternative, as the latter may apply only if the former does not. This interpretation allows us not only to consider that the scopes of application of the two immunities are not the same, but also to leave behind the traditional approach according to which the scope of application of immunity from jurisdiction is broader because it implies necessarily immunity from execution, and not the other way round too. As we will see, theoretically this conclusion has precise consequences for the subject matter of our work.

The development of national case law on immunity from execution followed that on immunity from jurisdiction with certain differences, in time (the development was slower[13]), materially (the scope of immunity from execution is still broader than that of immunity from jurisdiction), and in purpose (the purpose of immunity from execution is to prevent not the abstract possibility to suit a state but the adoption by a state of an authority action against the property of another state).

The literature and the most recent practice recognise the present rationale of immunity from execution not so much in the nature of an action (*iure imperii* or *iure gestionis*), already considered in the (logically prior) evaluation about immunity from jurisdiction, rather than in the intended use of the assets subject to enforcement[14]: the assets actually and effectively intended for the exercise of sovereign functions or the achievement of publicity purposes are immune. The ownership of the assets is instead irrelevant (unlike for immunity from jurisdiction).

Therefore, purposes become relevant for immunity from execution in both international conventions and state laws and practice, also because, as it does not refer to the activity but to the individual asset, it has a lesser – and however specific and concrete – scope of application. In particular, among the exceptions – detailed in exhaustive lists – to the general principle of immunity from execution,[15] national laws and international

---

[13] Italian and Swiss courts were the first to resolve in this sense, followed in the 1970s by French, German, English and Spanish courts (for a review see A. Atteritano, *Immunità dalle misure esecutive e cautelari*, in N. Ronzitti and G. Venturini, *Le immunità giurisdizionali degli Stati e degli altri enti internazionali*, n. 4 above, pp. 236–7).

[14] In this sense see: A. Reinisch, 'European Court Practice concerning State Immunity from enforcement measures' in [2006] EJIL 803–36, 804.

[15] The three traditional cases (i.e. in the 2005 UN Convention) are: (a) when the State has expressly consented to the taking of such measure, (b) when the State has allocated or earmarked property for the satisfaction of the claim which is the object of that proceeding, and (c) when it has been established that the property is specifically in use or is intended for use by the State for other than government non-commercial purposes and is in the territory of the State of the forum, provided

conventions include (which is of our concern here) the 'property in use for commercial purposes'. For example, according to the 2005 United Nations Convention on Jurisdictional Immunities of States and their Properties, post-judgement measures are admitted only if 'it has been established that the property is specifically in use or intended for the use by the State for other than government non-commercial purposes and is in the territory of the State of the forum'.[16]

The conditions provided by the Convention for the exercise of compulsory measures are more restrictive than those provided in the 1991 ILC Draft Articles on which the Convention is based.[17] In fact, the ILC proposal version only required 'assets serving commercial purposes'; the final text in the Convention has added to the objective factor another – and much heavier – subjective one, because the intention of a state to decide on an asset cannot be assumed, it must be explicit. The burden of proof is heavier also under an objective profile: an asset may be subject to enforcement measures not when it serves commercial purposes but when it is specifically used or intended for use for other than government non-commercial purposes. Apparently, at procedural level, the principle of the evidence that an asset is used for commercial purposes or is intended for use for other than government non-commercial purposes, is different. The psychological – i.e. subjective – component that characterises the latter makes the outcome of the assessment even more uncertain.

The 2005 UN Convention is certainly essential, however, – also with respect to immunity from execution – it is only in part the codification of a state practice; it indeed represents a progressive development, for instance, where it differentiates enforcement measures depending on whether adopted as provisional measures or on the merits.[18] However,

---

that post-judgement measures of constraint may only be taken against property that has a connection with the entity against which the proceeding was directed.

[16] Art. 19 of the UN Convention on State Immunity also clarifies that 'post-judgement measures of constraint may only to be taken against property that has a connection with the entity against which the proceeding was directed'.

[17] This with reference to both pre-judgement measures (including precautionary measures) and post-judgement measures. The former are actually barred without the prior consent of the defendant state (while in the ILC proposal they were subject to the same terms as post-judgement measures). Art. 18 of the 1991 ILC Draft Articles on Jurisdictional Immunities of States and their Properties provided for three main exceptions from enforcement immunity, the last one being that 'assets [are] serving commercial purposes, [are] present in the forum State and [are] connected with or linked to the underlying claim or defendant entity'.

[18] Pre-judgement measures of constraint are admitted only if and to the extent to 'the State has allocated or earmarked property for the satisfaction of the claim

we cannot assume that the Convention makes a rule out of the current practice, not even when it makes the enforcement of measures subject to the condition that the property serves 'commercial purposes' in the formulation just explained.

What the practice of states admits is, more simply, that enforcement measures are allowed only if the property serves non-sovereign purposes.[19] The problem is to transfer this abstract concept into reality and define and identify the scope of property to decide whether it is used for sovereign purposes or not. While some broad categories of property immune from enforcement – on certain conditions – can be recognised (embassy premises, cultural centres, information offices, military property, embassy accounts), others are more controversial. Being aware of these uncertainties, we may now deal with the issue of the immunity from jurisdiction and from execution applicable to sovereign wealth funds.

4 APPLICATION OF STATE IMMUNITY TO SWFS

We will now turn to the application of state immunity to SWFs and understand if and how an SWF can be identified with a state; immunity can apply only in this case. The analysis should concern both activities and assets, as they are both relevant for the purposes of immunity from jurisdiction and from execution.

4.1 Attribution to a State of the Activities and Ownership of SWF Assets for Immunity Purposes

The attribution to a state of an action or asset is a pre-requirement to assess the applicability of immunity. The exercise of sovereign functions (the only ones eligible for protection by restricted or functional immunity) is reserved to a state, which may then delegate them to agencies or entities acting with a more or less powerful formal and functional autonomy.

---

which is the object of that proceeding' (Art. 18 (b), 2005 UN Convention on State Immunity).

[19] For a review of the practice on this issue see A. Reinisch, n. 14 above, p. 808. There is no uniformity about a second (nexus) requirement, as national laws do not provide for such a requirement (UK SIA), or qualify the nexus requirement in different ways, such as a connection to the property and the underlying claim (US FSIA, but also French Courts, as in *Sonatrac* case), or as a connection between the property and the defendant state entity (ILC Draft Articles).

In order to assess whether a SWF's action or asset may enjoy immunity (from jurisdiction or from execution, respectively) we will need to figure out whether the action is attributable to (and the asset owned by) a state or a 'separate entity, distinct from the executive organs of the government of the state and capable of suing and being sued'.[20] To determine if the entity is sufficiently independent from the state, its incorporation, functions, powers and activities, as well as its relationship with the state should be examined. Of course, the definition is meaningful and the classification relevant with specific reference to the issue of immunity.

The classification becomes relevant for the granting of immunity with respect to international agreements and national law and practice. However, such relevance may differ from time to time and have different effects on jurisdiction and enforcement. A further analysis is therefore required.

4.1.1 International treaties

Starting from international law, the 2005 UN Convention establishes that 'State' means:

> '(i) the State and its various organs of government, (ii) constituent units of a federal State or political subdivisions of the State which are entitled to perform acts in the exercise of sovereign authority, and are acting in that capacity, [and above all] (iii) agencies or instrumentalities of the State or other entities, to the extent that they are entitled to perform and are actually performing acts in the exercise of sovereign authority of the State, and (iv) representatives of the State acting in that capacity' (Art. 2).

However, there is a difference between the first assumption and the others (i.e. between a state and other entities) in terms of jurisdiction and of enforcement. As to the former, states and various organs of government benefit from immunity *ratione personae*, which is therefore assumed, save for specifically stated exceptions, while other entities benefit from immunity *ratione materiae*, subject to proof of effective exercise of the sovereign authority of the state. As to enforcement, which presupposes the absence of immunity from jurisdiction (and hence the existence of a commercial activity), the difference is more blurred, because the property, of the state or of the separate entity, is in any case subject to enforcement measures only when it is intended for commercial activities.

---

[20] This definition becomes relevant both in the United Kingdom State Immunity Act 1978 s. 14(1) and the 1972 European Convention on State Immunity (Art. 27, and para. 107–9 of the Explanatory Note).

This is the contribution to definitions given by the Convention. As far as the applicable discipline is concerned, Article 10.3 of the Convention deals with the case in which a state does not act directly but through a separate entity. In particular:

> '[W]here a State enterprise or other entity established by a State which has an independent legal personality and is capable of: (a) suing or being sued; and (b) acquiring, owning or possessing and disposing of property, including property which that State has authorised it to operate or manage, is involved in a proceeding which relates to a commercial transaction in which that entity is engaged, the immunity from jurisdiction enjoyed by that State shall not be affected'.

Therefore, the involvement of a SOE or a SWF in a dispute relating to a commercial transaction does not impact on the immunity of the state that is not responsible for the transaction and whose property may not be subject to execution.[21]

Finally, and relevant for our research, Article 15 of the Convention states that a state cannot invoke immunity from jurisdiction before a court of another state in a proceeding relating to its participation in a company or other collective body, if that body (a) has participants other than states or international organisations, and (b) is incorporated or constituted under the law of the state of the forum or has its seat or principal place of business in that state.[22] Therefore, the rule of law assumes in absolute terms that the activity carried out by the state with respect to its participation in an enterprise is a 'commercial activity'. The beneficiaries of the rule are evidently SOEs, however its scope of application is seemingly broad enough to include SWFs as well. Therefore, according to Article 15 of the Convention, sovereign fund investments in host state companies are 'commercial activity' and as such they are not subject to immunity.

Also the 1972 European Convention, notwithstanding its well-known limits in terms of application,[23] is a useful interpretation tool. Article 27

---

[21] The Annex to the Convention, with respect to Art. 19, clarifies that 'Article 19 does not prejudge the question of "piercing the corporate veil", questions relating to a situation where a State entity has deliberately misrepresented its financial position or subsequently reduced its assets to avoid satisfying a claim, or other related issues'.

[22] Even in this case, immunity can be invoked by a State if the States concerned have so agreed or if the parties to the dispute have so provided by an agreement in writing or if the instrument establishing or regulating the body in question contains provisions to that effect (Art. 15.2).

[23] A small number of signatures and, above all, of ratifications has been gathered, therefore we may assume it will not come into force.

expressly excludes from the definition of 'contracting State' 'any legal entity of a contracting State which is distinct thereof and is capable of suing or being sued, even if that entity has been entrusted with public functions'. As a consequence, proceedings may be instituted against those entities in the same manner as against a private person. However, 'the courts may not entertain proceedings in respect of acts performed by the entity in the exercise of sovereign authority *(acta jure imperii)*' unless 'in corresponding circumstances, the courts would have had jurisdiction if the proceedings had been instituted against a Contracting State'.

As described in the explanatory note of the 1972 European Convention on State Immunity (para. 108), a legal entity is not defined by the criterion of legal personality alone, for even a state authority may have legal personality without constituting an entity distinct from the state. On the contrary, a dual test comprising (1) distinct existence separate and apart from the executive organs of the state, and (2) capacity to sue or be sued, i.e. the ability to assume the role of either plaintiff or defendant in court proceedings, has been considered more reliable. As examples of legal entities the explanatory note of the Convention refers to political subdivisions or state agencies, such as national banks or railway administrations. Those entities may not enjoy a more favourable treatment than a contracting state. Furthermore, some provisions of the Convention, i.e. those laying down special rules for proceedings to which one of the parties is a state (Arts 16–19), those dealing with the obligation to comply with a judgement or a settlement (Arts 20–22), and those prohibiting execution in the territory of the state of the forum (Art. 23), do not apply to such entities.

Therefore, this convention too differentiates separate entities from states not so much from the point of view of immunity from jurisdiction (in both cases subject to the verification of the commercial nature of the activity) than from the point of view of immunity from execution; in particular, it excludes the assumption of immunity from execution for the property of the separate entity, the actual and material destination of which will have to be assessed (i.e. commercial or to the exercise of sovereign authority).

4.1.2 National laws and practices

As to national laws, the UK State Immunity Act grants to separate state entities immunity both of jurisdiction and of enforcement only for activities carried out in the exercise of sovereign authority, while they don't enjoy immunity in commercial activities.[24]

Differently, the US Foreign Sovereign Immunities Act definition (FSIA)

24 Section 14(2), (3), United Kingdom State Immunity Act 1978.

of 'state' includes 'a political subdivision of a foreign state or an agency or instrumentality of a foreign state'. An agency or instrumentality of a foreign state is defined as 'a separate legal person, corporate or otherwise, that is an organ of a foreign state or political sub-division thereof, or a majority of whose shares or other ownership interest is owned by a foreign state'.[25] Under FSIA, 'commercial activity' is defined as a 'regular course of commercial conduct or a particular commercial transaction or act'. The definition, although general, gives relevance to the nature of the activity and not to the purpose.

Finally, as for immunity from execution, FSIA states that any property of an agency or instrumentality of the state which engages in commercial activity is subject to enforcement if the claim relates to an activity for which it enjoys no immunity from jurisdiction, irrespective that the property is used for commercial or sovereign purposes.[26] These rules, that served as inspiration for the lawmakers of other nations,[27] take the start from the assumption (absolute in certain countries, *iuris tantum* in others) that the separate entities are engaged in a commercial activity, as such not immune.

4.1.3 SWFs and state immunity practice

So far we have described the international (conventional) and national laws. In the practice, in those countries where the matter is ruled mostly by case law, there is a trend to keep for separate entities the typical distinction by nature of activities (for immunity from jurisdiction) and intended use of property (for immunity from execution).[28]

---

[25] 28 U.S.C. § 1603 (a) and (b). The practice shows a broad interpretation of the term 'agency or instrumentality', as those entities 'could assume a variety of forms, including state trading corporation, a mining enterprise, a steel company, a central bank, an export association, a department of ministry' (H.R. Rep. N. 94-1487, at 15–16 (1976)). US Courts considered several factors to determine whether an entity is an organ of a foreign state (i.e. the ownership and management of the entity; whether the entity performs a public activity; whether the foreign state created the entity for a national purpose; whether the entity is actively supervised by the state; the entity treatment under the foreign state's law (see M. Granne, *Defining 'Organ of a Foreign State' Under the Foreign Sovereign Immunity Act of 1976*, working paper).

[26] Section 1610(b), United States Foreign Sovereign Immunity Act 1976.

[27] See s. 35(2), Australia Foreign States Immunities Act 1985 (ILM1986 p. 715); s. 15(3), Pakistan State Immunity Ordinance 1981; s. 16(3), Singapore State Immunity Act 1985; s. 15(2), South Africa Foreign State Immunities Act 1981.

[28] In this sense *National Iranian Oil Company Revenues from Oil Sales Case*, Federal Republic of Germany, Federal Constitutional Court, 12 April 1983, 65 ILR 215, 243.

Apparently, there is not a long-standing and consolidated practice for immunity from jurisdiction for SWFs as yet. Hence, according to the information provided in the preceding paragraphs, we should refer to the practice that is to some extent 'closer', i.e. the one applied to SOEs and central bank funds. Regards to the former, all the information available give a clear indication that SOE activities qualify as commercial and are therefore not immune,[29] even when state-owned companies are considered agencies or instrumentalities.[30] Only whether its activities are considered sovereign acts, the company can benefit from immunity unless it is waived.

Regards to the latter, there is a sharp contrast between the general exemption recognised to central banks funds by international treaties and the restrictive approach adopted by some national courts. Indeed, the 2005 UN Convention considers central bank funds as typically non-commercial property, as it exempts from execution measures 'property of the central bank or other monetary authority of the state'.[31] The reason for such a specific rule in international conventions lies probably in the fact that the assets held by a central bank may represent a state's foreign exchange/foreign currency reserves or the assets held by it in the course of the conduct of the monetary policy or other credit operations. The safety and liquidity of those assets represent a priority in the management of public resources. Recent state laws go in the same direction.[32]

---

29 SOEs have separate legal personality and the capacity to sue and be sued; accordingly, they operate independently from the state (UN Convention, Art. 27). In the *Sarriò* case (*Kuwait v. X*, Swiss Federal Tribunal, 24 January 1994, and *Sarriò S.A. v. Kuwait Investment Authority* [1996] EWCA Civ 575, rev'd [1997] UKHL 49), the Court stated (and the court of appeal confirmed) that Kuwait could not invoke immunity provided that KIA (a Kuwaitian SOE) had an autonomous status; was an independent public authority; had brought suit in its own name in proceedings in England and Spain, irrelevant being that investments were made to benefit the state. Again, in the *Sonatrach* case, (*Société Sonatrach v. Migeon*, French Court of Cassation, 1 October 1985, 77 ILR 525) the Court found that 'the assets of public entities, distinct from the foreign state, whether or not enjoying legal personality, which are part of a group of assets which have dedicated to activities in the private law sector, may be seized by all creditors of the public entity'.

30 *Dole Food Co. v. Patrickson*, 538 US 468 (2003).

31 A similar exemption can be found in the ILA Draft Convention, as Art. VIII(c)3 prohibits execution if 'the property is that of a State central bank held by it for central banking purposes'.

32 Chinese and French laws (of 2005 and 2006, respectively) grant central banks a reinforced immunity: the Chinese law provides for absolute immunity from execution for the property of central banks, while the French law grants central banks stronger but not absolute immunity: execution is admitted if the property is part of 'a patrimony used for a principal activity of a private law nature'.

States' practice is not equally standardised; in some cases national courts denied such a general exemption and required a specific evidence that the central bank property served public purposes.[33] In other cases, the central bank was considered as a separate legal entity, so that its funds could not be used to satisfy the debt of a third party (the State).[34] In other cases again the central bank was not considered as an emanation of the state entitled to invoke immunity, and its funds were judged not immune from injunction.[35] Lastly, in other cases the central bank was considered at the same level as a state and immunity was granted only in case of actual and material use of the property for governmental non-commercial use.[36]

However, we may consider that central bank accounts too fall within the recent general trend of courts – which will be probably supported by the recent new laws – to presume the public purpose of property, or at least to place a high burden on plaintiffs by endorsing a quasi-presumption in favour of the sovereign purposes of state accounts.[37]

---

33 There is a different burden of proof, according to the courts.

34 *Ambassade de la Fédération de Russie en France v. Société NOGA*, Cour d'Appel, Paris, 1st Chamber, section A, 10 August 2000 [2001] 128 JDI 116. Similarly, recent cases in US courts: *EM Ltd. v. Republic of Argentina*, 473 F.3d 463 (2d CIR 2006); *LNC Invs. Inc. v. Banco Central de Nicaragua*, 228 F.3d 423 (2d Cir. 2000).

35 *Trendtex Trading Corporation v. Central Bank of Nigeria*, 13 January 1977 [1977] 2 WLR 356, 64 ILR 111 (CA).

36 In *République socialiste du people arabe de Lybie-Jamahirya v. Actimon SA*, Tribunal Fédéral Suisse, 24 April 1985, ATF 111 Ia 62; 82 ILR 30, at 35, the Court refused to exempt central bank funds unless it was specifically demonstrated that that property served public purposes, stating that 'a plea of immunity is inadmissible, in respect of money and securities, unless the documents or specified sums have been designated for the performance of such tasks'. Similarly, *Banque centrale de la République de Turquie v. Weston Compagnie de Finance et d'Investissement SA*, Tribunal federal Suisse, 15 November 1978, ATF 104 IA 367, 65 ILR 417, and *Central Bank of Nigeria*, Landgericht, Frankfurt, 2 December 1975 [1976] Neue Juristische Wochenschrift 1044, 65 ILR 131. In *Foreign Trade Institute Bank Account*, Landgericht, Hamburg, 26 March 1981, 65 ILR 209, the Court denied the immunity because of the private function (and purpose) of the foreign trade institute. Again, in *Weston Cie de Finance et d'Investissement, S.A. v. Ecuador*, 823 F. Supp. 1106 (S.D.N.Y. 1993) the Court stated that funds in a central bank account were not immune because they were not 'held for its own account', as they were used to finance commercial transactions of private parties.

37 In *The Philippine Embassy Bank Account Case* (Bundesverfassungsgericht, 13 December 1977, 46 BVerfG 342; 65 ILR 146, at 186), the German Constitutional Court stated that 'the executing authorities of the receiving State to require the sending State, without its consent, to provide details concerning the existence or the past, present or future purposes of funds in such an account would constitute interference, contrary to international law, in matters within

The high fragmentation of the national practice with respect to entities – central banks – usually independent from states but holding typically sovereign functions, lead us to foresee possible ambiguous answers also for SWFs, which are not all of the same type, as these hold sovereign functions but carry out investment activities that are now being conventionally regarded as 'commercial'.

The only two cases involving an SWF do not help in finding unambiguous responses. Indeed, in the *Sarriò* case[38] the English court judged irrelevant the fact that investments were made by the fund to benefit the state. Conversely, in the *AIG/Republic of Kazakhstan* case,[39] the English court considered relevant the purpose of an SWF of accumulating assets in the public interest, and granted the invested assets (managed by the Kazakhstan national bank) immunity from execution, because (s. 92) 'the dealings [were] all part of the overall exercise of sovereign authority by the Republic of Kazakhstan'.

4.2 The 'Tax Exemption' Factor

It is in this wide and variegated scenario that some states expressly exempt SWFs from paying taxes.[40] The issue of SWF tax exemption was studied

---

the exclusive competence of the sending State'. Similarly, *M.K. v. State Secretary for Justice*, Raad van State, President of the Judicial Division, 24 November 1986, 94 ILR 357 at 360, *Banamar-Capizzi v. Embassy of the Republic of Algeria*, Italian Court of Cassation, 4 May 1989, 87 ILR 56, at. 60 (according to which 'the funds in question appear to be devoted to financing the expenses necessary to fulfil sovereign purposes. Therefore any attempt to check if such funds are effectively used in whole or in part for those purposes would inevitably result in an undue interference in the affairs of the diplomatic mission'), and *X. v. Brazil*, Landgericht, Frankfurt am Main, 23 May 2000 [2001] Recht der Internationalen Wirtschaft 308. See also *AIG Capital Partners Inc. and Another v. Kazakhstan* [2005] EWHC 2234 (Comm) 129 ILR 589, where the court, applying s. 14(4) of the UK SIA, found that the property of central banks shall not be regarded as in use for commercial purposes. Hence, according to the court, the property is immune from execution regardless of whether it is used for commercial purposes. Contra: *Condor and Filvem v. Minister of Justice*, Italian Constitutional Court, 1992, n. 329; *Abbott v. South Africa*, Spanish Constitutional Court, 113 ILR 411 (1992).

[38] *Kuwait v. X*, Swiss Federal Tribunal, 24 January 1994, and *Sarriò S.A. v. Kuwait Investment Authority*, [1996] EWCA Civ 575, rev'd [1997] UKHL 49.

[39] *AIG Capital Partners Inc. and Another v. Kazakhstan* [2005] EWHC 2234 (Comm) 129 ILR 589.

[40] In USA and the UK the exemption applies to both commercial and non-commercial transactions, and to both portfolio and controlling investments. Other states grant an exemption limited to non-commercial investments: in Canada

only recently;[41] in the past, the 'sovereign' nature of funds owned by states was unquestioned, and justified tax exemption according to a common practice founded on the generally accepted principle that one government does not tax another.

In particular, section 892 of the US Internal Revenue Code (USIRC, last revised in 1986) makes a traditional distinction in international tax law between commercial activity, which is taxed at the source, and passive portfolio investing, generally taxed at the residence. Therefore, in section 892(a)(1) of USIRC, the income of foreign governments received from stocks, bonds, other domestic securities, financial interests held in the execution of governmental financial or monetary policy, and interests on U.S. bank deposits are exempt from taxation. However there is an exception made in (a)(2), according to which immunity does not apply to any income derived from a commercial activity. In such a case the sovereign fund's taxed income will be treated as if the fund were a corporation of its state.

In this case too, the main issue lies, on one hand, in the definition of 'foreign government', and on the other in the notion of 'commercial activity'. As for the former, the USIRC gives a broad definition of foreign government for tax purposes, as it encompasses both governmental departments or agencies and separate legal entities controlled by the foreign sovereign entity (such as state-owned or state operated pension funds, sovereign wealth or stabilisation funds, and state-owned enterprises).[42]

---

and Australia only passive portfolio investments are not subject to tax; in France foreign state income from portfolio investments is exempt by law, while foreign direct investments can be granted exemption by the Ministry of Finance. Other states (such as Germany, Switzerland, Poland and Norway) treat foreign states like private investors.

41 For recent studies dedicated specifically to this matter see: M. Melone, 'Should the United States Tax Sovereign Wealth Funds?' [2009] *Boston University International Law Journal* 143–225; V. Fleischer, 'A Theory of Taxing Sovereign Wealth' [2009] *New York University Law Review* 440–513; M. Desai and D. Dharmapala, *Taxing the Bandit Kings*, working paper (available at: ssrn.com/abstract=1265058 (accessed 29 March 2011)).

42 The definition does not instead include central banks, subject to a specific rule (s. 895) providing tax exemption for foreign central banks (only) of issue investing in obligations of the United States (i.e. Treasury bonds). The definition of foreign government (granting immunity) changes according to national laws: Australia requests that the agency 'be owned and controlled by the government and not engaged in commercial activities'. Canadian laws grant exemption to agencies or SWFs pursuing a public/humanitarian (not commercial) objective. In UK foreign agencies are exempted if they constitute

As for the latter, US regulations define as commercial activities all activities conducted 'with a view towards the current or future production of income or gain'. It also specifies that investments in stocks, bonds, and other securities are not commercial activities unless one is a 'dealer' in securities or engaged in an active banking, financing or similar business.

Hence, we can assume that in the United States, the notion of foreign government is, for tax purposes, broader than the one provided in the rules on state immunity, while on the contrary the notion of commercial activity is more restricted than the one provided in the state immunity practice. As a consequence, non-controlling stakes, including strategic equity investments, are treated as portfolio investments, and are therefore not considered as 'commercial activity'. We may conclude, all the more so, that passive portfolio investments by a foreign sovereign entity (meaning by that sovereign wealth funds too) are not taxed.

The underlying reason for tax exemption is now subject matter of discussion in the United States,[43] also due to the fact that the amendment to section 892 adopted in 1986, which introduced taxation in case of commercial activities, was aimed at reducing tax exemption for state-owned enterprises. According to some commentators, SWFs are not the direct recipients of the rule only because they were not then such active players in the global economic scene.

The exemption of SWFs' activities from taxation does not directly affect the related but different question of state immunity. The notions of state and commercial activity are different, and each instrumental to a different purpose. Also the purpose of the activity may or may not be relevant depending on the context. However, this gives even more uncertainty to the analysis. In fact, if SOEs are not to be considered immune due to being non-sovereign entities engaged in a typically commercial business, this is not true for SWFs, that do have a sovereign function and whose business, instrumental to such function, qualifies expressly – even if only for tax purposes – as a non-commercial one. This implies a case by case assessment of whether state immunity actually applies to each sovereign wealth fund.

'an integral part' of the government, while separate entities have been excluded from exemption.

43 See Joint Committee on Taxation, Economic and U.S. Income Tax Issues Raised by Sovereign Wealth Fund Investment in the United States, JCX-49-08 1-2 (17 June 2008).

4.3 SWFs, State Immunity and Competition Law: The Need to Overcome a Misunderstanding

An almost undisputed matter is related to the applicability of competition law to SWFs' investments. The question often asked is whether SWFs can invoke state immunity to be exempted from European competition law. From this starting point, many questions could arise: whether the scope of application of immunity and of competition rules overlaps; whether absolute immunity (for those states still recognising it) can also apply to competition rules; which definition of foreign state and commercial activity may apply to competition in states that recognise a relative immunity; whether a difference between portfolio investments and FDI can apply to competition rules, and, if so, what are its effects. Few observers focused on this relationship and admitted that competition cases (almost all in EU) do not apply immunity to foreign countries or to foreign-government-controlled-entities.[44]

I think that this question, asked in that way, is totally misleading. Immunity doesn't apply to competition cases.[45] SWFs, as all other entities, will be subject to competition rules if they are undertakings in the pursuit of an economic activity. Both 'undertaking'[46] and 'economic activity'[47]

---

44 D. Gaukrodges, *Foreign State Immunity and Foreign Government Controlled Investors*, OECD Working Papers on International Investments, 2010/2 (OECD Publishing, 2010).

45 In *Aluminium Imports* (Commission, case IV/26.870, OJ 1985 L92/1) the Commission stated that 'the applicability of [Art. 101 TFEU] since it relates to trading activities, is not defeated by claims of sovereign immunity'.

46 As for the definition of undertaking, it has been applied to an investment fund in Case C-67/96 *Albany International v. Stichting Bedrijfspensioenfonds* [1999] ECR I-5751, 21 September 1999, where the court stated that 'a sectoral pension fund of the kind at issue in the main proceedings engages in an economic activity in competition with insurance companies. In those circumstances, the fact that the fund is non-profit-making [...is] not sufficient to deprive the sectoral pension fund of its status as an undertaking within the meaning of the competition rules of the Treaty (p. I-5888, points 84–6).

47 As for the definition of economic activity, it includes all activities carried out in the market on equal terms with other undertakings. The only exception admitted is when the entity operates in the exercise of official authority or when it accomplishes a public authority's task: in Case C-30/87 *C. Bodson v. SA Pompes Funèbres Régions Libérées SA* [1988] ECR I-2479, 4 May 1988, the Court stated that 'article [101 of TFEU] does not apply to contracts for concessions concluded between communes acting in their capacity as public authorities and undertakings entrusted with the operation of a public service' (p. 2512 n. 18). Similarly, Case C-231/03 *Consorzio Aziende Metano v. Comune di Cingia de' Botti* [2005] ECR I-7287, 21 July 2005. In Case C-364/92 *SAT v. Eurocontrol* [1994] ECR

are defined by a consolidated competition practice, according to which competition law applies to states and agencies (SWFs included) whether they do not exercise their official, public authority. Hence, competition law does not apply: to anti-pollution surveillance in the public interest (*Diego Cali & Figli*); to the maintenance and improvement of air navigation safety (*Eurocontrol*); to the concessions contracts concluded by local municipalities acting in their capacity as public authorities (*C. Bodson v. Sa Pompes Funèbres*).

It is the activity carried out by the company, the municipality, the agency, even the state, that matters. And the activity can be exempted from the application of competition law whether in the exercise of official authority, in the public interest, performing state's essential tasks. It seems to be a stricter and more rigorous classification than that of non-commercial activities relevant for immunity purposes. So, an investment fund hardly fits in this definition. It is an undertaking because it engages in an economic activity in competition with other entities (as the court stated

---

I-43 at p. I-64 n. 17) the Court found that Eurocontrol carried out, on behalf of its member states, tasks in the public interest aimed at contributing to the maintenance and improvement of air navigation safety. The specific acts in question (the collection of route charges) were not separable from other activities, so that, taken as a whole, Eurocontrol's activities were typically those of a public authority and were not of economic nature. In Case C-113/07 *Selex sistemi integrati SpA v. Commission of the European Communities and Organisation européenne pour la sécurité de la navigation aérienne* (*Eurocontrol*) 29 March 2009, p. I-2207, the court stated that Eurocontrol was engaged in 'acts in the exercise of official authority' and was therefore not an undertaking. In *Diego Calì & Figli v. Servizi ecologici Porto di Genova SpA* [1997] ECR I-1547, 18 March 1997, the court stated (p. I-1587 n. 16–23) that 'as regards the possible application of the competition rules of the Treaty, a distinction must be drawn between a situation where the State acts in the exercise of its official authority and one where it carries out economic activities of an industrial or commercial nature by offering goods or services on the market (Case 118/85 *Commission v. Italy* [1987] ECR 2599 paragraph 7). In that connection, it is of no importance that the state be acting directly through a body forming part of the state administration or through a body to which it has conferred special or exclusive rights. . . . In order to make the distinction between the two situations referred to above, it is necessary to consider the nature of the activities carried on by the public undertaking or body on which the state has conferred special or exclusive rights .... The anti-pollution surveillance for which SEPG was responsible in the oil port of Genoa is a task in the public interest which forms part of the essential functions of the state as regards protection of the environment in maritime areas. Such surveillance is connected, by nature, aim and rules it is subject to, with the exercise of powers relating to the protection of the environment which are typically those of a public authority. It is not of an economic nature justifying the application of the Treaty rules on competition (case C-364/92 *SAT Fluggesellschaft v. Eurocontrol* (1994) ECR I-43 paragraph 30).'

in *Albany*), and carries out an economic activity (investment). Purposes do not matter in competition law; and the irrelevance of this subjective element, (typical of SWFs), is what makes it impossible to apply immunity criteria in this field.

4.4 SWF Models and Immunity: A Five-step Analysis

It seems clear from these premises that we cannot determine, in abstract terms and preventively, whether a SWF may enjoy immunity from jurisdiction or from execution. This assessment, considering the various types of funds, forms of investment, purposes sought, must be done on a case by case basis. Therefore it may be useful to adopt a method where the decisive distinctive factors may be identified for each fund. The method we propose is based on five steps.

4.4.1 SWF legal structure, governance and accountability

The first step is assessing whether the SWF is directly related to a state or is a separate entity, with a certain degree of independence, or again a mere state owned company. As we have seen in Chapter 2 there is not a single fund category – on the contrary, the variety of their forms is one of the main obstacles to a standard definition. There are funds without an autonomous legal personality (in Russia, Mexico, Canada/Alberta, Chile and Norway – managed by central banks), others that belong to monetary authorities, controlled by the Ministry of Finance, an agency or the central bank (Sama in Saudi Arabia, Safe Investment Company in China, the Investment Portfolio of the Hong Kong Monetary Authority), others again are entrusted to administrative authorities (for instance, the Kuwait Investment Authority runs two funds), others are sovereign wealth enterprises, vehicles of investments owned and controlled by funds (CIC in China), others are separate legal entities (Qatar, UAE/ADIA, Australia, Temasek of Singapore). Therefore, the following aspects should be reviewed for each type of fund: legal personality (where existing, and in such case whether of private or public law), incorporation (SWFs are sometimes incorporated as a result of laws, sometimes provided for by national constitutions), function, power, activities, governance, relation with the state, in order to verify if and to what extent fund activities may be ascribed to the state. For the purpose of investigating the possible immunity from jurisdiction or from execution a classification may be presented to differ funds by incorporation (as part of a state or having independent legal personality) and management (by the government or by independent state agencies). Hence the usefulness of the definition and classification proposed in Chapter 2.

4.4.2 SWF purposes

Second step: verifying the purpose (sovereign or commercial) of the fund. Purposes may be multiple, e.g. insulate the budget and economy from excess volatility in revenues; help monetary authority sterilise unwanted liquidity, build up savings for future generations; use the money for economic and social developments. Funds may also pursue macroeconomic and financial objectives: fiscal stabilisation funds reduce the impact of volatile fiscal revenues or foreign exchange receipts; saving funds create a store of wealth for future generations so that they can benefit from the (non-renewable) natural resources after their depletion; development funds allocate resources for funding priority socio-economic projects, such as infrastructures; the activity of pension reserve funds, or reserve investment corporations is also aimed at meeting specific public purposes. According to the Santiago GAPPs, SWFs are established by the general government for macroeconomic purposes, and are created to invest government funds to achieve financial objectives, employing a wide range of investment strategies with a medium- to long-term timescale. They serve a different objective than, for example, reserve portfolios held only for traditional balance of payments purposes. They may include reserve assets, but not all reserve assets are regarded as SWFs. Investment strategies are relevant here, apart from objectives, as closely related to the latter.[48] A review of objectives and strategies will obviously provide useful directions about the purpose of a fund in order to ascertain its relevance for immunity from jurisdiction and, above all, for immunity from execution. We may infer from all this that certain purposes may be directly related with the exercise of state sovereignty or at least with the exercise of public functions. After all, there seem to be more analogies than differences with the requirements for the immunity granted to central banks (in a broad fashion under international conventions and with more difficulties under national laws).

4.4.3 SWF financing practice

Third step: in the absence of clear guidance in the establishing laws, statutes etc., financing and drawing rights practices may be useful, as they depend directly on fund purposes: funding may be based on raw material price surpluses compared to pre-defined targets (stabilisation funds), on specific given objectives (pension funds) or be discretionary. Funding

---

[48] The World Bank defined SWFs as 'long-term investment funds, typically for both income and intergenerational wealth transfer' (Services for Sovereign Wealth and Commodity Fund Managers, at the World Bank website).

rules may be based on the occurrence of financial deficits, on specific public funding requirements, on the reduction of raw material prices compared to a given target (stabilisation funds), on balance of payment requirements, on future liabilities forecasts (pension funds).

4.4.4 SWF investment nature

Fourth step: as for the objective element (SWF activity for immunity from jurisdiction and SWF property for immunity from execution) reviewing the actual investments of the fund in order to ascertain if they may enjoy immunity from jurisdiction. What arises from international agreements and national case law leads to think that, if viewed in function of recognising immunity, SWF investments are considered as having a commercial nature. If the nature of individual actions is the only parameter, exemption from jurisdiction should be excluded. However, fund actions should be viewed at a higher level, that includes the whole of investments. Taking into account the 2005 UN Convention, this would allow for a careful consideration of the degree to which the purpose factor will be used by states as an instrument to guarantee immunity.

The analysis must also take the reference context into account. SWFs are new entities through which states regain full international economic sovereignty and operate with tools similar, under certain respects, to those used by private entities, yet pursuing typically sovereign purposes. This is obviously relevant also for the purposes of immunity, viewed under the functional profile. In these cases the state does not act as a private entity but as the 'bearer' of its sovereignty and exercises it also in the economic scenario. After all, the now prevailing notion of restricted immunity is not incompatible with that of functional immunity. This is relevant whenever there is a reference to the institutional objectives pursued by the state and is one of the basic assumptions for changing the rationale of immunity, which is no longer aimed at protecting actions *iure imperii* but the independence and autonomy with which the state pursues its institutional purposes.[49] In fact, immunity is granted when: (i) a state acts abroad as an international entity; (ii) a state acts in its own territory as the holder of authority of *imperium* of the laws of which it is a bearer; and (iii) a state carries out functions related with public and institutional purposes. This is obviously the most complex stage of the analysis, that will use, among other things, the results obtained from the investigations made in the three previous steps.

---

[49] Italian Court of Cassation S.u. 16 December 1987, n. 9322; and Cass. 9 May 1988, n. 3468.

4.4.5 SWF asset purposes

Fifth step: with regard to immunity from execution, reviewing the purpose of the asset (sovereign functions). The purpose of SWF assets is the same as that of the SWF itself. In fact, the investment implies its instrumentality to the objectives of the investing fund. However, two levels of purpose may be assumed: an immediate one and an indirect one. The immediate purpose is economic: to make greater profits. And it cannot be any different, because it is the only one allowed for SWF investments according to the Santiago GAPPs (any other purpose must be stated expressly). However, the immediate profit is in turn functional to the end purpose of the fund. In the same way, the activity of a central bank generates profits that are used to minimise risks: a stabilisation fund operates pursuing quite similar purposes, in theory. Therefore, if the direct and immediate purpose is relevant for the Santiago principles, we cannot exclude that the ultimate purpose of each single investment may be relevant for immunity from execution. In this view, SWFs are public sovereign entities, pursuing public goals. The practice of states and international agreements allow for this interpretation, that besides already applies to central banks.[50]

4.5 Conclusions

These are the five steps of the analysis we suggest. A further consideration should be added. As we have seen, SWFs are a modern development of the ways in which states manage their reserves. This evolution should be viewed in parallel to the present gradual reduction of the application of the principle of immunity (now restricted) on the basis of function; a development which brought forth a significant change in the rationale of state immunity, that has shifted from a corollary of sovereignty to a measure to protect states' institutional functions. These functions operate in different ways and therefore require different forms of protection, depending on whether they are threatened by host state measures or aimed at

[50] Two approaches may be followed. One is followed, for instance, by the Italian Courts on tort law. State activities are activities that express state sovereignty and therefore enjoy immunity from jurisdiction. Matters related to reporting, i.e. cases of application, are *iure privatorum* and do not enjoy immunity (neither of jurisdiction nor of enforcement). It remains to be seen what would be the consequence of this approach in the actual practice: wouldn't it mean recognising immunity in abstract terms but not in the practice? To the fund but not to its actions or property? What would be the use? The other approach is the one (e.g. military installations) where the activity in itself is immune and therefore so are all individual actions.

guaranteeing to the fund a freedom of operation which its competitors do not have. If we consider these differences, we may assume a different level of applicability (and strength) of immunity in respect of measures adopted by host states and investments made by funds.

The difference is relevant, both on subjective terms and for the recipients, as well as for the theoretical rationale of immunity. In the former case it would challenge host state measures justified by the fact that SWFs, as sovereign entities, have benefits not available to others and might use them for other than economic purposes. In this case, immunity would cancel measures adopted in respect of funds exactly for their sovereign nature; being grounded on this assumption, these measures find greater difficulties in overcoming the obstacle of immunity. For this form of immunity that we defined as 'passive' we should assume a 'strong' protection, improved by the reason of the measure it is claimed against, and might apply to all cases of passive investments by the funds. Conversely, the protection of immunity from host state measures would be weaker in the case of foreign direct investments (not portfolio ones) of SWFs, in the case of take-over of foreign companies, or again in the case of investments made through public enterprises. In fact, in these cases SWFs would operate as a SOE: the take-over of an enterprise would hardly be justified as a long-term investment of the fund. This form of 'strong immunity' assumed for the protection of SWF investments from host state measures would apply mostly at enforcement level.

The system works in a different manner, always with respect to immunity from execution, for 'active immunity', i.e. the actions performed by the funds in breach of the rules of the state hosting the investment. In these cases, the very reason for applying principles of non-discrimination with other operators that lead, for 'passive immunity' to protecting an investment from the specific limit imposed on 'sovereignty', calls for preventing a fund from committing actions prohibited to its 'competitors' because illegal.

As repeatedly stated earlier in these pages, these assumptions cannot be done in abstract terms and preventively, but on a case by case basis. We should then ask what will happen in all those cases where immunity does not apply, and in particular what form of protection for SWF foreign investments can be found. The research should continue from this point onwards, to verify whether the protection provided for in BITs may apply. This is what the next chapter deals with.

6. SWFs and bilateral investment treaties

1. AN UNDISCOVERED RELATIONSHIP

We have seen in the previous chapters that sovereignty and purposes, that we believe are the SWFs main features, are critical elements for SWFs immunity protection too. Whether immunity can not apply, because of the reasons mentioned in Chapter 5, SWFs should protect their investments by means of international arbitration, if a bilateral investment treaty (BIT) between their home state and the state that challenged their investment is in force and so provides for. Hence, we should also investigate if sovereignty and purposes play a role in the relationship between SWFs and BITs.

So far, the issue of SWF investment protection through BITs has been scarcely dealt with in literature.[1] The reason for this lack of interest might lie in the fact that as for now no SWF investments have been arbitrated. However, this is not enough to conclude that the issue will not arise in the near future. In fact, the phenomenon of SWFs is relatively recent in the dynamics and dimensions described above; therefore we have reason to believe that BITs might have a significant impact on decision-making and on the management of state investments. In the absence of a multilateral agreement on investments, BITs could guarantee both an adequate *continuum* in the states' relations and a reciprocity in investments guarantees.

Our analysis of the relationships between BIT and SWF investments starts from a review of current BITs in order to assess their relevance for SWF investments (Chapter 6, section 2.1). The theoretical analysis is then tried out by reviewing the BITs stipulated by the states holders of the most important SWFs; it will let us understand whether and to what extent the BITs in force are taken in (prior) consideration by SWFs willing to invest in a certain country (Chapter 6, section 2.2).

---

[1] At the time of writing (January 2011) there appear to be no studies on this specific matter.

Then our research will focus on the main BIT models to assess whether they are adequate and effective in protecting SWF investments (Chapter 6, section 3). For instance, a clear and precise definition of the term 'nationals of a contracting state' to identify the owner and invoke the protection of the investment made, is of essence in order to understand whether a SWF may enjoy or not protection under a BIT.

Another aspect we will attempt to assess relates to the fact that SWFs make mostly foreign investments that sometimes qualify as foreign direct investments – FDI, more often as portfolio investments, depending on whether they imply taking control of the target company or not. This difference leads to many consequences (it might be relevant, as we have seen, under the profile of immunity); therefore, it may be interesting to see if it is also relevant under the profile of protecting the investment in the host state by means of a BIT. Again, the notion of investment may help, because certain BITs make express reference to the control of enterprises, that therefore becomes relevant in itself (Chapter 6, section 3.2.1).

Another profile that deserves more insight is that of the exemptions host states can invoke to limit SWF investments on an exceptional basis. These restrictive measures that we classified in Chapter 4 could be considered, on certain conditions, as (indirect) expropriations, ruled in general terms, that impose adequate indemnification according to international law, which in certain cases the BITs expressly refer to (Chapter 6, section 3.2.2).

The ultimate purpose of our research on the relationship between BITs and SWFs is to formulate proposals to improve BIT efficacy in their current re-negotiation or in the negotiation of new ones. Indeed, a (re)negotiating process will be necessary in Europe, now that the Lisbon Treaty grants the European Union exclusive competence to abolish restrictions to foreign disinvestments.[2] The new comprehensive European international investment policy, illustrated in details by the European Commission in a recent Communication (COM (10) 343 final) requests both a new EU BIT model and transitional arrangements for bilateral investment agreements currently in force between member states and third countries.[3]

---

[2] Art. 207 of the Treaty on the Functioning of the European Union (TFEU) includes foreign direct investments as one of the areas covered by the commercial policy of the Union, that is an area of EU exclusive competence pursuant to Art. 3(1) of TFEU.

[3] See the proposal for an *ad hoc* EU Regulation, establishing traditional arrangements for bilateral investment agreements between member states and third countries (COM (10) 344 final).

Table 6.1 SWF home states and bilateral investment treaties

	China	Republic of Korea	UAE	Qatar	Libya	Kuwait	Singapore	Norway	Russ Feder
Albania	1993	2004							
Algeria		2001							
Argentina	1992	1996							200
Australia	1988								
Austria	1985	1991	2001		2002	1996			199
Bahrain	1999								
Bangladesh		1988							
Barbados									
Belarus		1997							
Belgium	1984	1978			2004	2000			198
Belize	1999								
Benin	2004								
Bolivia	1992	1996							
Bosnia Herzegovina	2005								
Botswana	2000								
Brazil		1995							
Brunei	2000	2003							
Bulgaria	1989					1997			
Burkina Faso		2005							
Cambodia	1996	1997					1996		
Cameroon	1997								
Canada									198
Chile	1994	1999						1993	
China		1992		1999		1985	1985	1985	
Colombia									
Congo		2005							
Costa Rica	1999	2002							
Cote d'Ivoire	x								
Croatia	1993	2005				1997			
Cuba	1995								
Cyprus									199
Czech Republic	2005	1995	1994			1996	1995	1991	
Denmark	1985	1988				2002			
Djibouti	2003								
Ecuador	1996								
Egypt	1994	1996					1997		199
El Salvador		1998							
Estonia	1993							1992	
Ethiopia	1998					1996			199
Finland	2005	1996	1996			1996			
France	1985	1979	1991	1996		1989	1975		198
Georgia	1993								

zuela	Kazakhstan	Australia	Algeria	Brunei	Malaysia	Taiwan	Chile	Iran	Nigeria
93		1995					1991		
							1996		
					1985		2000	2001	
								2001	
94									
								1995	
	1998		2002				1992		
						1999			
00							1994		
95									
	1999								
					1994				
96									
93		1996			1992				
		1988		2000	1990		1994	2000	
							2001		
97							1996		
							1994	2000	
							1996		
95		1994	2000		1996		1995		
94			2005		1992		1993		
93							1993		
	1993	2001			1997		1999	X	2000
							1996		
					1998				
			2005		1988		1993		2005
01	1998		1993		1975		1992	2003	1990

	China	Republic of Korea	UAE	Qatar	Libya	Kuwait	Singapore	Norway	Russ Feder
Germany	2003	1987	1997	1996		1994	1973		19
Ghana	1989								
Greece	1992	1995							19
Guatemala		2002							
Guyana	2004								
Honduras		2001							
Hong Kong		1997							
Hungary	1991	1989				1989	1997	1992	19
Iceland	1994								
India		1996							
Indonesia	1994	1994					1990	1991	
Iran	2000	2006							
Iraq						1964			
Israel		2003							
Italy	1986	1992	1995			1987			19
Jamaica	1994	2004							
Japan	1988	2003							19
Jordan	x	2004				2001	2004		
Kazakhstan		1996				1997			
Korea	1992								
Kuwait	1985	2005							
Kyrgyzstan									
Lao People's	1993	1996							
Latvia	2004	1997						1992	
Lebanon	1997	2006				2002			20
Lithuania	1993	1993				2003		1992	19
Madagascar	2005								
Malaysia		1989	1991					1984	
Mali									
Malta					1973				
Marshall Islands									
Mauritania		2005							
Mauritius							2000		
Mexico		2000							
Mongolia	1991	1991					1995		
Morocco	1995	2001				2001			
Myanmar	2001								
Netherlands	2004	2005				2001	1973		19
New Zealand	1988								
Nicaragua		2001							
Nigeria		1997							
Norway									19
Oman		2004							

ezuela	Kazakhstan	Australia	Algeria	Brunei	Malaysia	Taiwan	Chile	Iran	Nigeria
996	1992		1996		1996		1997	1965	2000
					1997				
	2002		2000				1996	2002	
							1996		
							1996		
		1993							
	1994	1992			1993		1997		
							2006		
	1996	1999							
		1993	2000		1994		1999		
	1996								
990	1994		1991		1988				
			1996		1994				
					1996			1996	
	1997								
					1995				
		1995							
					1998		1999	1997	
995		2002							
	1996						1992		
			1996						
						1999			
		X							
					1995				
					2002			2001	
993	2007		X		1972		X		1994
							X		
							1996		
					1984		1993		
				1998					

	China	Republic of Korea	UAE	Qatar	Libya	Kuwait	Singapore	Norway	Russi Federa
Pakistan	1989	1990				1983	1995		
Panama		2002							
Papua New Guinea									
Paraguay		1994							
Peru	1994	1994					2003	1995	
Philippines	1992	1996							X
Poland	1998	1990						1990	
Portugal	1992	1996			2003				199
Republic of Korea	2005			1999		2004			199
Republic of Macedonia									
Romania	1994	1994						1991	
Russian Federation	2006	1991						1995	
Saudi Arabia		2002							
Senegal		1985							
Slovakia	1991	2005						1991	199
Slovenia	1993								
South Africa		1995							
Spain	1992	1994							199
Sri Lanka	1986	1980					1980	1985	
Swaziland	1998								
Sweden	1982	1997							199
Switzerland	1987	1971	1999	2004	2004	2000	1978		199
Tadjikistan		2005							
Thailand	1985	1989							200
Trinidad and Tobago	2004	2002							
Tunisia	2004	1976							
Turkey	1990	1994		2001					199
UAE		2004							
Uganda	2004								
UK	1986	1978	1993				1975		199
Ukraine		1996							199
Uruguay	1993								
USA									199
Uzbekistan		1992							
Venezuela									
Viet Nam	1992	1993					1992		

ezuela	Kazakhstan	Australia	Algeria	Brunei	Malaysia	Taiwan	Chile	Iran	Nigeria
		1998							
							1996		
		1991							
96							1995		
96		1995			1995		2000		
		1995					1995		
		1992					1995		
94			2004				1995		
	1996		2001	2003	1989		1999	2006	1997
					1999				
		1994	1994				1995		
					2000				
							1998	1997	
97	1995		1996		1996		1991	2004	2002
		2002						2000	
						1998			
96	2004				1979		1993		
94	1994		2005		1978		2002	1998	2003
						1996			
							1998		
	1992		X		2000		1998	1996	1996
					1991				
96	1995				1988		1997		1990
							1995		
97		2001			1995		1995		
	1994								
							1993		
		1991			1992		1999		

Note: Dates indicate the year of entry into force of the treaties; 'X' indicates that a treaty has been signed, but is still not in force.

2. BILATERAL INVESTMENT TREATIES AND THEIR RELEVANCE FOR SWF INVESTMENTS

BITs are the instruments by which two states agree to safeguard investments in the territories of the signatory countries. BITs guarantee substantive and procedural rights to foreign investors. The former include: a 'minimum standard treatment', considered (depending on the treaty and still on the country area) as a treatment of foreign investment not less favourable than the one accorded under international law, or the most favoured nation treatment, or again the national treatment; guarantees of appropriate compensation (depending on the cases, adequate, prompt and effective – the so-called Hull formula, or just and equitable compensation which represent the fair value of the investment expropriated) in case of expropriation (considered as an ultimate measure); assurances of non-discriminatory measures and of full investment protection and security. The BITs procedural rights give investors an instrument to enforce the substantive right, arbitrating directly with the state for a violation of the treaty. The BITs dispute settlement resolution clauses provide (depending on the treaties) for an ad hoc tribunal, sometimes on the basis of UNCITRAL rules, more often on the ICSID basis.

The number of stipulated BITs has been increasing lately, and so has the number of controversies raised under them; therefore the matter is starting to have significant proportions.[4] The even more recent phenomenon of SWFs has set itself into this situation.

2.1 Theoretical Analysis

Under the theoretical aspect, there are no studies about the relationships between BITs and SWFs. This is not surprising, if we think that SWFs (in the forms and dimensions described in the previous chapter) have come out only very recently.

2.1.1 BITs and FDI relationship

The studies in literature – starting from the 2000s – generally focus on the relationships between BITs and foreign direct investments (FDI). Therefore they are a valuable starting point, even knowing that the result of the analysis will have to be fine-tuned for SWFs according to the scope of application of our study. While this scope is objectively broader (SWF

---

[4] There are more than 2600 BITs in force, and almost 300 arbitrations opened.

investments are not limited to FDI – that imply take-over of the target company – but include also portfolio investments – that do not), it is subjectively narrower (as it is limited to the investments of SWFs alone).

Unfortunately, this starting point gives more doubts than certainties.[5] In fact, the literature is split between those that consider that BITs have scarce influence on FDIs,[6] and those that consider them important, if not decisive.[7] There are various arguments in support of either theory, that highlight different aspects of the quantitative and qualitative analysis. Therefore, the existence and the strength of a causal relationship between BITs and FDI remains disputed.

What can be said with reasonable certainty is that the existence or not of a BIT is relevant for the purpose of investing in a state, but its relevance is relative, as it depends on other factors that come into play in these options, e.g. size of the internal market, gross domestic product of the host country, pre-existing levels of investment, degree of market liberalisation, sector-specific or securities (or antitrust) domestic laws, levels of domestic investment, size and growth rate of the host-country market, availability of raw materials or labour. All these factors play a different role, depending on: the country one wishes to invest in (and hence domestic rules, growth prospects, political risk matter); the type of intended investment (FDI or portfolio investment); the business area of the target enterprise (industry, finance); and the economic situation. All these factors suggest considering aggregate aspects of economy, politics and law. Therefore we may conclude that generalisation is inappropriate and that each case should be

---

5 For a recent story of the discussion see S. Frank, 'Foreign Direct Investment, Investment Treaty Arbitration, and the Rule of Law' [2007] *Global Business & Development Law Journal* 337–73, esp. 348–54.

6 M. Hallward-Driemeier, *Do Bilateral Investment Treaties Attract Foreign Direct Investment? Only a Bit-and they could bite*, World Bank working paper, 2003; M. Sornarajah, 'State Responsibility and Bilateral Investment Treaties' [1986] *Journal of World Trade L.* 79–98; J. Salacuse and N. Sullivan, 'Do BITs really work?: An Evaluation of Bilateral Investment Treaties and Their Grand Bargain' [2005] *Harvard International Law Journal* 67 *ff*; UNCTAD, *Bilateral Investment Treaties in the Mid-1990s*, UNCTAD/ITE/IIT/7, sales n. E98.II.D.8-10 (1998); J. Tobin and S. Rose-Ackerman, 'Foreign Direct Investment and Business Environment in Developing Countries: The Impact of Bilateral Investment Treaties', in *Yale Law and Economics Research Paper* no. 293, 2005.

7 E. Neumayer and L. Spess, *Do Bilateral Investment Treaties Increase Foreign Direct Investment in Developing Countries?* (World Development Paper, 2005); D. Swenson, 'Why Do Developing Countries Sign BITs?' [2005] *U.C. Davis Journal of International Law and Policy* 131–54; P. Egger and M. Pfaffermayr, 'The Impact of Bilateral Investment Treaties on Foreign Direct Investment' [2004] *Journal of Comparative Economy* 788–804.

reviewed, according to the applicable BITs and the specific investment, to see whether the presence (or absence) of the BIT is relevant or not.

2.1.2 . . . and its relevance to SWFs' investments

This conclusion, valid for the relationships between BITs and FDIs, may also apply to SWF investments, with one simplification and two corrections. The simplification is that so far SWFs have made portfolio investments, more linked to the nature of these funds that make medium-to-long-term investments and as such are less interested in direct management. This allows to give value to certain factors compared to others. For example, a portfolio of financial investments in Indian banks (like that of the Government of Singapore Investment Corporation – CIG) presupposes a careful evaluation of the political risk, of securities laws, of levels of domestic investment, of the size and the growth rate of the host-country market. A portfolio investment in airlines (Temasek holds shares in Chinese airlines) implies specific knowledge of the development of the specific domestic regulatory framework.

So far the simplification. As to corrections, SWFs are above all informed investors who make financial rather than industrial investments and are interested in long-term returns. Therefore they will focus most on typical long-term indicators and give less importance to contingent information. Another correction factor derives from the fact that SWFs are perfectly aware of whether their home state ratified a BIT with a country they are considering to invest in. In addition, their 'sovereign' nature also allows them to steer the government towards the negotiation of BIT with the countries they wish to invest in, in order to maximise the security of their investments. This imbalance does not adversely affect the market – on the contrary, if well used it might improve international relationships and exchanges even further. In fact, the protection given by BITs guarantees higher standards compared to multilateral treaties, (now limited to the regional level), that are always a consequence of a broad compromise. Therefore, we may reasonably assume that the existence or negotiation of a BIT is more relevant for a SWF than for an investor that cannot exercise political lobbying, or can do it only indirectly.

2.2 SWFs' Home States' Practice

Two pieces of information emerge from a preliminary review of the practice. First, SWF home states have ratified few BITs. Second, many of the BITs ratified by SWF home states are with developing countries, where evidently SWFs feel they should be more protected. This first impression confirms the need for further insight.

Among the home states of the biggest SWFs, United Arab Emirates ratified 11 bilateral investment treaties,[8] Qatar 8,[9] Libyan Arab Jamahiriya 6,[10] Kuwait 23,[11] Saudi Arabia 9,[12] Singapore 20,[13] Norway 15,[14] the Russian Federation 29,[15] Venezuela 23,[16] Kazakhstan 21,[17] Australia 21,[18] Algeria 18,[19] Brunei Darussalam 3,[20] Malaysia 34,[21] Taiwan province

---

[8] UAE ratified bilateral investment treaties with Lebanon, Malaysia, Morocco, United Kingdom, Czech Republic, Austria, Finland, France, Germany, Italy and Switzerland.

[9] With China, Egypt, Morocco, Germany, Turkey, France, Korea and Switzerland.

[10] With Malta, Morocco, Austria, Belgium and Portugal.

[11] With Bulgaria, China, Ethiopia, Hungary, Jordan, Kazakhstan, Morocco, Czech Republic, Austria, Belgium, Croatia, Denmark, Finland, France, Germany, Italy, Iraq, Lebanon, Lithuania, Pakistan, Switzerland, Netherlands and Republic of Korea.

[12] With Belgium, Malaysia, Austria, France, Germany, Italy, Republic of Korea and Switzerland.

[13] With China, Egypt, Hungary, Mauritius, Mongolia, Pakistan, Sri Lanka, Czech Republic, Cambodia, France, Germany, Netherlands, United Kingdom, Viet Nam, Peru, Indonesia, Jordan and Switzerland.

[14] With Chile, China, Estonia, Hungary, Indonesia, Latvia, Lithuania, Malaysia, Slovakia, Czech Republic, Peru, Poland, Romania, Russian Federation and Sri Lanka.

[15] With Argentina, Cyprus, Egypt, Ethiopia, Hungary, Lebanon, Lithuania, Philippines, Sweden, Turkey, Thailand, Ukraine, United States of America, Switzerland, United Kingdom, Slovakia, Austria, Belgium, Canada, France, Germany, Greece, Italy, Japan, Netherlands, Norway, Portugal, Republic of Korea and Spain.

[16] With Bolivia, Brazil, Chile, Costa Rica, Ecuador, Peru, Barbados, Lithuania, Uruguay, Paraguay, Czech Republic, Canada, Denmark, France, Germany, Italy, Netherlands, Portugal, Spain, Sweden, Switzerland and United Kingdom.

[17] With Bulgaria, Egypt, Hungary, India, Iran, Republic of Korea, Kuwait, Malaysia, Netherlands, United Kingdom, Turkey, United States of America, Belgium, France, Germany, Greece, Italy, Spain, Sweden and Switzerland.

[18] With Argentina, Mexico, Chile, China, Czech Republic, Egypt, Hong Kong Special Administrative Region of China, Hungary, India, Indonesia, Lao People's Democratic Republic, Lithuania, Pakistan, Papua New Guinea, Peru, Philippines, Poland, Romania, Sri Lanka, Uruguay and Vietnam.

[19] Belgium, Czech Republic, Denmark, France, Germany, Greece, Indonesia, Italy, Jordan, Turkey, Romania, Mali, Finland, Netherlands, Portugal, Republic of Korea, Spain and Switzerland.

[20] China, Oman and Republic of Korea.

[21] Chile, China, Egypt, Ethiopia, Ghana, Hungary, Indonesia, Jordan, Kazakhstan, Kyrgyzstan, Lebanon, Mongolia, Netherlands, Norway, Peru, Spain, Switzerland, Viet Nam, United Kingdom, Uruguay, United Arab Emirates, Morocco, Saudi Arabia, Czech Republic, Austria, Cambodia, Denmark, Finland, France, Germany, Italy, Republic of Korea, Sweden and Turkey.

of China 5,[22] Chile 49,[23] Iran 19,[24] Nigeria 10,[25] China 108, Republic of Korea 96. A comparative review of the BITs ratified by the home states of the main SWFs is in the table at pages 118–23.[26]

The analysis of this practice – content of treaties, partner states – gives useful hints for reflection. One significant figure is the low number of bilateral investment treaties ratified by SWF home countries. Except for China, and the Republic of Korea, other SWF home states do not seem to consider BITs as an ordinary instrument for the protection of their foreign investments. It is surprising, for instance, to see that the Russian Federation has entered into just 23 bilateral investment treaties. And it is no less surprising that the UAE have stipulated 11, and the Libyan Arab Jamahiriya 6. At first sight, it seems that the states owning the most important SWFs do not feel that the existence of a BIT is any relevant for the protection of their investment. This aspect should be subject to further verification.

Another thing to consider is that most home states of the main SWFs have ratified agreements mainly with countries that offer good investment opportunities. It is therefore surprising that none among the home states of the main SWFs has ratified a bilateral investment treaty with the United States (only China, Russia and Kazakhstan did). Singapore, for one, didn't, although in 2008 alone it stipulated some of the most relevant acquisitions for that year in the US.[27]

The information about the countries with which SWF home states have

---

22 Thailand, Belize, The former Yugoslav Republic of Macedonia, Marshall Islands and Swaziland.

23 Argentina, Australia, Austria, Belgium, Bolivia, Brazil, China, Colombia, Costa Rica, Croatia, Cuba, Czech Republic, Denmark, Ecuador, Egypt, Finland, France, Germany, Greece, Guatemala, Honduras, Hungary, Indonesia, Republic of Korea, Lebanon, Malaysia, Netherlands, New Zealand, Nicaragua, Norway, Panama, Paraguay, Peru, Philippines, Poland, Portugal, Romania, El Salvador, South Africa, Spain, Sweden, Switzerland, Tunisia, Turkey, United Kingdom, Ukraine, Uruguay, Venezuela and Vietnam,

24 Austria, Bangladesh, Belarus, China, Kazakhstan, Lebanon, Republic of Korea, Sri Lanka, South Africa, Thailand, Switzerland, Turkey, Morocco, Croatia, France, Germany, Greece, Republic of Korea and Spain.

25 Egypt, Turkey, United Kingdom, Finland, France, Germany, Netherlands, Republic of Korea, Spain and Switzerland.

26 The table is based on UNCTAD figures taken from http://www.unctadxi.org/templates/DocSearch.aspx?id=779 (accessed 30 March 2011).

27 Temasek Holdings acquired on January 2008 Merrill Lynch stocks for a value of $4400 billion, and on July 2008 stocks for a total amount of $3400 billion; the Government of Singapore Investment Corporation (GIC) invested in Citigroup in 2008 $6800 billion.

bilateral investment treaties becomes more relevant if weighed against the countries where the SWFs have made their biggest investments. In spite of scarce information on the matter, if we look at recent data, and particularly at 2008 figures (the year when SWF investments came to the forefront), the ten biggest investments were made by SWFs in China, Switzerland, United States, United Arab Emirates, United Kingdom, Sweden. All countries with a high number of bilateral investment treaties into force.[28] If we cross-refer the data (even though these are partial because they relate to the ten biggest transactions of 2008) for investments made and BITs effective between the home state of the investor SWF and the host state, we see that the investment in China was an internal one (by the China Investment Corporation),[29] as was the one in the UAE (by the Mubadala Development Company[30]); the investments in Switzerland were made by Government of Singapore Investment Corporation (there has been a bilateral investment agreement into force between Singapore and Switzerland since 1978);[31] those in the United States were made by China and Singapore (China does have a BIT with the USA, Singapore does not); the investment in the United Kingdom was made by the Qatar Investment Authority (there is no BIT between Qatar and the United Kingdom),[32] the investment in Sweden was made by the Dubai International Financial Centre – DIFC – (no BIT here as well).

---

[28] China 120, Switzerland 111, USA, UK and Sweden 51, UAE 11.

[29] About one-third of Chinese funds investments are aimed at supporting internal development projects; the remaining two-thirds are used for foreign transactions. For example, CIC has invested $3 billion in 2007 in the American fund Blackstone, $5 billion to purchase 9.9% of Morgan Stanley.

[30] Mubadala Investment Company has also recently invested in the Italian companies Piaggio Aero Industries (where it holds 25%) and Ferrari (5%), in the US fund Carlyle (where it holds 7.5%) and in the US-based Advanced Micro Devices (8%).

[31] Singapore has two main funds. One, Government of Singapore Investment Corporation (CIG), has a very broad portfolio, ranging from an equity investment in Westin Paris to financial investments in India, in the Budapest airport, in the Swiss bank UBS or in the US bank Citigroup. The other one, Temasek Holding, invests 38% of its assets in Singapore and the rest abroad, more than 40% in Asia and 20% in non-Asian OECD countries. It holds equity investments in the DBS Group, in the Barclays bank (2.1%), in Chinese companies (including an airline), in the Russian bank VTB, in the Indian group INX-Media.

[32] Qatar Investment Authority is particularly active in the United Kingdom and in other European countries. It holds more than 20% in the London Stock Exchange, 10% in the Swedish stock exchange (Nordic Exchange OMX), 5.1% in the French group Lagardère, 25% in the British supermarket chain Sainsbury's, and equity investments in Middle Eastern banks.

If we exclude internal investments, that evidently serve to meet peculiar logics, the biggest investments made in 2008 were targeted to companies in Europe or in the US, countries that offer a series of guarantees to foreign investors. Apparently it was for this reason that the existence of a BIT was not considered decisive in the choice of the investment. We may assume, in particular, that the investments in Western financial institutions (among the main investment targets) were made by SWFs regardless of the existence of a BIT between the home and the host state.

This is confirmed by the fact that if we broaden the scope of our survey from the biggest transactions to all the known transactions made between 2007 and 2010, the SWFs of UAE, China, Singapore, Korea and Qatar have invested in financial institutions mostly in the United Kingdom, United States and Switzerland.[33] Among these home states, only China has a BIT with the United States; China, Korea, UAE and Singapore (not Qatar) have a BIT with the United Kingdom; all these home states have a BIT with Switzerland. Again, we see that there is no uniformity about the United States; in all other cases the relationship between BITs and SWF investments is significant. This relationship is even clearer if we differentiate the investments into financial activities and manufacturing activities: in the case of the former, the existence of a BIT between SWF home state and host state is materially irrelevant.[34] Investments in manufacturing

[33] SWF transactions in 2007 involving financial institutions were the following: ICD (Dubai) in May invested $1.2 billion in HSBC (UK); CIC (China) in June acquired 9.9% of Blackstone (US); CDB (China) in July acquired 3.1% of Barclays (UK); Temasek (Singapore) in July acquired 2.1% of Barclays (UK); Mubadala Development Fund (Abu Dhabi) in September acquired 7.5% of Carlyle (US); ADIA (Abu Dhabi) in November acquired 4.9% of Citigroup (US). In December 2007 CIC (China) acquired 9.9% of Morgan Stanley (US); GIC (Singapore) 9% of UBS (Switzerland); Temasek invested $5 billion in Merrill Lynch (US); IC Korea invested $2 billion in Merrill Lynch; Temasek (Singapore) acquired 18% of Standard Chartered (UK). In January 2008, Kuwait IA invested $2 billion in Merrill Lynch (US); GIC (Singapore) acquired 3.7% of Citigroup (US); KIA (Kuwait) 1.6% of Citigroup; in February, QIA (Qatar) acquired 1% of Credit Suisse (Switzerland). In July, Temasek (Singapore) acquired 3% of Barclays (UK) and invested $3 billion in Merrill Lynch (US); QIA (Qatar) acquired 9.4% of Barclays. Finally, between October and November 2008 Qatar Holding invested $8.8 billion in Credit Suisse (Switzerland) and acquired 12.7% of Barclays (UK).

[34] For example, KIA (Kuwait) invested in Citigroup; GIC (Singapore) invested in Citigroup, in UBS, in Rosen Real Estate Securities (US); ADIA (Abu Dhabi) invested in Citigroup and in the US private equity companies Apollo Management and AP Alternative Assets; SAFE (China) invested in Visa Inc., in Commonwealth Bank of Australia, in National Australia Bank, in Australia and New Zealand Banking Group, in the private equity TPG, in Aviva (UK); Temasek (Singapore) invested in Merrill-Lynch, in Barclays Bank, in Standard Chartered; CIC (China)

enterprises or in infrastructures are instead made almost always in countries where the SWF home state has ratified a BIT.[35]

This is less indicative, albeit more or less uniform, in the case of SWF investments in developing countries. The lower reliability of the analysis owes to the relative transparency of fund transactions, as these arise almost completely when performed in Western countries but are much less visible when performed in developing countries. Based on accessible information, the Kuwait Investment Authority invests mostly in developing countries in the area (Lebanon, Bahrain, Jordan),[36] and Kuwait has bilateral investment treaties with all these countries. Singapore funds invest in Hungary and China, countries with which Singapore has BITs; however, they also invest in Indian (and US) banks in the absence of BITs with those countries. The Libyan Investment Authority invests mostly in North Africa and the Middle East and, among European countries, in Italy.[37] Interestingly, the Norwegian SWFs conditioned an investment in India to the entry into force of the BIT between Norway and India.[38]

We may therefore confirm, although with greater prudence considering the scarcity of information about SWF investments in developing

---

invested in Morgan Stanley, in Barclays Bank, in Blackstone and JC Flowers (private equity); SAMA (Saudi Arabia) invested in UBS; QIA (Qatar) invested in Credit Suisse, in Barclays Bank, in the London Stock Exchange; ICD (Dubai) invested in Marfin Investment Group Holdings, in Standard Chartered, in the London Stock Exchange, in Nasdaq-OMX, in Och Ziff.

[35] For example, KIA (Kuwait) invested in BP (UK), SAFE (China) invested in BP, in TOTAL, in Royal Dutch Shell, in BG Group, in Veolia, in Sanofi Aventis; ICD (Dubai) invested in BHP Hilton, in Almatis, in EADS, in Mauser, in MGM Mirage, in Travelodge, in ESPA International, in Inchcape Shipping Services, in Alliance Medicale; ADIA (Abu Dhabi) purchased a direct share of London Gatwick Airport; QIA (Qatar) invested in BHP Hilton, in Cegelec, in Lagarère, in Casino de Cannes, in Sainsbury's, in Suez Environment, in Veolia Environment, in German railways (jv with Deutsche Bahn), in Volkswagen, in Harrods; Mubadala (Abu Dhabi) invested in Ferrari, in FIAT, in Piaggio Aero Industries; ADIA (Abu Dhabi) invested in Mediaset; GIC (Singapore) invested in West Quai Shopping Centre, in Roma Est Shopping Centre, in British Land; Temasek (Singapore) invested in the construction of new cities in China. In all those cases the SWF invested in a country with the guarantee of a BIT between his home state and the host state.

[36] For the rest it holds small equity interests in Daimler-Benz (7%), BP (3%), Citigroup (6%) and Merrill Lynch (5%).

[37] In Italy it has acquired interests in FIAT and, more recently, in Unicredit Bank.

[38] See L. Catà Backer, 'Sovereign Wealth Funds as regulatory chameleons: the Norwegian Sovereign Wealth Funds and public global governance through private global investment' [2010] *Georgetown Journal of International Law* 425–500, 480 *ff*.

countries, that there is a trend whereby funds do pay attention to the existence of BITs with the countries of nationality of target companies, especially when the investment is in an enterprise, while the presence of BITs is considered less decisive if the investment target is a bank.

Another relevant piece of information is the date of BIT ratification and coming into force. It is reasonable to expect that older agreements follow a one-way rationale while more recent ones adopt a policy of balancing investment flows in an increasingly reciprocal manner, or are at least more negotiated. In line with this trend, certain countries (the US and Canada above all) have started to renegotiate existing BITs and stipulate new ones on the basis of new models, much more detailed compared to the current practice.

This is important for the purpose of assessing the content of the agreements, which is the subject matter of the following paragraphs.

3. THE MAIN BIT MODELS. ASSESSMENT OF THEIR EFFICACY WITH RESPECT TO SWF INVESTMENTS

Bilateral Investment Treaties are characterised by a common pattern, both in structure and content, that may be summarised as follows: the first part contains subjective and objective definitions (the investors and investments benefiting from treaty protections are defined); the second part defines the investors' substantive rights (minimum standard treatment, most favoured nation treatment, national treatment, right to compensation in case of expropriation, etc); the third part is dedicated to procedural rights, including dispute settlement instruments. The last part provides for final provisions on effective date and termination. If the skeleton is the same, the various models now in use differ in certain points, only apparently of detail.[39]

[39] The literature is split between those who give relevance to the aspects in common to the BITs and those who point out their differences. In certain cases, the former even assume that multilateralisation is taking place because of the similarities among many BITs (S.W. Schill, *The Multilateralization of International Investment Law: the Emergence of a Multilateral System of Investment Protection on the Basis of Bilateral Treaties* (SIEL Inaugural Conference Paper, 2008). The latter point out at jurisdictional conflicts that are becoming more and more evident as the number and relevance of controversies started under BITs increase. See, in this sense, G. Sacerdoti, *The Proliferation of BITs: Conflict of Treaties, Proceedings and Awards*, Bocconi University – Institute of Comparative Law 'Angelo Sraffa' (I.D.C.) – Legal Studies Research Paper Series; S.D. Frank, 'The Legitimacy Crisis

3.1 Existing Models

Let us first review the characteristic features in common to the BITs and then the most significant differences. One thing in common to all BITs is certainly the structure of the treaty: the first part for definitions, the second part for substantive rights, the third part for procedural rights and the fourth part for final provisions. However, as soon as we start reviewing the contents, we understand that each BIT is a treaty of its own, being the result of a specific negotiation between two states. It is therefore hard, already from a preliminary review, to give credit to the theory that the multiplication and standardisation of bilateral treaties is giving rise to a kind of multilateralisation.[40]

3.1.1 Definitions

Let us take definitions: the definition of investment, for which examples are used in order to have as broad a concept as possible;[41] that of investor, defined broadly both for natural persons and legal persons.[42] As for the

in Investment Treaty Arbitration: Privatizing Public International Law Through Inconsistent Decisions' [2005] *Fordham Law Review* 1521–1625.

[40] S. W. Schill, *The Multilateralization of International Investment Law: the Emergence of a Multilateral System of Investment Protection on the Basis of Bilateral Treaties*, n. 39 above.

[41] According to most BITs the term 'investment' means every kind of asset. It includes specifically – for the purposes of our work – shares in, and stock, bonds and debentures of, and any other form of participation in, a company or a business enterprise. These are indeed typical investments – although only portfolio investments – of SWFs, and therefore certainly fall within the scope of application of BITs. For a broad interpretation of the concept of investment in the ICSID case law see Case 1996, *FEDAX N.V. v. Republic of Venezuela* (ICSID Case No. ARB/96/3(1), ICSID, Decision on Jurisdiction issued on 11 July 1997; *Salini Costruttori S.p.A. and Italstrade S.p.A. v. Jordan*, ICSID Case No. ARB/02/13 (Italy/Jordan BIT). – Decision on Jurisdiction, 9 November 2004.

[42] As a general rule, the provision is as follows (or quite similar): the term 'nationals' shall comprise with regard to either Contracting Party: (i) natural persons having the nationality of that Contracting Party in accordance with its laws; (ii) legal persons constituted in accordance with the law of that Contracting Party; (iii) legal persons controlled directly or indirectly, by nationals of that Contracting Party, but constituted in accordance with the law of the other Contracting Party (Bolivia–Netherlands BIT of 1992). Other BITs, when referring to legal persons constituted in the state, sometimes specify that their legal personality is irrelevant, sometimes specify that the treaty does not apply to the branches of companies constituted in third countries (Singapore–Germany BIT of 1973).

latter, some treaties require, in order for companies to benefit from treaty protection, not only the ownership but also the control by a national (other BITs give relevance to the place of incorporation or to the 'real seat'). Apparently, the notion of control opens up a frontier in terms of dispute resolution, as arbitration case law on the matter is extremely variegated.[43] The analysis is not made any easier by the fact that, according to certain BITs, minority, non controlling or indirect shareholders have *jus standi* before arbitration tribunals.[44]

3.1.2 Standard treatment and allowed host state restrictive measures

There are differences among the various BITs also with reference to the minimum standard treatment accorded to foreign investments. The differences lie not so much in the various models applied but (mostly) in host state (recipient) territories. In the Latin American region, the echoes of the 'Calvo clause' still shape a protectionist approach in favour of national investors. In most other BITs instead the non-discrimination of foreign

---

[43] For example, the ICSID case law recognises control where foreigners own a majority of the shares of the enterprise concerned (see *Klòckner v. Cameroon* (ICSID Case No ARB/81/2) Decision on Annulment, 3 May 1985; *Liberian Eastern Timber Corporation (LETCO) v. Republic of Liberia*, ICSID Case No. ARB/83/2, Decision on Rectification, 17 June 1986; *Vacuum Salt Prod., Ltd. v. Ghana*, ICSID Case No. ARB/92/1, Award of 16 February 1994). The rule has two important caveats: the effective foreign control may be not only direct but also indirect (*Société Ouest Africaine des Bétons Industriels (SOABI) v. Senegal* ICSID Case No. ARB/82/1, Award on Merits of 25 February 1988), and the national controlling the local company may have dual nationality, one of the nationalities being that of the host country.

[44] The negative answer given by ICJ in *Barcelona Traction* is often overruled because related to diplomatic protection, and hence not applicable to a BIT dispute. In *CMS v. Argentina*, ICSID Case no. ARB/01/8, Award, 12 May 2005 the Tribunal not only made a distinction between diplomatic protection and individual investors' direct right of action, but also stated that a new rule had developed under customary international law, according to which allowing claims by even minority or not-controlling shareholders is a result of a *lex specialis* now so prevalent that can be considered the general rule 'certainly in respect of foreign investments and increasingly in respect of other matters'. Furthermore, as the text of the ICSID Convention does not define the term 'investment', the tribunal concluded that the investments covered by the Convention were not only those owned by a majority or controlling shareholders. The relevance of minority shareholders is in many BIT ratified by home states of important SWFs. See, for example, Art. 1 of the BIT between China and France of 1985; Art. 1 of the BIT between UAE and France of 1995; Art. 1 of the BIT between Singapore and the Netherlands (1973); Art. 1 of the BIT between Qatar and Germany (1999); Art. 1 of the BIT between China and Switzerland (1987).

investors is based on the principle of the most favoured nation.[45] A few treaties into force (but almost all new BIT models) make express reference to the minimum standard accorded under international law.[46]

Again, we may look for our purposes here at the definition of expropriation, that in certain BITs is expressly broadened to include indirect investments,[47] and the terms for its exercise.[48] There are also differences among the various BITs with respect to the compensation in case of expropriation, which is sometimes qualified as 'prompt, adequate and effective' (the Hull formula), some other times as 'just and equitable compensation which represents the fair market value of the investments expropriated'. The same happens with compensation for losses, where generally restitution, indemnification, compensation no less favourable than that which the contracting party accords to its nationals or companies or to nationals or companies of any third state are provided.[49]

3.1.3 Dispute settlement resolution

As to dispute settlement mechanisms, BITs provide that controversies be settled between the parties to the treaty (states) regards to its

---

[45] The Most Favoured Nation clause in BITs follows this general formulation: neither contracting party shall subject in its territory nationals or companies of the other contracting party as regards their activities in connection with investments, including the effective management, use or enjoyment of such investments, to a treatment less favourable than that accorded to its own nationals or companies, or to national or companies of any third state as regards their activities in connection with investments.

[46] So are the new BIT models of Canada (2004), USA (2004), Norway (2007) and Germany (2008).

[47] Some treaties expressly provide for direct expropriation, which entails the actual taking of ownership by direct means, including the loss of all, or almost all, useful control over property. Others admit also indirect taking, where the measure deprives the owner of the substantial benefits of the property, without formally expropriating him. A kind of indirect taking is a regulatory expropriation, where a measure is taken for regulatory purposes, but has an impact on the economic value of the investment sufficient to be considered an expropriation.

[48] It appears to be unanimously recognised that foreign-owned property may not be expropriated, or subject to a measure equivalent to expropriation, unless four conditions are met: (1) the measure is for a public purpose; (2) it is taken in accordance with applicable laws and due process; (3) it is non-discriminatory; (4) it is accompanied by compensation.

[49] Of course there is the exception, for EU members, that the Agreement shall not be construed so as to oblige the contracting party to extend to the nationals or companies of the other the benefit of any treatment, preference or privilege which may be extended by the former contracting party by virtue of a customs union or a free trade area or a common external tariff area or a monetary union.

interpretation, and between the investor and the host state regards to any dispute arising from alleged treaty breaches.

As to the second aspect, the most relevant one for our purposes, BITs often provide for alternative dispute settlement procedures. In particular, usually a national or company that is a party to an investment dispute may submit it for resolution under one of the following alternatives: (i) to the administrative tribunals of the party to the dispute; (ii) in accordance with any applicable, previously agreed dispute-settlement procedures, (iii) after three (or often six) months have elapsed form the date the dispute arose, the dispute may be submitted (a) to the Centre (ICSID), (b) to the Additional Facilities of the Centre,[50] (c) in accordance with the UNCITRAL Arbitration Rules, (d) if agreed by both parties to the dispute, to any other arbitration institution or in accordance with any other arbitration rules.

The investors' faculty to select among alternative systems has generated certain practical problems, for example in the activation of multiple mechanisms that settle disputes in different manners. There are various ways to overcome these difficulties in the practice. In certain cases BITs include a fork-in-the-road clause,[51] which may however be easily circumvented;[52] in other cases they impose the so-called 'no U-turn clause'.[53] Another way to avoid *litis pendens* is in the new 2007 Norwegian BIT model that contains a requirement regarding exhaustion of national legal remedies. In the Norwegian model, the application of the requirement is limited to a three-year period; if the investor has not reached a settlement pursuant to national law within three years, he can institute international dispute settlement.

---

[50] The ICSID arbitration is available if both states are parties to the ICSID Convention. If only one state is party to the Convention, then the ICSID Additional Facility may apply, often offered in the BIT as an option.

[51] With that clause, some agreements force the investor to decide *ab initio* whether the dispute shall be adjudicated in domestic tribunals or through international arbitration. Once the dispute is submitted to either forum, the election shall be definitive. An example of this clause is in Art. IX.3 of the BIT between Indonesia and Chile (1999), according to which 'Once the investor has submitted the dispute to the competent tribunal of the Contracting Party in whose territory the investment was made or to international arbitration, that election shall be final'.

[52] The so-called fork-in-the-road clause aims at preventing *litis pendens*; but this is the case only if there is identity of the parties, object and cause of action in the proceeding pending before two or more tribunals (ICSID award in *S.A.R.L. Benvenuti & Bonfant v. Congo*, 21 I.L.M. 740 a). Therefore, the clause barely applies.

[53] The no-U-turn approach provides the investor with the possibility of making a final decision at a later stage, even after having submitted the dispute to the tribunals of the host country. The investor is allowed to opt for international arbitration as long as domestic tribunals have not rendered a final judgement.

3.2 Renegotiation Under Way

The recent increase in the number of BITs stipulated and ratified and the consequent increase in the number of arbitrations led many states to revise their BIT models in order to better specify certain definitions, provide for additional investors' rights, add other general safeguard clauses. Useful in this sense was the indirect experience of the NAFTA, that led the US and Canada to revise, albeit each in a different manner, their own models.

3.2.1 The notion of investment

We may detect the following main differences (compared to the past) in the new models. First, the notion of investment, once broadened to encompass any type of asset, is now built around specific limits, e.g. based on a detailed list that tends to be increasingly exhaustive.[54] The notions of investor[55] and of state, that are particularly relevant in our work, did not receive equal attention.

---

[54] A 'closed-list' definition is in Art. 1139 of NAFTA. In these cases the notion of investment expressly excludes: (a) claims to monies that arise only from (i) commercial contracts for the sale of goods or services by a national or enterprise in the territory of a party to an enterprise in the territory of another party; or (ii) the extension of credit in connection with a commercial transaction, such as trade financing, and (b) an order entered in a judicial or administrative action. An example of this is the list given in the Canadian 2004 BIT model, according to which investment means: an enterprise, an equity security of an enterprise; a debt security of an enterprise (but only where (i) the enterprise is an affiliate of the investor, or (ii) the original maturity of the debt security is at least three years. It does not include a debt security, regardless of original maturity, of a state enterprise), a loan to an enterprise, an interest in an enterprise that entitles the owner to share in income or profits of the enterprise; an interest in an enterprise that entitles the owner to share in the assets of that enterprise on dissolution, other than a debt security or a loan excluded from other subparagraphs; real estate or other property, tangible or intangible, acquired in the expectation or used for the purpose of economic benefit or other business purposes; interest arising from the commitment of capital or other resources in the territory of a Party to economic activity in such territory, such as under (i) contracts involving the presence of an investor's property in the territory of the Party, including turnkey or construction contracts, or concessions, or (ii) contracts where remuneration depends substantially on the production, revenues or profits of an enterprise. 'Investment' does not mean (i) claims that arise solely from commercial contracts for the sale of good or services or (ii) the extension of credit in connection with a commercial transaction, (iii) any other claims to money that do not involve the kinds of interests set out above.

[55] The absence of innovative aspects in the contributions arises for instance from the new 2008 German BIT model, which defines as investor (for companies) any juridical person and any commercial or other company or association with or without legal personality which is founded pursuant to the law of the Federal

3.2.2 Host state measures and indirect expropriation

Second, the wording of various substantive treaty obligations has also been revised. For our purposes here, the international minimum standard of treatment was specified in detail in accordance with international law.[56] Indirect expropriation also was defined: it means measures having effect equivalent to nationalisation or expropriation.[57] Treaties often propose a distinction between direct and indirect expropriation or, alternatively, between expropriation and measures equivalent to nationalisation or expropriation. Indirect expropriation includes measures short of physical taking that may amount to taking in that they result in the effective loss of management, use or control, or a significant depreciation of the value, of the asset of a foreign investor.[58] Some particular types of such takings

---

Republic of Germany (FRG) or the law of a Member State of the European Union or the European Economic Area and is organised pursuant to the law of the FRG, registered in a public register in the FRG, or enjoys freedom of establishment as an agency or permanent establishment in Germany, which, in the contest of entrepreneurial activity is the owner, possessor or shareholder of an investment in the territory of the other contracting state, irrespective of whether or not the activity is directed at profit. The definition of investing company in the new 2006 French BIT model is precise: any legal person constituted on the territory of one contracting party in accordance with the legislation of that party and having its head office on the territory of that party, or controlled directly or indirectly by the national of one contracting party, or by legal persons having their head office in the territory of one contracting party and constituted in accordance with the legislation of that party.

56 The reference to the international minimum standard of treatment in accordance with international customary law includes both the notions of fair and equitable treatment and full protection and security. Art. 5 of the new Norwegian BIT model recognises that the investors' right to fair and equitable treatment and full protection and security is based on the international minimum standard of customary public international law, which specifies the lowest threshold for treatment of foreigners. Art. 5 of the new Canadian BIT model states that Each Party shall accord to covered investments treatment in accordance with the customary international law minimum standard treatment of aliens, including fair and equitable treatment and full protection and security. The concept of 'fair and equitable treatment' and 'full protection and security' do not require treatment in addition to or beyond that which is required by the customary international law minimum standard of treatment of aliens.

57 See Art. IV of the World Bank Guidelines on the Treatment of Foreign Direct Investment of 1992 (referring to expropriations or measures which have similar effect), or Art. 13(1) of the Energy Charter Treaty (measures having effect equivalent to nationalisation or expropriation), or Art. IV(2) of OECD Draft Multilateral Agreement on Investment (MAI) stating that a contracting party shall not expropriate or nationalise directly or indirectly an investment or take any measure having equivalent effect.

58 This is the definition given by G. Christie, 'What constitutes a taking of

have been called 'creeping expropriations' (i.e. foreign divestment of shares of a company; interference in the right of the management; appointment of managers; excessive or arbitrary taxation),[59] while others are defined as 'regulatory takings' (i.e. a state legislative or administrative measure).[60] The focus of the discussion is that, if almost any governmental measure could be construed as an act of interference in the business of a foreign investor, it should be distinguished between regulatory measures that have to be compensated and measures that do not need a compensation. To evaluate the difference, attention should be paid to the character of the government action,[61] to its economic impact,[62] and to reasonable investment expectations.[63]

---

property under international law?' [1962] *British Yearbook of International Law* 307–16; R. Dolzer, 'Indirect expropriation of alien property' [1986] *ICSID Review* 41–65; B. Weston, 'Constructive takings under international law: a modest foray into the problem of creeping expropriation' [1975] *Virginia Journal of International Law* 103–75. A different classification is proposed by A. Newcombe, in 'The Boundaries of Regulatory Expropriation in International Law' [2005] *ICSID Review* 1–57, which classifies international expropriation in three ways: (i) direct or indirect expropriation; (ii) arbitrary deprivations that cannot be justified by the exercise of state police powers to protect public order or morals, human health or the environment; (iii) cases where the state has abrogated a previously granted permission and the investor is deprived of its investment.

[59] A creeping expropriation is the 'slow and incremental encroachment on one or more of the ownership rights of a foreign investor that diminishes the value of the investment. The legal title to the property remains vested in the foreign investor, but the investor's rights of use of the property are diminished as a result of the interference' (*Taking of Property*, UNCTAD Series on issues in international investment agreements, New York and Geneva, 2000).

[60] Regulatory takings are 'those takings of property that fall within the police powers of a State, or otherwise arise from State measures like those pertaining to the regulation of the environment, health, morals, culture or economy of a host country' (*Taking of Property*, n. 59 above).

[61] Among the distinctions proposed, J. Sax ('Takings and the police power' [1964] *Yale Law Journal* 36–76), argued that non-compensation may be justified where the state is not acting as 'enterpriser' but as mediator between different and conflicting property rights. A. Newcombe (n. 58 above) refers to the benefits and harms criteria, according to which if the government acquires public benefits (a national park, a highway) it should pay for them, but if it is acting to protect the public from harms associated to the use of property (pollution, health effects) no compensation should be paid. Others (S. Rose-Ackerman and J. Rossi, 'Disentangling Deregulatory Takings' [2000] *Virginia Law Review* 1435–95) distinguished between government as purchaser and government as policy-maker in the context of utility regulation; only in the first case – government acting as a purchaser – compensation should be paid.

[62] An investment has been expropriated when the foreign investor suffered a

Therefore, the boundaries of indirect expropriation have not yet been clearly outlined. Besides, developing countries have no interest in outlining it in absolute terms, nor do developed countries that have much regulatory legislation in areas such as antitrust, corporate, securities, environment and planning, and are reluctant about transferring the review of these matters to international courts. The notion will therefore depend from time to time on the definition provided by the BIT, on its relationship (and compatibility) with the ICSID Convention (where chosen) or with UNCITRAL rules.

What is clear is that indirect expropriation is lawful if it meets certain conditions, as it should be: (i) done for public purpose, (ii) not discriminatory; (iii) proportionate;[64] (iv) accompanied by the payment of a compensation;[65] and (v) subject to judicial review (due process).

These changes have emerged from the recent practice. The new US and Canadian BIT models (but also some recent BITs signed by Japan or the Republic of Korea) define in detail the principle of fair and equitable treatment and its relation to the international minimum standard of treatment, and the scope of the concept of indirect expropriation as well.

3.2.3 Essential security and prudential financial measures

Concerning another issue introduced by the new models, a fundamental new development is that many recent BITs emphasise that investment protection must not be pursued at the expense of other legitimate public interests; this is the conceptual basis for general treaty exemptions, referred not only to taxation and regional economic integration, but also to essential security, prudential measures for financial services, public order, protection of health, safety and national resources, cultural diversity (the last one limited to BITs negotiated by Canada and France).

---

substantial deprivation. Obviously, all the debate is focused on when a deprivation can be considered 'substantial'.

[63] The question of legitimate expectation is linked to the risk allocation. The debate is focused in evaluating when a foreign investor is legitimate expecting a certain return from the investment, and what the amount (or the percentage) of this return could be.

[64] The proportionality test is aimed at guaranteeing that state measures do not deprive investors of their investments unless the measure is reasonably necessary to protect an essential public interest.

[65] The standard compensation issue is proposed, based on the Hull standard (prompt, adequate and effective compensation), or on the 'full market value' standard, or the 'appropriate compensation' standard; or the book value standard (consisting either in the net book value or in the updated book value, or in the tax value).

The first two new exemptions (essential security and prudential financial measures) are particularly relevant to our research,[66] as shown in Chapter 4. In fact, the security interest clauses are one of the most critical aspects of national law systems that can be opposed against SWF investments, due to their general content and their asserted enforceability at the host state's discretion.

Arbitration procedures have also been changed on the basis of

---

[66] Art. 18 of USA BIT new model states that '[n]othing in this Treaty shall be construed: (i) to require a Party to furnish or allow access to any information the disclosure of which it determines to be contrary to its essential security interests, or (ii) to preclude a party from applying measures that it considers necessary for the fulfilment of its obligations with respect to the maintenance or restoration of international peace or security, or the protection of its own essential security interests'. Also the 2007 Norwegian BIT model makes certain exceptions from the agreement for measures implemented on the basis of necessary security measures. The formulations are derived from Art. XIV *bis* of GATS, except that the term 'military sector' from GATS is replaced by the more wide-ranging term 'defence and security sector[s]' in the model agreement. This term reflects the provision's purposes more precisely, while clarifying the increasingly unclear distinction between defence interests and security interests. Indeed, Art. 26 of the model (Security Exemptions) states that: 'Nothing in this Agreement shall be construed:

i to require any Party to furnish any information, the disclosure of which it considers contrary to its essential security interests; or
ii to prevent any Party from taking any action which it considers necessary for the protection of its essential security interests: (a) relating to investment in defence and security sector[s]; (b) relating to fissionable and fusionable materials or the materials from which they are derived; (c) taken in time of war or other emergency in international relations; or
iii to prevent any Party from taking any action in pursuance of its obligations for the maintenance of international peace and security, including under the United Nations Charter'.

According to Art. 10 (General Exemptions) of the 2004 Canadian BIT model, each party may adopt or maintain reasonable measures for prudential reasons, such as the protection of investors, depositors, financial market participants, policy-holders, policy-claimants, or persons to whom a fiduciary duty is owed by a financial institution; ensuring the integrity and stability of a party's financial system. Furthermore, each party may take any actions that it considers necessary for the protection of its essential security interests, (i) relating to the traffic in weapons, ammunition and implements of war and to such traffic and transactions in other goods, materials, services and technology undertaken directly or indirectly for the purpose of supplying a military or other security establishment, (ii) taken in time of war or other emergency in international relations, or (iii) relating to implementation of national policies or international agreements expecting the non-proliferation of nuclear weapons or other nuclear explosive devices.

arbitration experience and are now more detailed with reference to greater and more substantial transparency in arbitration proceedings, open hearings, publication of related legal documents, possibility for representatives of the civil society to submit *amicus curiae* briefs to arbitration tribunals.

3.3 The Efficacy of Existing Models in Protecting SWF Investments

After reviewing the practices followed by the states in bilateral treaties and the recent innovations proposed, we may consider the efficacy of existing treaties and new models for SWF investments. The adequacy of treaties is considered under four respects. First, in subjective terms, it should be seen whether the notion of state and that of 'national of the other contracting party' are detailed enough and allow to classify a SWF as an investor or not. This assessment is important because it determines from the beginning whether BITs are an instrument that SWFs may use to protect their investments from host state measures taken against them. Second, it should be concluded if and to what extent BITs classify host state measures as indirect expropriations. This will allow us to consider whether a restrictive state measure may imply or not a compensation for the SWF. Third, the impact of general exemptions in the new models of some Western states should be studied. In fact, the reference, among others, to the security interest (and its alleged self-judging character) and to prudential measures might exclude BIT application to SWF investments in the most important cases. Lastly, the adequacy of existing BITs should be weighted with respect to dispute settlement resolution clauses; in fact, the mandatory jurisdiction of national courts or a fork-in-the-road provision might be particularly detrimental in certain cases, given the not only public but also 'sovereign' nature of the investor.

3.3.1 The state as an investor

As to the first question, so far the arbitration practice has brought to light difficulties in ascertaining the nationality of legal entities, from time to time on the basis of place of incorporation, location of the company's seat (real seat or place of business) or nationality of its owner or control.[67] But the issue of an investor state has not yet been addressed. In fact, if the investor is a state, BITs – and the related DSR mechanisms – do not apply.

[67] As a general principle ICSID Tribunals apply the criterion of incorporation or seat rather than control: see *Southern Pacific Properties v. Egypt* (ICSID Case no. ARB/84/3, Decision on Jurisdiction, 27 November 1985), and *Kaiser Bauxite v. Jamaica* (ICSID Case no. ARB/74/3, Decision on Jurisdiction, 6 July 1975). However, different criteria agreed by the parties are taken in consideration by the

The problem is a dual one. On one hand, the notion of state should be defined for BIT purposes. On the other, the limits of how this definition can apply to home states should be analysed, in order to verify not so much whether an action may be attributed to a host state, but the applicability of the treaty, which is based on the assumption that the claim is raised by an investor and not by a state (unless it provides so expressly, a BIT cannot apply to a dispute between states, as might be the case of a 'sovereign investor'). In other words, we should evaluate what relevance should be given to the fact that a SWF is controlled by a state – or is even the state itself.

As to the former side of the problem, BITs do provide a definition of state. Of course it relates to the host state. In this case, we should verify whether and to what extent the conduct of government agencies, government-owned companies, state enterprises, administrative or judicial courts can be attributed to the host state and thus become the basis for a claim. The criteria usually followed are those of 'structural' and 'functional' tests. The structural test takes into account the structure of the entity, including legal personality, ownership and control; the functional test considers the character, purposes and objectives of the functions performed by the entity. The two tests are often used together.[68]

As to the latter side of the problem, we should verify the applicability by similarity of this definition to a 'national of another contracting state', which is the other party to a state in a BIT. Now, the notion of national of another contracting state, referred not to a natural but to a legal person, is a very varied one, because – as we have seen – it sometimes refers to the place of incorporation, sometimes to the actual seat, sometimes to the nationality of owner or control. However, in the practice of treaties or in past arbitration awards, the difference between public or private control of the legal person is never relevant. Therefore, state-owned entities can legitimately claim a violation of the BIT; the same should be true for SWFs, the difference between the two vehicles being irrelevant for this purpose. A difference could arise where the SWF has no legal personality, being an entity not separate from the state (this is the case of Norway, Russia,

---

tribunals. It is the case if the parties agree to consider a legal entity constituted or having its seat in the host country as a foreign investor because of foreign control; see: *Liberian Eastern Timber Corporation (LEICO) v. Liberia* (ICSID Case no. ARB/83/2, Award, 31 March 1986) and *Klöckner Industrie-Anlagen GmbH and others v. Cameroon* (ICSID Case no. ARB/81/2, Award, 21 October 1983).

[68] See cases *Emilio Augustin Maffezini v. Spain* (ICSID Case no. ARB/97/7, Decision on Jurisdiction, 25 January 2000) and *Salini v. Morocco* (ICSID Case no. ARB/00/4, Decision on Jurisdiction, 23 July 2001).

Chile, Mexico, Saudi Arabia, etc.). In all these cases, the capability of a SWF to raise a claim under a BIT will depend much on the text of the BIT; in fact, in certain cases there is an express provision whereby a 'national of another contracting party' is not necessarily a legal person;[69] certain BITs ratified by the home states of major SWFs even qualify expressly the state government as 'investor'.[70] If, on the contrary, the BIT makes no express reference to the state as investor, the recall to 'national' as 'any juridical person'[71] actually prevents BIT measures from being claimed by a fund that lacks independent legal personality and coincides with a state. In this case, the BIT cannot be enforced because the SWF does not meet the definition of 'national' of that particular BIT, and cannot be distinguished by the state.

3.3.2 Host state measures as indirect expropriations

As to the second question, it should be seen whether host state measures adopted in respect of SWFs as such fall within the scope of application of the BITs, being aware that no general answer can be given: it will depend on the characteristics of the measure adopted by the state and by the contents of the BIT governing the relationships between host state and SWF home state.

Two aspects should be considered here. On one side, we should verify

---

[69] For example, in the BIT between Kuwait and Germany of 1994, investor (in respect of the State of Kuwait) is also any entity, *with or without legal personality*, established in accordance with the laws of the State of Kuwait and having its seat in Kuwait, such as enterprises, cooperatives, partnerships, corporations, foundations, companies, firms, establishments, funds, organisations and business associations or similar entities, irrespective of whether their liabilities are limited or otherwise. The BITs between Singapore and China of 1985 qualifies as investor any 'company, firm, association or body, with or without personality, incorporated, established or registered under the laws in force in the Republic of Singapore'. See also the BIT between China and the Republic of Korea, and the BIT between the Republic of Korea and Germany of 1967 (Art. 8).

[70] In the BIT between Kuwait and Germany of 1994, investor (in respect of the State of Kuwait) is also: '(iii) the Government of the State of Kuwait acting either directly or indirectly through the Kuwait Investment Authority (KIA) or its offices abroad, as well as development funds, agencies or other similar government institutions having their seats in Kuwait'. Also the BIT between Kuwait and Italy of 1987, and the BIT between Kuwait and France of 1991 qualify as investor the government of Kuwait. The BITs between Qatar with Germany (1996), France and China all expressly qualify the Government of Qatar as an investor.

[71] For example Art. 25.1 of the ICSID Convention, that is a benchmark for BIT interpretation when controversies are submitted to courts according to the ICSID procedure.

whether the measure qualifies (in abstract terms) as a form of indirect expropriation. If it does, we should verify whether its application implies a compensation. On the other side, we should ascertain whether in the existing treaty between host state and SWF home state the definition of expropriation is broad enough to include indirect forms similar to those proposed or applied by host states in respect of SWFs.

The measures proposed in literature or taken by the states so far (see on this Chapter 4, section 2.4) may be classified into two main categories: preventive and repressive measures. The former prevent a SWF from making investments, the latter aims at neutralising the effects of fund 'sovereignty'. When the law provides for both, the latter have a residual purpose as they only refer to investments that have already been made. In particular, certain measures apparently apply to all foreign investments but are specifically appointed to SWFs; others are aimed at regulating the investments made by sovereign entities. These include restrictions on foreign investments (applicable by means or preventive and repressive measures) in critical areas or strategic sectors, or for essential security interests. Other measures are fund-specific, such as those adopted in Australia, that apply where the initiative of the investor is not independent from the foreign government of the country the investor is based in, or where the nature of the investment is not only commercial;[72] or the measures provided for by Canadian laws, with rules on the foreign investments of state-owned enterprises (SOEs) under the Investment Canada Act, requiring that SOEs adhere to Canada standards of corporate governance.[73]

Other measures proposed in literature with express reference to SWFs consist of the suspension of voting rights for the shares held by a sovereign investor (which would cease to have effect if the shares are transferred to a non-sovereign entity),[74] or the setting of a limit for sovereign investors to the shares or quotas they may purchase, i.e. below the controlling majority,[75] or the disclosure of voting records. Other measures propose to remove the tax exemption enjoyed by SWFs.[76]

The above-mentioned measures, and also others equivalent, might in abstract terms qualify as indirect expropriations, as they result in the effective loss of management, use or control of the company, or in a significant depreciation of the value of the shares. Some of them set the foreign divestment of shares of a company; others interfere in the right of management

---

72 Ch. 4 above, s. 2.4.
73 Ibid.
74 Ch. 3 above, s. 1.3.
75 Ibid.
76 Ch. 5 above, s. 4.2.

or in the appointment of managers; others determine an arbitrary taxation. Conversely, other measures do not qualify as indirect expropriation, however broad such definition may be; a BIT or its dispute settlement resolution (DSR) instruments cannot apply to these measures.

For measures that in abstract terms qualify as forms of indirect expropriation one should verify if they can be followed by forms of compensation. In this case too, the analysis should be based on the criteria now most widely used; therefore, we should see if the host state adopts the measure acting as 'enterprise' or as a mediator between different and conflicting property rights; or if the government, by adopting that measure, acquires public benefits or protects the public from harms connected to the use of the property; or if the government act as a purchaser or as a policy maker. Whether the government acts as entrepreneur, acquires a public benefit, or acts as a purchaser, a compensation should be paid to the foreign investor. In this case too the amount of the compensation depends on the model provided by the applicable BIT, that will use one of the criteria mentioned above to ascertain the value of the asset upon expropriation.

So far, we have seen one side of the issue, i.e. the assessment of whether the state measure may represent an indirect expropriation. Let us now see the other side, i.e. whether the notion of expropriation in individual treaties is broad enough to include indirect expropriation and hence the host state measures we consider as such. A review of the BITs ratified by the home states of major SWFs shows a variegated practice, but the main trend seems to go towards broadening the scope of indirect expropriation. In some cases such broader meaning is apparently not allowed under the literal wording of the treaty;[77] in other cases the broader meaning is allowed sometimes on the basis of a notion of indirect expropriation,[78] sometimes on the basis of the admission of measures equivalent to expropriation or nationalisation,[79] that are sometimes even listed, although

[77] In that sense, Art. 3 of the BIT between the Republic of Korea and Germany of 1967.

[78] Art. 6 of the BIT between UAE and France of 1995 states that '[L]es Parties contractantes ne prennent pas de mesures d'expropriation ou de nationalisation ou toutes autres mesures, quelles qu'en soient la nature et le champ d'application, dont l'effet est de déposséder, directement ou indirectement les investisseurs de l'autre Partie des investissements leur appartenant.' Similar contents are in Art. 4 of the BIT between Singapore and France (1976), and Art. 4 of the BIT between Qatar and France.

[79] Art. 6 of the BIT between UAE and UK (1992) states that 'investments or investors of either Contracting party shall not be nationalized, expropriated or subjected to measures having the effect of dispossession, direct or indirect, or having effect equivalent to nationalization or expropriation'. The same provision

without limitation.[80] In certain cases even both criteria are present, which gives rise to several interpretation problems.[81] The actual solution will then depend on these variables. In any case, the possibility to qualify a measure as indirect expropriation and obtain compensation therefore is not a satisfactory solution for SWFs, as their aim is not obtaining a compensation but being free to make investments. State measures, be they any form of indirect expropriation or not, are an effective and major deterrent to SWF investments.

We may add that the exemptions from the application of BIT rules provided for in some treaties (and in all the most significant new models) and that refer to general exemptions (including the essential security interest) might override the question of whether state measures against SWFs qualify as indirect expropriations; in this case it would not be a matter of considering whether a compensation is mandatory or not, but of excluding the application of the entire BIT. Which leads us to reviewing the third aspect.

3.3.3 SWF and BIT general exemptions

The third aspect concerns the role ascribable to general exemptions – and particularly to those relevant to the essential security clause – that are starting to appear in standard and new BIT models.

---

is in: Art. 5 of the BIT between Singapore and UK (1975); Art. 4 of the BIT between China and France of 1985; in Art. 5 of the BIT between China and the Netherlands; Art. 5 of the Republic of Korea/China BIT of 1992; in Art. 7 of China/Switzerland BIT of 1987; Art. 5 of Korea/Argentina BIT of 1996; Art. 5 of Korea/India BIT of 1996; Art. 6 of Singapore/China BIT of 1985; Art. 4 of Qatar/China BIT (referring to 'similar measures); in Article 4 of Kuwait/Germany BIT of 1994. Art. 4.2 of the BIT between Qatar and Germany pays attention to the effect; it states that investments by investors of either Contracting party shall not be expropriated, nationalised or subjected to any other measure the effect of which would be tantamount to expropriation or nationalisation.

[80] The BIT between UAE and Italy states that investment will not be directly or indirectly expropriated, nationalised, frozen or submitted to measures having the same effects as nationalisation or expropriation, including taxation, mandatory sale of an investment in whole or in part, deprivation of its management or control. The BIT between Kuwait and France (1991) clarifies (in the protocol) that 'les dispositions de l'article 7 [expropriation] s'appliquent à toute mesure directe ou indirecte d'expropriation, de nationalisation ou à toute autre mesure de dépossession, telle que le gel ou le blocage des avoires, la vente forcée de tout ou partie de l'investissement ou autre mesure similaire d'effect équivalent'.

[81] The BIT between Kuwait and Italy states that 'the investments of both contracting states or of any of their legal or individual persons will not be directly or indirectly nationalised or expropriated nor subject to measures having the same effects as nationalisation or expropriation'.

These clauses do not release a state from responsibility and hence from the obligation to pay a compensation. They go well beyond this, excluding BIT application *tout court*. Therefore, they propose in bilateral treaties the questions we already faced in Chapter 4 (section 3.2) about the security exemptions in domestic law, i.e. the vagueness of these clauses, also considering the uncertain qualification of essential security interest, and the risks deriving from the alleged self-judging character of essential security provisions. At present there are not many treaties re-negotiated on these bases and to the best of our knowledge none of the BITs ratified by the main home states of SWFs has recently re-negotiated BITs containing these provisions. Therefore there is no immediate threat; however this is an important factor in the progress of the practice, a major element of uncertainty in a juridical system that has built the trust of states exactly on the certainty of relationships.

3.3.4 BITs, SWFs and dispute settlement mechanisms

The fourth aspect concerns the adequacy of the existing dispute settlement mechanism for the disputes that SWFs may raise against the restrictive measures adopted by host states in their respect. The BITs ratified by the home states of the major SWFs, in case of dispute between the investor and the other contracting party, provide for the submission of the controversy to the ICSID tribunal or, if not applicable, to an *ad hoc* tribunal;[82] or alternatively to national court or to ICSID or another international tribunal;[83] or to an *ad hoc* tribunal.[84]

The practice reviewed, although limited to the home states of the main SWFs, is variegated and does not allow us to define a standard path. This is probably due, among other things, to the fact that the BITs of the states that today invest directly through SWFs are based on Western models; we have seen only recently multiple different models and a greater freedom of negotiation that, strangely enough, is likely to generate greater uniformity

[82] Art. 11 of Qatar–Germany BIT; Art. 8 of Kuwait–Germany BIT; Art. 11 of Qatar–France BIT; Art. 11 of Kuwait–France BIT; Art. 8 of Singapore–UK BIT; Art. 8 of UAE–UK BIT; Art. 9 of UAE–France BIT; Art. 10 of China–The Netherlands BIT (with a no-U-turn clause); Art. 9 of China–Korea BIT.

[83] Art. 10 of UAE–Italy BIT; Art. 8 of Kuwait–China BIT; Art. 9 of Kuwait–Italy BIT; Art. 9 of Korea–India BIT; Art. 8 of China–France BIT; Art. 9 of the BIT between Qatar and China states that if the dispute cannot be settled within a period of six months from the date on which it occurred, it shall be settled at the request of either party by the competent court in the country in whose territory the investment was made. If neither party chooses to settle the dispute by the competent (national) court, either party shall be entitled to submit it to arbitration.

[84] Art. 13 of the BIT between Singapore and China.

in the results, based on investment flows (i.e. on international relationships) that are no longer one-way. However, the process of 'normalisation' of relationship is still a long one, and will include the re-negotiation of existing treaties.

4. FINAL REMARKS

SWFs make informed investments, taking care to protect their investments by virtue of BITs stipulated between home states and recipient states that host SWF investments. This is especially true for industrial investments. Financial investments follow a totally different logic and are guaranteed by sound international regulations. This situation applies to investments in Europe, North America, Japan, but also in countries that are quickly reaching Western-like levels of development (Brazil, Russia, India, China) and in still developing countries. Rather than by region, the distinction is by sector, depending on whether the investment is a financial or an industrial one.

A discussion apart should be reserved to the role of the United States, that have not entered into any BIT with almost none of SWF home states but are recipients of the main investments. Indeed, the rule also applies to the US, that host SWFs investments almost exclusively in financial institutions, while SWFs industrial investments are very few. Probably this is due to the absence of BITs with SWF home states and to internal rules that in the last two years have become more detailed and (for now, only potentially) restrictive. We may therefore conclude that there is a relationship between SWF investments and BITs, and while it is direct for all industrial investments it is not decisive for investments in financial institutions, that are in any case guaranteed by a series of international rules and standards.

Having ascertained, in theory and in practice, the existence of a relationship between SWF investments and BITs, we tried to weigh the efficacy of existing BITs with respect to the specific requirements called for by the investments made by sovereign entities. In the first place, we questioned whether SWFs can avail themselves of the instruments and guarantees offered by BITs. We saw that in certain cases the treaties ratified by SWF home states provide expressly that the government is the main investor; in other cases we may assume that this is not excluded. In many other BITs, instead, the possibility that the national of other contracting party is the state itself or a government agency is not allowed, or at least any dispute, being between two states, would not be resolved under the BIT.

We then questioned whether the measures threatened or adopted by host states, or proposed in literature in respect of SWFs may qualify as indirect expropriation, and therefore allow SWFs – which as we have seen at least in certain cases have legal capacity of their own – to take action aimed at obtaining protection of their investment. However, such protection is limited to a compensation, which is equitable (although in various forms according to the formula chosen in each BIT), but which cannot certainly be satisfactory as it compromises the certainty of investment that is the main guarantee at international level. Another risk of losing investor trust in BITs might derive from a massive use of certain new BIT models that carry general exemption clauses which usually include those relating to the essential security interest. The uncertainty of the BIT instrument casts a shadow over the entire system.

7. Conclusions

1. CONCLUSIONS

The quick growth of sovereign wealth funds, only temporarily slowed down by the economic crisis of 2008, is one of the most interesting recent matters of international law, for a series of reasons: because it is new; because it reverses the usual trend of financial flows and investments between states (so far mostly one-way) and therefore calls for more insight on the actual implementation of the mechanisms of reciprocity that have so far remained theoretical; because it poses questions that cannot be adequately answered by the multilateral agreements now in force, that are showing all their inadequacy; because it brings international law back to the 'primeval' state of bilateral relationships between states and demands a review of national law systems as well; because it demonstrates the inseparable cross-relationship between international law and national law, with actions in one system that have direct consequences in another, and with actions brought indifferently before national and international courts as the expression of a 'global' law; because it forces experts and international institutions into unconvincing connections between legal and ethical obligations, whereby states and SWFs are supposed to abide by voluntary codes of ethics that do not provide for material sanctions; because it is an example of the way in which states regain their financial sovereignty at international level to prevent, or at least to handle global and quickly evolving phenomena faster than the political path would; because it converts states from regulators of domestic economy into international operators, players in markets they have contributed to creating and that now they cannot regulate by themselves; because it affects many areas of international law, from the regulation of foreign investments to the protection of state immunity, from WTO multilateral discipline to bilateral treaties on investments, to dispute settlement mechanisms, and calls for broader and more systematic considerations.

Regarded by many at its beginnings (2007) as a form of state capitalism, the symbol of a return to the past, foreign state investments have been partially re-positioned in context (and reappraised) after the economic crisis started in 2008 and which SWF investments have contributed to ease, acting as market stabilisers. In fact, the crisis forced many states to intervene in their domestic economies to save national enterprises (especially in the financial sector) with forms of state capitalism that have affected market freedom and were justified only as being allegedly temporary. In this work we have chosen to leave contingent factors aside and focus on the structural aspects of the phenomenon, weighing its relationships with the law.

In our research we have tried to separate, divide, classify, in order to understand how the case can be studied, as a whole, from a legal point of view. We have seen that quite different entities with different structures fall under the umbrella of the general definition of SWFs. These entities must necessarily be separated under some respect in order to be reviewed, to determine which rules are the most appropriate to regulate their activities, to identify the most appropriate measures to protect their investments from unjustified hostile actions by host states.

Therefore, in Part I of this work we have intended to place the phenomenon within the context of current law mechanisms (Chapter 1) and provide a definition and a classification for SWFs (Chapter 2). Chapter 1 views the SWFs alongside the wider category of FGCI (Foreign Government Controlled Investments), following the same *ratio* as between 'genus' and 'family'. Then the reasons of their recent advent are investigated, as well as the criticism and concerns that they have engendered, many of which are due to SWFs being mistaken with SOEs in definition and classification.

For this reason we have focused on the question of defining and classifying SWFs. The definition we provide in Chapter 2 is functional, instrumental to our research. Therefore, we do not wish to assert that other definitions found in literature or in the practice are not useful; we simply believe it is the one that highlights best the profiles we have deemed important for the purposes of our research. Therefore, we have concluded that an appropriate definition of SWF might be the following: 'funds established, owned and operated by local or central governments, with investment strategies including the acquisition of equity interest in companies listed in international markets operating in sectors considered strategic by their countries of incorporation'.

This definition provides a guiding light in our proposal for a classification of funds which is not based on principles useful for other purposes such as, for example, origin of resources (commodity or non-commodity), investment strategies, or investment areas (finance or industry). Nor are we interested in distinguishing among SWFs and other close categories like central banks, pension funds, public enterprises, investment capital funds. We are in fact well aware that the SWF category is not a 'monolithic' one, and that therefore certain types of sovereign funds are more similar to other entities (e.g. some of them are run by central banks, others run central banks themselves), and that there might be exchange and co-operation between SWFs and other entities (e.g. one SWF may use a SOE, a pension fund may be converted into an SWF, etc.). We rather decided to work out a classification based on *criteria* that play a role in our research, and these are: presence of an autonomous legal personality, i.e. formal separation of the SWF – hence the importance of governance – from the state (which is relevant for immunity and for investment protection through BITs); purpose of activity (which is important for immunity, as not only the commercial nature of the activity but its purpose too may be relevant in certain cases and on certain terms). For a better approach to their classification, we qualified SWFs as a 'genus' that includes different 'species'. In turn, the SWF 'genus' belongs to the 'family' of FGCI (foreign government-controlled investors), which in turn belongs to the 'order' of Foreign Investments.

On the basis of the definition and the classifications proposed, in Part II we identify and review in detail the rules applicable to SWFs, under two respects. First (Chapter 3) we explain the forms of regulation of fund activity suggested in literature and those adopted by certain states. We also try to see whether and to what extent can we rely on international multilateral regulations, and see that the novelty, and above all the peculiarity of the case make the multilateral rules adopted in international treaties such as WTO or the codes of ethics developed by the OECD inapplicable, or however totally inadequate. We also recognised that all the regulatory measures adopted (such as the code of conduct known as the 'Santiago principles') can only be voluntary and do not provide for any sanction in case of breach. Therefore, SWFs remain subject to national measures. Our research contains suggestions for a regulatory solution whereby Santiago's GAPPs and OECD codes should be converted into international benchmarks which home states and host states respectively may use as reference, and make measures conditional on the compliance with them, or apply them in BITs.

The second part of Part II (Chapter 4) is dedicated to the measures that host states may adopt to counterbalance SWFs activities. We first propose the solutions suggested in literature, then review the measures adopted – or being discussed – by the states and, in the end, make our alternative proposals. As to the solutions suggested in literature, we highlight those profiles that set most limits to the freedom of investment guaranteed by international law in various forms under WTO agreements or OECD codes. As to the solutions adopted by the states, we highlight the risk deriving from general exemptions, and among these the essential security exemption in particular, more and more often the rationale of domestic measures. We then make our alternative proposals, characterised by measures that on one hand provide proper guarantees to host states and on the other are not penalising for those home states that wish to invest by means of SWFs. In particular, we propose both substantive and procedural solutions, limited in any case to the definition of principles; proper rules in fact may only be identified on a case by case basis. In substantive terms, host states should define clearly their general exemptions clauses, based on essential security, public order, public security, public interest, strategic industry, safeguard of critical infrastructures. In procedural terms, the regulation should be consistent with three basic principles: predictability (of the timeframe and outcome of the evaluation of the investment); transparency (of the exemptions applied and on the risk assessments that justify such exemptions); confidentiality.

Part III of our research (Chapters 5 and 6) deals with two crucial factors that have not been investigated so far in literature and are closely related to each other. They both refer to the bilateral relationships between states, the only ones applicable today considering the inadequacy of multilateral instruments, and concern the forms of guarantee that SWFs may avail themselves of to protect their foreign investments.

In Chapter 5 we consider whether SWFs may enjoy immunity from jurisdiction or from execution with respect both to the measures adopted by host states on individual investments, and to the illegal actions that SWFs might commit in connection with the investment (i.e. as shareholders). We assume a 'strong' and a 'weak' form of protection, that differ according to the kind of investment (portfolio investment or FDI, implying taking of control), or depending on whether the protection applies in reaction to a state measure (we call it 'passive immunity') or to protect fund activities ('active immunity'). Most of the distinctions are however based on SWF characteristics, which take particular relevance here, to show that the possibility to use or not state immunity – and in case how and with what 'strength' – depends much on the SWF and on how it is structured. The definition and classification of SWFs developed in Chapter 2 are useful here.

In Chapter 6 we investigate an issue 'reciprocal' – and somehow alternative – to state immunity, i.e. what other forms of protection may be used by SWFs where they cannot invoke immunity. In this case too the answer can only be abstract and not universal, because it will depend on: (i) the existence or not of a BIT between the host state and the SWF's home state; (ii) BIT contents, with reference for example to the notion of 'national of the other contracting party' (definition that may or may not apply to the investor state, as the case may be); (iii) the BIT's scope of definition of indirect expropriation (that might include many of the state measures described in literature as an instrument for regulating SWF activities); and (iv) the instruments chosen for the settlement of controversies (e.g. the option for ICSID arbitration will imply an interpretation of the BIT compatible with the ICSID Convention). Under this aspect too, the focus is on the different application of the discipline to each SWF.

The analysis of many controversial aspects of the SWF phenomenon leads to one answer: it is actually impossible and in any case useless to group all SWFs into one single category. SWFs should be considered as a 'genus' in a broader 'family' formed by Foreign Government-Controlled Investors (FGCI). Within the SWF 'order' there may be several different 'species' by structure and characteristics, to which a different discipline and different rules will apply from time to time.

Hence the utility of the definition of each 'species', including hybrid ones, that will allow to distinguish between objectively different (even very different) situations and to normalise a discipline that would otherwise appear inconsistent, due to not being always applicable or applicable each time in a different manner.

Therefore, all the attempts to make all the various types of SWF and the similar 'orders' of foreign state investments (like SOEs) subject to one single discipline, one single form of regulation, are proved unreasonable. The minimum common denominator of SWFs is really minimum (they are investment funds, sovereign). And it is relatively simple for a SWF to invest using different instruments belonging to different 'orders' so as to circumvent the specific regulations applicable to SWFs. At the same time, the objective of those who claim to make not the SWF 'order' but the FGCI 'family' (regardless of the form used) subject to one single discipline is too ambitious. In fact, the only element in common might be that the economic action is performed by a state, which is honestly not enough: a state may take action in many forms, the sovereign factor may be neutralised in many ways, and therefore an individual action may actually not fall within a category, however broad and general it may be.

Therefore, the only plausible answer is: admit that we must abandon the perspective of a general, one-size-fits-all regulation. The solution will be, both at international and at national level, an administrative or judicial one. The actual case must be looked at. There may be cases where a SWF identifies with the state because it lacks a legal personality of its own, and may therefore invoke state immunity from execution if the investment is in the territory of states that give relevance to the purpose of the investment. In other cases, a SWF may qualify as foreign investor (because it has legal personality or because the underlying treaty qualifies expressly the state as an investor) and will therefore be allowed to protect its investment with the instruments provided for by the BIT existing between the SWF's home state and the host state, and, if unsuccessful, it will be allowed to avail itself of one of the dispute settlement mechanisms provided for by the BIT, often as an alternative, that recognise the jurisdiction of national courts or of international arbitration boards. The possibilities are many, and depend on the various combinations of requirements which we considered as distinctive and that led us to classify four 'species' of SWF, described in Chapter 2, section 3.

The best solution for the protection of SWF investments will have to be sought in the actual circumstance, on a case by case basis. Therefore it is important to focus on all the factors we have identified, i.e. sovereignty and purposes, but also fund characteristics, type of investment made, measure adopted by the host state, internal practice of host states about immunity, existing bilateral treaties between SWF home state and host state in terms of investors' substantive and procedural rights. All those elements should be screened to give an answer to each different case.

Bibliography

Aimehaiza, M., *The Impact of the Growth of Sovereign Wealth Funds*, Paper prepared for the Arab Financial Forum, 2009.

Aizenmam, J. and G. Reuven, *Sovereign Wealth Funds: Stumbling Blocks or Stepping Stones to Financial Globalization?*, FRBSF Economic Letter, 2007-38.

Aizenmam, J. and G. Reuven, 'Sovereign Wealth Funds: Stylized facts about their Determinants and Governance' (2009) 12(3) *International Finance* 351–86.

AAVV, *293° Rapport d'Information Sur Les Fonds Souverains, Révélateurs De Nos Propres Faiblesses*, prepared for the French *Assemblée Nationale* by the 'Délégation de l'Assemblée Nationale pour l'Union Européenne', 2008.

Arangio-Ruiz, G., 'Le Domaine Réservé – L'Organization Internationale et le Rapport entre Droit International et Droit Interne', in Académie de Droit International, *Recueil des Courses*, 225 (1990 IV).

Audit, M., *Is the Erecting of barriers Against Foreign Sovereign Wealth Funds Compatible with International Investment Law?* Paper prepared for the Society of International Economic Law (SIEL) Conference, July 2008.

Avendaño, R. and J. Santiso, *Are Sovereign Wealth Funds' investments politically biased? A Comparison with mutual funds,* available at www.oecd.org/dataoecd/43/0/44301172.pdf.

Balding, C., *Framing Sovereign Wealth Funds: What we Know and Need to Know,* Working Paper, January 2009.

Balding, C., *A Portfolio Analysis of Sovereign Wealth Funds,* Working Paper, University of California, Irvine, 2008.

Barbary, V. and E. Chin, *Testing Time: Sovereign Wealth Funds in the Middle East and North America and the Global Financial Crisis* (Monitor, 2009).

Barysch, K., S. Tilford and P. Whyte, *State, money and rules: An EU policy for Sovereign investments,* Centre for European Reform essay, 2008.

Bassan, F., 'Una Regolazione per i Fondi Sovrani' [2009] *Mercato Concorrenza Regole* 95–132.

Bassan, F., 'Host States and Sovereign Wealth Funds, between National

Security and International Law' [2010] *European Business Law Review* 165–201.

Bassanini, F. and E. Reviglio, *New European Institutional Long Term Financial Instruments for a Strong, Sustainable and Balanced Global Growth*, Paper prepared for the Eurofi Financial Forum, September 2009.

Bassanini, F. and E. Reviglio, *Union bonds and new financial instruments for European Growth*, IlSole24Ore, 16 February 2010, p. 2.

Bech, R. and M. Fidora, *The Impact of Sovereign Wealth Funds on Global Financial Markets*, European Central Bank Occasional Paper 91, 2008.

Behrendt, S., *Sovereign Wealth Funds and the Santiago Principles: Where Do They Stand?*, Carnegie Papers 22 (May) (Washington, Carnegie Endowment for International Peace, 2010).

Bernstein, S., J. Lerner and A. Schoar, *The Investment Strategies of Sovereign Wealth Funds*, FEEM Working Paper 25/2009.

Berrigan, J., M. Bertoldi and C. Bosma, *New Perspectives on Sovereign Asset Management*, (London Central Banking Publication, 2008).

Battacharjee, S., *National Security with a Canadian Twist: The Investment Canada Act and The New National Security Review Test,* Columbia FDI Perspectives, Vale Columbia Center of Sustainable International Investment, no. 10, July 2010.

Blundell-Wignall A., Hu Hu-Wei and J. Yermo, *Sovereign Wealth and Pension Fund Issues*, OECD Working Paper on Insurance and Private Pensions, no. 14, 2008.

Bordoni, M., 'Default nel Debito Pubblico e Immunità dello Stato Estero dalla Giurisdizione Civile' [2005] *Rivista di Diritto Internazionale* 1031–1077.

Bortolotti, B., V. Fotak, W. Megginson and W. Miracky, *Sovereign Wealth Fund Investment Patterns and Performance*, FEEM Working Paper, 22/2009.

Buhi, J., '*Negocio de China*: Building Upon the Santiago Principles to Form an Effective International Approach to Sovereign Wealth Fund Regulation' [2009] *Hong Kong Law Journal* 197–216.

Butt, S., A. Shivdasani, C. Stendevad and A. Wyman, 'Sovereign Wealth Funds: a Growing Force in Corporate Finance' [2008] *Journal of Applied Corporate Finance* 73–83.

Caner, M. and T. Grennes, *Sovereign Wealth Funds: The Norwegian Experience,* Working Paper, November 2008.

Catà Backer, L., 'The Private Law of Public Law: Public Authorities as Shareholders, Golden Shares, Sovereign Wealth Funds and the Public Law Element in Private Choice of Law' [2008] *Tulane Law Review* 1801–1868.

Catà Backer, L., 'The Norwegian Sovereign Wealth Fund: Between Private and Public' [2009] *Georgetown Journal of International Law* 1271–1280.

Catà Backer, L., 'Sovereign Investing in Times of Crisis: Global Regulation of Sovereign Wealth Funds, State Owned Enterprises and the Chinese Experience' [2010] *Transnational Law and Contemporary Problems* 1–144.

Catà Backer, L., 'Sovereign Wealth Funds as Regulatory Chameleons: the Norwegian Sovereign Wealth Fund and Public Global Government Through Private Global Investment' (2010) 41(2) *Georgetown Journal of International Law* 425–499.

Cehajic, S., *Sovereign Wealth Funds: Contingent Risks and a Laissez-Faire Approach Complemented with a 'Just in Case' Reactive Regulatory Framework*, Working Paper, 2009.

Chalamish, E., *Protectionism and Sovereign Investment post Global Recession,* Paper prepared for the 2009 OECD Global Forum on International Investment.

Chalamish, E., *Rethinking Global Investment Regulation in the Sovereign Wealth Funds Era*, paper prepared for the ASIL International Economic Law Research, 2009.

Chao, C., 'The Rise of Global Sovereign Wealth Funds', in *Modern Bankers*, V.10, 2006.

Chao, C. and X. Ping, *Sovereign Wealth Funds, Macroeconomic Policy Alignment and Financial Stability,* Working Paper, China Investment Corporation, 2008.

Chao, C., *The Theoretical Logic of Sovereign Wealth Funds,* Working Paper, China Investment Corporation, 2009.

Chhaochharia, V. and L.A. Laeven, *The Investment Allocation of Sovereign Wealth Funds,* Working Paper, 2009.

Christie, G., 'What Constitutes a Taking of Property under International Law?' [1962] *British Yearbook of International Law* 307–316.

Clark, G. and A. Monk, *The Oxford Survey of Sovereign Wealth Funds' Asset Managers,* Working Paper, July 2009.

Clark, G. and A. Monk, *Nation-state Legitimacy, Trade, and the China Investment Corporation,* Working Paper, 2010.

Cohen, B., *Sovereign Wealth Funds and National Security: the Great Trade-off*, Paper presented at the annual meeting of the ISA's 50th Annual Convention, New York, 2010.

Couturier, J., D. Sola and P. Stonham, 'Are Sovereign Wealth Funds "White Knights"?' [2009] *Qualitative Research in Financial Markets* 142–151.

Cox, C., *The Rise of Sovereign Business*, Speech, December 2007.

Crawford, J., 'Execution of Judgements and Foreign Sovereign Immunity', in [1981] *American Journal of International Law* 404–422.
Curto, S., 'Sovereign Wealth Funds in the Next Decade', in O. Canuto and M. Giugale (eds.), *The Day after Tomorrow* (2010), pp. 239–249.
Das, U., Y. Lu, C. Mulder and A. Sy, *Setting up a Sovereign Wealth Fund: Some Policy and Operational Considerations*, IMF Working Paper, WP/09/179.
Delacour, C., *Les Fonds Souveraines – Ceux Nouveaux Acteurs de l'Economie Mondiale* (Paris, 2009).
Demarolle, A., *Report to the Government of France on Sovereign Wealth Funds*, 2008.
Denza, E., 'The 2005 UN Convention on State Immunity in Perspective' [2006] *International and Comparative Law Quarterly* 395–8.
Desai, M. and D. Dharmapala, 'Taxing the Bandit Kings' (2008) 118 *Yale Law Journal Pocket* 98.
de Vido, S., 'La recente giurisprudenza comunitaria in materia di golden shares: violazione delle norme sulla libera circolazione dei capitali o sul diritto di stabilimento?', in [2007] *Diritto del commercio internazionale* 861–891.
Dewenter, K., X. Han and P. Malatesta, 'Firm Values and Sovereign Wealth Funds' [2010] *Journal of Financial Economics* 256–278.
Dickinson, A. *et al.* (eds.), *State Immunity: Selected Materials and Commentary* (2004).
Dolzer, R., 'Indirect Expropriation of Alien Property' [1996] *Foreign Investment Law Journal* 41–65.
Doran, M., O. Prost, R. Pogrel and H. Parmentier, 'Sovereign Wealth Funds: The rapidly evolving landscape' [2009] *PLC Magazine*.
Drezner, D., 'Sovereign Wealth Funds and the (in)security of Global Finance' [2008] *Journal of International Affairs* 115–30.
Egger, P. and M. Pfaffermayr, 'The Impact of Bilateral Investment Treaties on Foreign Direct Investment' [2004] *Journal of Comparative Economy* 788–804.
Epstein, R. and A. Rose, 'The Regulation of Sovereign Wealth Funds: The Virtues of Going Slow' [2009] *University of Chicago Law Review* 111–34.
Fernandes, N., *Sovereign Wealth Funds: Investment Choices and Implications around the World,* EFA 2009 Bergen Meeting Paper.
Fiechter, J., 'The French Strategic Investment Fund: A Creative Approach to Complement SWF Regulation or Mere Protectionism?' (2010) *Journal of Applied Economy* 59 – 77.
Fleischer, V., 'A Theory of Taxing Sovereign Wealth' [2009] *New York University Law Review* 440–513.

Fleischer, V., 'How Should We Tax the Sovereign Wealth?' [2008] *Yale Law Journal, Pocket* 93–7.

Fotak, V., B. Bortolotti and W. Megginson, *The Financial Impact of Sovereign Wealth Fund Investments in Listed Companies*, Working Paper, University of Oklahoma, 2008.

Fox, H., *The Law of State Immunity*, 2nd edn. (Oxford, 2008).

Fox, H., 'In Defence of State Immunity: Why the UN Convention on State Immunity is Important' [2006] ICLQ 399–406.

Fox, H., 'International Law and Restraints on the Exercise of Jurisdiction by National Courts of States', in M.D. Evans (ed.), *International Law* (2003) 357 *ff.*

Fox, I., P. del Vecchio, O. Kayum, C. Gatenio, J. Blackburn and D. Wolfson, *Do Sovereign Wealth Funds Best Serve the Interest of their Citizens?*, Working Paper, University of Chicago Graduate School of Business, 2008.

Frank, S., 'Foreign Direct Investment, Investment Treaty Arbitration, and the Rule of Law' [2007] *Global Business & Development Law Journal* 337–73.

Frank, S., 'The Legitimacy Crisis in Investment Treaty Arbitration: Privatizing Public International Law Through Inconsistent Decisions' [2005] *Fordham Law Review* 1521–1625.

Gardiner, R., 'UN Convention on State Immunity: Form and Function' [2006] ICLQ 407–410.

Gaukrodges, D., *Foreign State Immunity and Foreign Government Controlled Investors*, OECD Working Papers on International Investments, 2010.

Gelpren, A., 'Sovereignty, Accountability, and Wealth Fund Governance Conundrum' [2011] *Asian Journal of International Law*, forthcoming.

Gelpren, A., *A Sovereign Wealth Turn*, Rutgers School of Law-Newark, Research Paper Series, paper no. 025.

Georgiev, G., 'The Reformed CFIUS Regulatory Framework: Mediating Between Continued Openness to Foreign Investment and National Security' [2008] *Yale Journal of Regulation* 125–134.

Gilson, R. and C. Milhaupt and J. Curtis, 'Sovereign Wealth Funds and Corporate Governance: a Minimalist Response to the New Mercantilism' [2009] *Stanford Law Review* 1345–69.

Granne, M.A., 'Defining "Organ of a Foreign State" Under the Foreign Sovereign Immunity Act of 1976' [2008] *UC Davis Law Review* 1–56.

Greene, E.F. and B.A. Yeager, 'Sovereign Wealth Funds – A Measured Assessment' [2008] *Capital Markets Law Journal* 247–74.

Griffith-Jones, S. and J. Ocampo, *Sovereign Wealth Funds: a Developing*

Country Prospective, paper prepared for the workshop on the Sovereign Wealth Funds (Andean Development Corp., London 2008).

Guaccero, A. and E. Pan and M. Chester, 'Investimenti stranieri e fondi sovrani: forme di controllo nella prospettiva comparata USA – Europa' [2008] *Rivista delle società* 1359–1394.

Hafner, G. and U. Kohler, 'The United Nations Convention on Jurisdictional Immunities of States and their Property' [2004] *Netherlands Yearbook of International Law* 3–49.

Hafner, G. and L. Lange, 'La Convention des Nations Unies sur les Immunités Juridictionnelles des Etats et de Leurs Biens' [2004] *Annuaire Français de Droit International* 45–76.

Hallward-Driemeier, M., *Do Bilateral Investment Treaties Attract Foreign Direct Investment? Only a Bit – and they could bite*, World Bank Working Paper, 2003.

Hammer, C. and P. Kunzel and I. Petrova, *Sovereign Wealth Fund Current Institutional and Operational Practices*, IMF Working Paper 2008/254.

Hildebrand, P., *The Challenge of Sovereign Wealth Funds*, Report to the International Centre for Monetary and Banking Studies, 2007.

Hsu, L., 'SWF, Recent US legislative changes, and Treaty Obligations' [2009] *Journal of World Trade* 451–477.

IMF, *Sovereign Wealth Funds – A Work Agenda* (2008).

International Working Group of Sovereign Wealth Funds, *Sovereign Wealth Funds: Generally Accepted Principles and Practices*–Santiago Principles, International Monetary Fund, 2008.

Jen, S., *How Big Could Sovereign Wealth Funds Be By 2015?*, Morgan Stanley, May 2007 Report.

Jen, S., *The Definition of a Sovereign Wealth Fund*, Morgan Stanley, March 2007 Report.

Johnson, S., *The Rise of Sovereign Wealth Funds* (2007).

Karolyi, G. and R. Liao, *What is different about Government-Controlled Acquirers in Cross-Border Deals?*, Cornell University Working Paper, 2010.

Keenan, P.J., 'Sovereign Wealth Funds and Social Arrears' [2009] *Virginia Journal of International Law* 431–72.

Keenan, P.J. and C. Ochoa, 'The Human Rights Potential of Sovereign Wealth Funds' [2009] *Georgetown Journal of International Law* 1151–1189.

Keller, A., 'Sovereign Wealth Funds: Trustworthy Investors or Vehicles of Strategic Ambitions?' [2009] *Georgetown Journal of Law and Public Policy* 333–72.

Kern, S., *Sovereign Wealth Funds – State investment on the rise*, Deutsche Bank Research, 2007.

Kimmitt, R., 'Public Footprints in Private Markets – Sovereign Wealth Funds and the World Economy' [2008] *Foreign Affairs* 119–30.

Knill, A., B. Lee and N. Mauck, *'Sleeping with the Enemy' or 'An Ounce of Prevention': Sovereign Wealth Fund Investment and Market Instability,* Working Paper, 2009.

Kotter, J. and U. Lel, 'Friend or Foes? Target Selection Decision of Sovereign Wealth Funds and their Consequences' *Journal of Financial Economics*, forthcoming.

Kurtz, J., *Adjudging the Exceptional at International Law: Security, Public Order and Financial Crisis*, paper presented at the Annual Meeting of the Society of International Economic Law (SIEL), 15–17 July 2008.

Lavelle, K.C., 'The Business of Governments: Nationalism in the Context of Sovereign Wealth Funds and State-Owned Enterprises' [2008] *Journal of International Affairs*, 2008 131–47.

Le Borgne, E. and P. Medas, *Sovereign Wealth Funds in The Pacific Island Countries: Macro-Fiscal Linkages,* IMF Working Paper 07/297.

Lee, Y., 'A Reversal of Neo Colonialism: The Pitfalls and Prospects of Sovereign Wealth Funds' [2009] *Georgetown Journal of International Law* 1103–49.

Lyons, G., *State Capitalism: The Rise of Sovereign Wealth Funds*, Standard Chartered Global research, 2007

Lhaopadchan, S., 'The Politics of Sovereign Wealth Fund Investment: The Case of Temasek and Shin Corp.' [2010] *Journal of Financial Regulation and Compliance* 15–22.

Mahajan, K.A. and V. Subhramanium, 'Sovereign Wealth Funds – An opinion for India' [2009] *Company Law Journal* 124–36.

Marchick, D. and M. Slaughter, *Global FDI Policy: Correcting a Protectionist Drift*, Council Special Report, US Council on Foreign Relations, 2008.

Mattoo, A. and A. Subramanian, *Currency Undervaluation and Sovereign Wealth Funds: a New Role for the World Trade Organization*, Working Paper 08-2, Peterson Institute, 2008.

McGregor, L., 'State Immunity and *Jus Cogens*' [2006] ICLQ 437–46.

Melone, M., 'Should the United States Tax Sovereign Wealth Funds?' [2009] *Boston University International Law Journal* 143–225.

Mezzacapo, S., *The So-called 'Sovereign Wealth Funds': Regulatory Issues, Financial Stability and Prudential Supervision* (Bruxelles, 2009).

Miracky, W., D. Dyer, D. Fisher, T. Goldner, L. Lagarde and V. Piedrahita, *Assessing the risks: The Behaviours of Sovereign Wealth Funds in the Global Economy* (Boston Monitor Group, 2008).

Mohi-Uddin M., *The Return of Sovereign Wealth Funds*, UBS Investment Research. Foreign Exchange Notes, 2010.

Monk, A., *Sovereignty in the Era of Global Capitalism: The Rise of Sovereign Wealth Fund and the Power of Finance*, Working Paper 2010.

Monk, A., *Recasting the Sovereign Wealth Fund Debate: Organizational Legitimacy, Institutional Governance and Geopolitics*, Working Paper, 2008.

Neumayer, E. and L. Spess, *Do Bilateral Investment Treaties Increase Foreign Direct Investment in Developing Countries?,* World Development Paper 2005.

Newcombe, A., 'The Boundaries of Regulatory Expropriation in International Law' [2005] *ICSID Review* 1–57.

Newcombe, A. and L. Paradell, *Law and Practice of Investment Treaties* (The Hague, 2009).

Nouvel, Y., 'Les Entités Paraétatiques Dans la Jurisprudence du CIRDI', in Leben C., *Le Contentieux Arbitral Transnational Relatif à l'Investissement – Nouveaux Développements* (Paris/Anthemis, LGDJ, 2006) 32 *ff.*

O'Brian, J., 'Barriers to Entry: Foreign Direct Investment and the regulation of Sovereign Wealth Funds' [2008] *International Law* 1234–40.

O'Neill, J. and E. Nielsen and S. Bahaj, *In Defence of Sovereign Wealth Funds,* Goldman Sachs Global Economics Paper no. 167, 2008.

OECD, *International Investment Perspectives: Freedom of Investment in a Changing World* (2007).

OECD, *Protection of 'Critical Infrastructure' and The Role of Investment Policies Relating to National Security*, Report, 2008.

OECD, *Transparency and Predictability for Investment Policies Addressing National Security Concerns: a Survey of Practices*, Report, 2008.

OECD, *Accountability for Security-related Investment Policies*, Report, 2008.

OECD, *Foreign Government-Controlled Investors and Recipient Country Investment Policies: a Scoping Paper* (2009).

OECD Investment Committee, *Sovereign Wealth Funds and Recipient Country Policies* (2008).

Park, D. and B. Estrada, 'Developing Asia's Sovereign Wealth Funds and Outward Foreign Direct Investments' [2009] *Asian Development Review* 57–85.

Plotkin, M., 'Foreign Direct Investments by Sovereign Wealth Funds: Using the Market and the Committee on Foreign Investment in the United States Together to Make the United States More Secure' (2008) 118 *Yale Law Journal*, pocket 88.

Popova, A., 'Sovereign Wealth Funds: To Be or Not To Be Is Not the

Question; Which One To Choose Is' [2009] *Georgetown Journal of International Law* 1191–1206.

Popova, A., 'We Don't Want to Conquer You; We Have Enough to Worry About: The Russian Sovereign Wealth Fund' (2008) 118 *Yale Law Journal*, pocket 109.

Prequin, E., *Sovereign Wealth Funds: SWFs Total Assets Continue to Grow*. Prequin Special Report, 2010.

Quadrio Curzio, A., *Sovereign Wealth Funds. A complete guide to state-owned investment funds* (Harriman House, 2010).

Quadrio Curzio, A. and V. Miceli, *I Fondi Sovrani – I Nuovi Attori della Finanza Mondiale: Opportunità o rischi?* (Bologna, 2009).

Razanov, A., *Sovereign Wealth Funds:Defining Liabilities*, Working Paper, State Street Global Advisor, 2007.

Razanov, A., 'Who Holds the Wealth of Nations?' [2005] *Central Banking Journal* XV/4.

Razanov, A., *What is 'Sovereign Wealth' Anyway?* AsianSIL Working Paper 2009/15.

Reed, B., 'Sovereign Wealth Funds: The New Barbarians at the Gate? An Analysis of the Legal and Business Implications of their Ascendency' [2009] *Virginia Law and Business Review* 97–138.

Reinisch, A., 'European Court Practice Concerning State Immunity From Enforcement Measures' [2006] *European Journal of International Law* 803–36.

Reinsberg, B., *Sovereign Wealth - No Fund. The decisive Role of Domestic Veto Players*, PIPE Working Paper 1/2009.

Reisen, A., *Organisation for Economic Co-Operation Development, How to spend It: Commodity and Non-Commodity Sovereign Wealth Fund*, OECD Development Centre Policy Brief 38, 2008.

Roeller, L. and N. Veron, *Safe and Sound: An EU Approach to Sovereign Investment.* Bruegel Policy Brief 08/2008.

Ronzitti, N. and G. Venturini, *Le immunità giurisdizionali degli Stati e degli altri enti internazionali* (Rome, 2008).

Rose, P., 'Sovereign Wealth Fund Investment in the Shadow of Regulation and Politics' [2009] *Georgetown Journal of International Law* 1207–37.

Rose, P., 'Sovereigns as Shareholders' [2008] *North Carolina Law Review* 83–150.

Rose-Ackerman, S. and J. Rossi, 'Disentangling Deregulatory Takings' [2000] *Virginia Law Review* 1435–95.

Roselli, A. and G. Mazzantini, *I Fondi Sovrani : a quanto ammontano e come si possono regolare? Opportunità e problemi*, ASTRID Working Paper, 2009.

Sacerdoti, G., 'Bilateral Treaties and Multilateral Investments on Investment Protection' (1998) 269 *Academie de Droit International, Recueil des Courses* 251–460.
Sacerdoti, G., *The Proliferation of BITs: Conflict of Treaties, Proceedings and Awards*, Bocconi Legal Studies Research Paper no. 07/02 (2007).
Salacuse, J. and N. Sullivan, 'Do BITs Really Work?: An Evaluation of Bilateral Investment Treaties and Their Grand Bargain' [2005] *Harvard International Law Journal* 67 *ff*.
Santino, J., *Sovereign Development Funds*, OECD Development Centre, *Policy Insights* no. 58, 2008.
Santino, J., *Sovereign Development Fund: Financial Actors in the Shifting Wealth of Nations*, OECD Emerging Markets Network Working Paper, 2008.
Sarkar, R., 'Sovereign Wealth Funds: Furthering Development or Impeding it?' [2009] *Georgetown Journal of International Law* 1181–90.
Sarkar, R., 'Sovereign Wealth Funds as Development tool for ASEAN Nations: From Social Wealth to Social Responsibility' [2010] *Georgetown Journal of International Law* 621–45.
Sax, J., 'Takings and the Police Power' [1964] *Yale Law Journal* 36–76.
Schachter, O., 'The Twilight Existence of Nonbinding Internationals Agreements' [1977] *American Journal of International Law* 296–304.
Schill, S., *The Multilateralisation of International Investment Law: the Emergence of a Multilateral System of Investment Protection on the Basis of Bilateral Treaties,* Paper presented at the SIEL Annual Conference, 2008.
Schmerler, C., 'Restructuring Sovereign Debt', in Schmerler and Silkenat (eds.), *The Law of Insolvencies and Debt Restructuring* (2006) 431–78.
Schreuer, C., *State Immunity: Some Recent Developments* (Cambridge, 1988).
Shai, B., J. Lerner, A. Schoar, *The Investment Strategies of Sovereign Wealth Funds*, Working Paper, Harvard University, 2009.
Shelton, D., 'Normative Hierarchy in International Law' [2006] *American Journal of International Law* 291–323.
Shemirani, M., *Investor State and the Rise of Sovereign Wealth Funds (SWFs)*, paper prepared for the ISA South Conference, 2009.
Shih, W., *Energy Security, GATT/WTO and Regional Agreements*, Paper prepared for the SIEL Annual Conference, 2008.
Siniscalco, D., 'Governi Alle Porte – Crisi del Credito e Fondi Sovrani' [2008] *Mercato, Concorrenza e Regole* 75–86.
Slavotsky, J., 'Sovereign Wealth Funds as Emerging Financial Superpowers: How U.S. Regulators Should Respond' [2009] *Georgetown Journal of International Law* 1239–69.

Sornarajah, M., 'State Responsibility and Bilateral Investment Treaties' [1986] *Journal of World Trade* 79–98.

Sun, T. and H. Hesse, *Sovereign Wealth Funds and Financial Stability: An Event Study Analysis.* IMF Working Paper 09/239 (2009).

Swenson, D., 'Why Do Developing Countries Sign BITs?' [2005] *U.C. Davis Journal of International Law and Policy* 131–54.

Tobin, J. and S. Rose-Ackerman, *Foreign Direct Investment and Business Environment in Developing Countries: The Impact of Bilateral Investment Treaties*, Yale Law and Economics Research Paper no. 293 (2005).

Truman, E., *Sovereign Wealth Funds: the Need for Greater Transparency and Accountability* (Peterson Institute for International Economics, 2007).

Truman, E., *Sovereign Wealth Funds Acquisitions and Other Foreign Government Investments in the United States: Assessing the Economic and National Security Implications,* Testimony before the Committee on Banking, Housing and Urban Affairs, United States Senate, 14 November 2007.

Truman, E., 'A Blueprint for Sovereign Wealth Fund Best Practices', in *Policy Brief* (Peterson Institute for International Economics, April 2008).

Truman, E., 'The International Monetary Fund and Regulatory Challenges', in *The International Spectator* (2010), 37–58.

Truman, E., *Sovereign Wealth Funds: Threat or Salvation?* (Peterson Institute for International Economics, 2010).

UNCTAD, Bilateral Investment Treaties in the Mid-1990s, UNCTAD/ ITE/IIT/7.

Weimer, C., 'Foreign Direct Investment and National Security Post-FINSA 2009' [2009] *Texas Law Review* 663–84.

Weiss, M., *Sovereign Wealth Funds: Background and policy issues for Congress*, Congressional Research Service – Report for US Congress, 2008.

Weston, B., 'Constructive Takings Under International Law: a Modest Foray into the Problem of Creeping Expropriation' [1975] *Virginia Journal of International Law* 103–175.

Index